T0399742

Considering Conservative Women in the Gendering of Modern British Politics

This volume examines how the British Conservative Party has appealed to women, the roles that women have played in the party, and the tense relationship between women's activism on the Right and feminism. Covering the period since the early twentieth century, each contribution questions assumptions about the reactionary response of the British Right, Margaret Thatcher's party, to women's issues and their political aspirations.

How have women been mobilized by the Conservative Party? What kind of party appeals has the British Conservative Party designed to attract women as party workers and voters? Developing successful strategies to attract women voters since 1918, and appealing to certain notional women's issues, and having produced the only two women Prime Ministers of the UK, the Conservative Party has its own special relationship with women in the modern period. The shifting status of women and opportunities for women in politics in modern Britain has been garnering more scholarly attention recently, and the centenary of women's partial suffrage in 2018, and Astor 100 in 2019, has done much to excite wider attention and public interest in these debates. However, the role of Conservative women has too often been seen as problematic, especially because of general assumption that feminism is only allied to leftist movements and political positions. This volume explores these themes through a range of case studies, covering the period from the early twentieth to the twenty-first century.

The chapters in this book were originally published as a special issue of the journal *Women's History Review*.

Clarisse Berthezène is Professor of Modern History at the University of Paris, France, and she has published widely on conservatism in Britain and abroad in the twentieth century, including *Training Minds for Ideas: Ashridge College, the Conservative Party and the Cultural Politics of Britain, 1929–54* (2015).

Julie V. Gottlieb is Professor of Modern History at the University of Sheffield, UK, and she has published extensively in the field of women and politics in the first half of the twentieth century, including *'Guilty Women', Foreign Policy and Appeasement in Interwar Britain* (2015).

Together the co-editors of this volume organised the Rethinking Right-Wing Women conference (2015, Oxford, UK) and together they have published a collective volume, *Rethinking Right-Wing Women: Gender and the Conservative Party, 1880s to the Present* (2017).

Considering Conservative Women in the Gendering of Modern British Politics

Edited by
Clarisse Berthezène and Julie V. Gottlieb

LONDON AND NEW YORK

First published 2021
by Routledge
2 Park Square, Milton Park, Abingdon, Oxon OX14 4RN

and by Routledge
52 Vanderbilt Avenue, New York, NY 10017

Routledge is an imprint of the Taylor & Francis Group, an informa business

© 2021 Taylor & Francis

British Library Cataloguing in Publication Data
A catalogue record for this book is available from the British Library

ISBN 13: 978-0-367-56965-5

Typeset in Minion Pro
by Newgen Publishing UK

Publisher's Note
The publisher accepts responsibility for any inconsistencies that may have arisen during the conversion of this book from journal articles to book chapters, namely the inclusion of journal terminology.

Disclaimer
Every effort has been made to contact copyright holders for their permission to reprint material in this book. The publishers would be grateful to hear from any copyright holder who is not here acknowledged and will undertake to rectify any errors or omissions in future editions of this book.

Contents

Citation Information

The chapters in this book were originally published in *Women's History Review*, volume 28, issue 2 (2019). When citing this material, please use the original page numbering for each article, as follows:

Introduction

Considering conservative women in the gendering of modern British politics
Clarisse Berthezène and Julie V. Gottlieb
Women's History Review, volume 28, issue 2 (2019), pp. 189–193

Chapter 1

'Does the right hon. Gentleman mean equal votes at 21?' Conservative women and equal franchise, 1919–1928
Mari Takayanagi
Women's History Review, volume 28, issue 2 (2019), pp. 194–214

Chapter 2

The Elusive Lady Apsley
Madge Dresser
Women's History Review, volume 28, issue 2 (2019), pp. 215–235

Chapter 3

Women in the organisation of the Conservative Party in Wales, 1945–1979
Sam Blaxland
Women's History Review, volume 28, issue 2 (2019), pp. 236–256

Chapter 4

Diana Spearman's role within the post-war Conservative Party and in the 'battle of ideas' (1945–1965)
Stéphane Porion
Women's History Review, volume 28, issue 2 (2019), pp. 257–276

Chapter 5

Housewives having a go: Margaret Thatcher, Mary Whitehouse and the appeal of the Right Wing Woman in late twentieth-century Britain

For any permission-related enquiries please visit:
www.tandfonline.com/page/help/permissions

Notes on Contributors

Clarisse Berthezène is Professor of Modern History at the University of Paris, France.

Sam Blaxland is Postdoctoral Fellow and Tutor in History at Swansea University, UK.

Beatrix Campbell is a journalist, writer, and political activist whose career spans the Campaign for Nuclear Disarmament, the Communist Party, the Women's Liberation Movement, Gay Liberation, and the Green Party.

Madge Dresser is (retired) Associate Professor in British Social History, University of the West of England, Bristol, UK.

Julie V. Gottlieb is Professor of Modern History at the University of Sheffield, UK.

Ben Jackson is Associate Professor of Modern History at the University of Oxford, UK, and a Fellow of University College, London, UK.

Stéphane Porion is Lecturer in British Political History at the University François Rabelais of Tours, France.

Jessica Prestidge is Parliamentary Researcher at the House of Commons, London, UK.

David Swift was former Kreitman Postdoctoral Fellow at Ben Gurion University of the Negev, Israel.

Mari Takayanagi is Senior Archivist at the Parliamentary Archives, London, UK.

Considering conservative women in the gendering of modern British politics

Clarisse Berthezène and Julie V. Gottlieb

ABSTRACT

The shifting status of women and opportunities for women in politics in modern Britain has been garnering more scholarly attention recently, and the centenary of women's partial suffrage in 2018 has done much to excite wider attention and public interest in these debates. However, the role of Conservative women has too often been seen as problematic, especially because of general assumption that feminism is only allied to leftist movements and political positions. This is the case despite the fact that there have been only two women Prime Ministers, and both Conservatives, and that the party has been highly successful at motivating and mobilising women at and outside election time. This special issue takes on the task of reconsidering, situating and nuancing the place of Conservative women in the story of women's political emancipation.

Introduction

'Shy Women Tories' or 'Bloody Difficult Women': the Enigma of British Conservative Women in the Twentieth Century

The 100th anniversary of the Representation of the People Act is an ideal moment to reflect on the history and take a more nuanced approach to Conservative women. How has the history of Tory women been different and set apart from that of their counterparts in other parties or in the women's movement? After pollsters failed to accurately predict the Conservative General Election victory in 1992, they, together with psephologists, proposed the theory of the 'Shy Tory Effect'. Those who voted Conservative were (and are) much less likely to publically admit their voting intensions. Are Conservative women the *Shy Tories* of gender and political history?

On various levels there are analogies to be drawn between the 'Shy Tory Factor' and the history and the historiography of women in the Conservative party.[1] First, Conservative women have been, comparatively speaking, hesitant about identifying themselves with feminism as an anti-establishment movement that aspires to overturn the socio-political and cultural structures of patriarchy. Conservative women have been more comfortable evoking the legacy of feminist campaigners in history and less so at identifying themselves with contemporaneous expressions of feminist activism and militancy. For example,

Margaret Thatcher acknowledged the debt of the women of her generation to the Edwardian suffragettes, but she expressed open contempt for the Women's Liberation Movement. As the first woman party leader, in 1978 Thatcher gave a speech celebrating the 50th anniversary of the Equal Franchise Act (1928). She noted how 'At the height of the Suffragette movement women chained themselves to the railings outside Number Ten Downing Street. Today, women are not content to be outside Number Ten looking in,'[2] and then proceeded to highlight the hand of the Conservative party had in many of the significant milestones in women's constitutional emancipation. Similarly, the present-day Conservative Women's Organisation reveres Emmeline Pankhurst, Emily Wilding Davison and other feminist pioneers with more and less direct links to the Conservative Party, but their support for contemporary incarnations of the women's movement is more circumspect.[3] That being said, the involvement of Tory women in various women's rights campaigns—from suffrage to more and fuller roles for women in public life—has not been sufficiently recognised and scrutinised. Arguably this is because 'Tory feminism' looks rather different from the women's rights agenda enmeshed with other party political cultures at the centre and on the Left. The emphasis for Conservative women (and some male supporters) is on women's duties and the legal and constitutional rights they require to animate the performance of their citizenship. As a further caveat, Tory feminism is not historically static and immutable, its malleability and evolution recently acknowledged, surprisingly, by the Mother of the House, Labour's Harriet Harman.[4]

Second, histories of the Conservative party have been reserved about women. On the one hand, the institutional or heavily biographical narratives have been written mainly by men, with varying degrees but usually limited interest in gender as a category of analysis. From the 1920s to the 1980s, there were more women than men within the Conservative party and the history of this very female (and feminised) party still needs to be written.

Third, feminist historians have also been reticent and often not so reserved about their reluctance to research Conservative women. Women's historians have been suspicious of making Conservative women the focus of their research, opting to research women and women's organisations that did credit to later incarnations of the women's movement. This makes sense given that feminist history as a practice and as a movement originated on the New Left in the 1960s and it has always been closely intertwined with social and sexual radicalism and activism.

The advent of Margaret Thatcher as first woman PM in the 1980s, together with the frontal attack on sixties radicalism inherent in Thatcherism, only reinforced the sense that Tory women were no part of the sisterhood. Indeed, for years, Conservative women were torn between being the *Shy Tories* of gender and political history, on the one hand, and the *Bloody Difficult Women* of politics on the other. The description of the only two women Prime Ministers in the history of Britain as 'bloody difficult women' made by Ken Clarke in his microphonic gaffe in July 2016 immediately went viral with women of all parties turning it into a compliment and calling for more 'BDW'.[5] What BDW presumably meant was being assertive and not being afraid to challenge others, the precise opposite of being shy.

What might appear as the structural concealment of Conservative women seems to stem from the formidable layers of contradictory clichés: most of the time Conservative women are either presented in an ancillary role of discreet sandwich-making and envelope-filling activities or as honorary men (literally the case when Margaret Thatcher entered the all-male Carlton Club in 1975) and bullying men at that. The result is that the impact of women's involvement with the British Conservative Party remains unclear, which is an important deficiency in our understanding not just of Conservatism but also of women's political activity in Britain more generally.

In recent years while the number of Conservative women in the House of Commons increased to 21%, the number of Conservative women at the grassroots level has been in sharp decline. The latest findings show that only five per cent of rank and file Tories are aged 18–24 and as many as 85% of those young adults Tories are male rather than female.[6] The decline in the female vote began under Margaret Thatcher's premiership. It is also under the first woman's premiership that the Conservative Women's National Advisory Committee (WNAC) campaigned for the first time against its own party to protect child benefit from Patrick Jenkin and Geoffrey Howe's 1980 budget cuts.[7]

Similarly, it is important to note here that in the 1970s, the Women's Liberation Movement was not affiliated to any political party in Britain. It is Margaret Thatcher's free market policies, monetarism in particular, along with cutbacks in social services that convinced many feminists to affiliate to the Labour Party. That the women's liberation feminists were persuaded to embrace the Labour party as a result of the success of the first female leader of the Conservative party was most ironic of course.[8]

It took the 1997 election defeat and the decline of female support for the Party in the 1990s for almost the first time in the twentieth century to result in a questioning of the Conservative Party's relationship with women. Historians were forced to look back to earlier, more successful periods to assess the importance of the women's vote but also to recognise that the link between conservatism and women wasn't necessarily a direct one. It had the effect of generating a greater scholarly engagement with the nature of Conservatism and it resulted in the recognition of the complexity of the Conservative party's electoral constituency.[9] While David Cameron's 'modernising' of the Conservative Party and Anne Jenkin's Women2Win organisation seem to have been successful in getting some women back into the party in 2015, the evidence shows that the politics of austerity under Theresa May have led to a severe drop in female voters.

What this special issue aims to do is to show the pivotal importance of female support for the Conservative Party and recognise that the Party was at times, such as in the inter-war period, successful at constructing political identities that appealed to women while at other times, less so. It also examines how the rise of market liberalism under Thatcher altered the gendered character of the traditional economic discourse of the Conservative Party and affected its female voters. This can only be done by historicising the party's relationship with women at the level both of practice and ideology. This leads us to the central question of the type of feminism Conservative women see themselves as espousing. In the words of Anne Milton, are they 'born-again feminists'?[10]

Feminist journalist and writer Beatrix Campbell—in a dialogue with Julie Gottlieb and to mark the thirtieth anniversary since the publication of her agenda-setting and ground-breaking study *Iron Ladies. Why Do Women Vote Tory?*,—aims to answer this question by reconsidering how Tory women's history has evolved since the 1980s, and especially how Thatcher's death and Theresa May's Premiership demand reconceptualization.

Moving back in time to the controversial decision by the Conservative government to support equal franchise, Mari Takayanagi then examines the role of Conservative women in the campaigns by women inside and outside Parliament between 1919 and 1928. She evaluates the role of female MPs including Astor and the Duchess of Atholl, considers the level of engagement by the Conservative Women's Advisory Committee and other Conservative women's organisations with this issue, and compares this to the role played by more overtly feminist pressure groups including the Equal Rights Political Campaign Committee.

Shifting from the general to the particular, Madge Dresser assesses the political significance of Bristol's first woman M.P., Lady Apsley (1895–1966) who held office between 1943–1945, and addresses the issue of her pre-war admiration for Hitler and the apparent contradiction between her explicit championing of patriarchal values and her advocacy of wider opportunities for women.

Sam Blaxland explores the role of women in the Welsh Conservative party from 1945 to 1979 and argues that, beneath the strong impression of a political culture still shaped by traditional gendered stereotypes, can be found a body of organisers 'exercising a considerable degree of organisational and social leadership ... demonstrate[ing] both agency and power'.

The period after the Second World War sees the more vocal emergence of proponents of the free-market. Stéphane Porion's article examines the career of Diana Spearman, a founding member of the Mont-Pèlerin Society in 1947, and an intriguing figure in Conservative politics in the period from 1945 to 1975, especially in the promotion of free-market ideology within Conservatism and the development of groups and think-tanks supporting this.

Margaret Thatcher and Mary Whitehouse have been described by Beatrix Campbell as 'populist heroines of the right', and an affinity between the two women was widely assumed throughout Thatcher's leadership. They were both suburban mothers with prominent handbags, calling for a return to the stabilising values of 'simpler times'. Their relationship, however, was far from straightforward. By examining this relationship alongside its public presentation, Jessica Prestidge considers their shared cultural resonances and enhances understanding of the late twentieth-century cultural and political contexts within which they operated.

Ben Jackson then investigates the gendered character of the economic discourse of the New Right in the Conservative Party in the 1970s and 1980s. He explores the largely sceptical response to feminist economic arguments made by key intellectuals and think tanks associated with the Conservatives in this period, and examines some of the ways in which ideas about gender nonetheless shaped Conservative economic ideas in this period, focusing on the New Right's use of economic justifications for traditional family structures and a gendered labour market (drawing on certain strands of Chicago economics) and on the centrality of consumption (often presented in highly gendered terms) to the vision of capitalism advanced by Thatcherites. The role of gender within the rise of the New Right in British Conservatism during this period exposes tensions between radically libertarian and more socially conservative versions of neo-liberalism; tensions which have still not been fully resolved by today's Conservative Party.

Following up on Ben Jackson's article, David Swift explores why, in the period between 1979 and 2005, Conservative women consistently denied that they were 'feminists' while at the same time supporting policies that could be understood as feminist. He suggests that after 2005 this position was reversed. This change occurred he argues because neo-liberal versions of feminism, which suited the Conservative Party's political and economic agenda became a more common element in public discourse.

Needless to say, against the backdrop of Theresa May's Premiership and coinciding with a period of reflection, nostalgia and renewed activism generated by the centenary of women's (partial) enfranchisement, this just the time to consider Conservative women reconsider the terms of debate.

Notes

1. Julie V. Gottlieb, blog on '"Shy Women Tories" in the History of Suffrage and Beyond', Vote100, 12 March 2018.
2. Margaret Thatcher, 'Speech celebrating 50th anniversary of equal female suffrage ("A Right to Vote"),' Margaret Thatcher foundation, July 3, 1978.
3. https://conservativewomen.uk/content/history
4. Anushka Asthana, 'Harriet Harman hails the rise of "Tory feminist" MPs', *The Guardian*, March 6, 2018.
5. Ken Clarke was caught on camera on Sky News on 5 July 2016 describing Theresa May as a 'bloody difficult woman' and comparing her to Margaret Thatcher who was so 'bloody difficult' that she earned the label of 'Iron Lady'. It was immediately turned into a compliment with many women describing themselves as 'BDW'. Damian Gayle, 'Britain needs "bloody difficult women" says Theresa May', *The Guardian*, July 9, 2016.
6. Tim Bale, Monica Poletti, and Paul Webb, 'Where have all the women goneThe Tories have a serious gender problem', *The Conservation*, March 15, 2018.
7. Report on the Working Party on Maternity Benefit, 1980 and Family Budget Proposals submitted to Geoffrey Howe for 1983 Budget, 1983, CC0 170/5/51.
8. Laura Beers, 'Feminist Responses to Thatcher and Thatcherism', in *Rethinking Right-Wing Women, Gender, Women and the Conservative Party, 1880 to the present*, ed. Berthezène and Gottlieb (Manchester University Press, 2017).
9. David Jarvis, G. E. Maguire, etc
10. Speech by Anne Milton MP, "Historical Perspectives on Tory Women," House of Lords, Westminster, March 5, 2018.

Disclosure statement

No potential conflict of interest was reported by the authors.

'Does the right hon. Gentleman mean equal votes at 21?' Conservative women and equal franchise, 1919–1928

Mari Takayanagi [iD]

ABSTRACT

This paper examines the role of Conservative women in the controversial decision by Stanley Baldwin's Conservative government to support equal franchise, placing it in the context of campaigns by Conservative women inside and outside Parliament between 1919 and 1928. It evaluates the role of female MPs including Nancy Astor and the Duchess of Atholl, Caroline Bridgeman and the Women's Unionist Organisation, pressure groups and local organisations. It gives an account of the issues debated, including whether the franchise should be equalised at age twenty-five or twenty-one. It sheds light not only on the subject of equal franchise, but also on the relationship between Conservative women and their party in this period.

Introduction: Conservative women and equal franchise

In 1918, the Representation of the People Act gave the Parliamentary franchise to virtually all men and to women over the age of 30 who met (or whose husbands met) the property qualification for the local government franchise. Ten years later, following a raft of unsuccessful attempts to achieve equal franchise via private members' bills, Stanley Baldwin's Conservative government finally passed the Equal Franchise Act 1928, which gave women the vote on the same terms as men.[1] The Equal Franchise Act was a milestone in equality legislation. Ray Strachey declared, 'With the passage of this Act the last glaring inequality in the legal position of women was abolished.'[2] Men and women now had the same qualifications to vote, based on residence, business premises, or being the husband or wife of a person with a business premise qualification. Women were also entitled to the university franchise if they had passed the examinations required, even if the university did not admit women to degrees.[3] The Act also equalised the local government franchise and other consequential issues.[4]

Historians of women's suffrage between 1918 and 1928 have tended to concentrate on the actions of non-party feminist groups.[5] There has also been work on the Conservative government's gradual acceptance of the need for equal franchise, despite press opposition to the 'flapper' vote.[6] Recent scholarship has examined the parliamentary process, placing equal franchise in the context of other legislation, including the Parliament (Qualification of Women) Act 1918, the Sex Disqualification (Removal) Act 1919, and the role played by the various private members' bills.[7] And there have been studies of Conservative women, and the Conservative party including their attitude to women, covering this period.[8] Mitzi Auchterionie's analysis of Conservative suffragists stops in 1914, however. Other relevant works such as Julia Bush's study of anti-suffragists, and Nicoletta Gullace's work on suffrage in the First World War, largely end with the passage of the Representation of the People Act 1918.[9] Studies of the early women MPs are also limited.[10]

An analysis of the role of Conservative women in relation to the specific issue of equal franchise, inside and outside Parliament, is lacking. This despite the crucial political and symbolic significance of the 1928 Act, which moved the female electorate from an apparently conservative-leaning group bound by age and property restrictions, to the unfettered femininity of all women, everywhere. The decision by the Conservative government to support equal franchise in 1927 was made in the absence of an official election manifesto commitment, amidst press hysteria about the 'flapper' vote, and in the teeth of opposition from many Cabinet ministers including Winston Churchill, who feared it meant the end of the Conservative party.[11] It hinged on the personal election pledge of Prime Minister Stanley Baldwin to Dame Caroline Bridgeman, Chair of the Women's Unionist Organisation in 1924; and a commitment made by the Home Secretary William Joynson-Hicks during an exchange with Nancy Astor in the House of Commons in 1925.

This paper will explore the role played by Conservative women in the path to equal franchise. It will consider in particular the contrasting positions of Astor and the Duchess of Atholl; the Women's Unionist Organisation; the role of Caroline Bridgeman; and follow Parliamentary progress towards the 1928 Act from 1925 onwards.

Astor in Parliament, 1920–1923

Of the 12 women elected to Parliament before 1929, one third were Conservatives.[12] These four were Nancy, Viscountess Astor, the first woman to take her seat in Parliament, MP for Plymouth Sutton 1919–1945; Mabel Philipson, MP for Berwick-upon-Tweed 1923–1929; Katharine, Duchess of Atholl, MP for Perth and Kinross 1923–1938; and Gwendolen, Countess of Iveagh, MP for Southend-upon-Sea 1927–1935. All four were elected for seats previously held by their husbands, although Atholl did not directly 'inherit' hers and in fact won it from a sitting Liberal MP.[13]

Of the four, only Astor was whole-heartedly in favour of equal franchise throughout the period up to 1928. In all the various debates and divisions on private members' bills on equal franchise between 1920 and 1928, Astor was consistently present, speaking and voting in favour every time, regardless of which party the bill had come from. This is particularly apparent in the early period up until 1923, when she was very much on her own as a Conservative woman in Parliament. As an American divorcee, a Christian Scientist, and a passionate advocate of temperance, Astor was also a very unusual Conservative woman, less inclined to toe the party line. She had no record of supporting women's suffrage before her election to Parliament, but once she was elected she found women wrote to her from all over the country, seeing her as 'their' MP, and unfailingly supported causes affecting women, children and equality throughout her long Parliamentary career.

The first occasion she supported equal franchise was during the debate on Labour MP Thomas Grundy's private member's bill on 27 February 1920.[14] It took place during the period of Conservative-dominated coalition government led by Liberal Prime Minister David Lloyd George, just a few days after Astor's maiden speech. She had not intended to speak, but she did:

> I only wish hon. Members could see the letters I have received since my maiden speech. It would be an eye-opener. There were thousands of them, and they were on a high level, and of such hope, both spiritual and material ... I would like to tell them that there is no reason to fear us. We are reasonable and we are not fanatics, and the people that fear us I cannot understand where they get it from. Fear never won anything.[15]

The Times recorded, 'she must have been glad that the House took her speech not as a curiosity but on its merits ... there was wit and some shrewd observation.'[16] *The Vote* was enthusiastic:

> All right-minded women will feel grateful to their spirited and fearless champion who, in these early days of her political experience, while still, in a sense, on trial in the House, sprang to her feet because she felt that she must.[17]

In the following division, the government allowed a free vote,[18] although they would have preferred it to be talked out.[19] Astor went into the lobby with Grundy, even at this early date not afraid to support a Labour MP's bill—a bold action for such a new Member. The bill was subsequently killed by hostile MPs in Standing Committee using wrecking amendments; Astor referred to this as, 'A most unnatural death!'[20]

The next opportunity came on a bill brought by a fellow independent-minded Conservative, Lord Robert Cecil, on 8 March 1922. As Cecil explained in the House:

> I have ventured to ... introduce the Bill under what is called the Ten Minutes Rule in order to give the House an opportunity of expressing in the Division Lobby who are for and who are against this proposal, and I have done so for this reason, that the Government has expressed great reluctance to put forward this reform.[21]

Cecil was a long-standing supporter of women's suffrage, and other women's equality issues.[22] Astor was not able to make a speech, as the Ten Minute Rule procedure only allows for one speech for and one against, but she still played a part by heckling Cecil's opponent Lieutenant-Colonel Archer-Shee, making four interjections in the space of the twenty minute debate. In the division the motion for the bill was passed by 208 votes to 60, with Astor voting in favour.[23] A year later, during Baldwin's Conservative administration, Astor was one of a cross-party group of named supporters of another Ten Minute Rule bill in April 1923, on which there was no division.[24] Astor was still the only Conservative woman MP at this point, before Mabel Philipson was elected in a by-election the following month.

Astor versus Atholl: Conservative women MPs, 1924

At the general election in December 1923 eight women were elected, including Astor, Philipson and the Duchess of Atholl. In the wake of the results, Astor described her previous five lonely years:

> I have tried for five years to get the Conservative Party right about the position of women. I have never been to a Conference where I have not been treated more like a poor relation than the only Unionist woman MP. I don't mind one scrap for myself, but I do care desperately for

social reform ... you cannot conceive how many women there are who have been Unionists all their lives, but are absolutely up against the Party ... [25]

Lady Frances Balfour wrote to Astor at this time, reflecting on the relative positions of the Conservative, Liberal and Labour parties in relation to women's suffrage:

> The whole women's question has been in the hands of Liberals, later Labour, since 1868 ... I admit a new generation has now come on who don't remember, but engraved on the heart of the older women, are the scars of that long fight. I cannot think of any Tory, save one, that was Lord Shaftesbury. Otherwise of John S. Mill to that great little woman still with us, Mrs Fawcett, they were all Liberals. And today it is the Tories who are abusing the women and their vote ... [26]

A Labour minority government led by Ramsay MacDonald was formed in January 1924. The equal franchise debate this session took place on Labour backbench MP William Murdoch Adamson's private member's bill in February 1924.[27] With Labour in power, and support for equal franchise declared by many individual Conservatives at the general election,[28] Adamson's bill came the closest to achieving equal franchise since 1919. For the first time there were female Labour MPs, two of whom (Susan Lawrence and Dorothy Jewson) acted as supporters of Adamson's bill, and Jewson used her maiden speech to second the bill. Adamson began his speech at second reading:

> The Press has named this Bill a Leap Year proposal, owing I suppose to the fact that it is being introduced on this, the 29th day of February. I rather think, however, that if it had been a Leap Year proposal, probably one of the lady Members of the House would have been in the fortunate position of putting it forward.[29]

This debate is significant in revealing fully for the first time in Parliament the differences of opinion between Conservative women MPs on this issue. Astor spoke in favour, arguing that support for equal franchise was consistent with Conservatism:

> It is a principle to which we are all pledged ... Some of the greatest champions of women's suffrage in the country have been members of the Conservative party. Social reformers in the Unionist party have always had a difficult time, but they have always won in the end, and we are very hopeful that sooner or later we shall either get rid of the others or convert them. We are not asking for any revolution.[30]

However, opposition came from the Duchess of Atholl, who moved a delaying amendment, asking for a conference to be held on the issue. Astor said of Atholl, 'she is like Canute, trying to keep the waves back.'[31] Atholl's action is well known to historians, but usually presented very simply as a vote against the principle of equal franchise.[32] Undoubtedly Atholl was anti-suffrage before 1918, and anti-feminist in this period, with little sympathy for women's organisations.[33] However examination of her speech shows a more nuanced position on equal franchise. She declared:

> This Bill is not merely, or even mainly, a Bill for equal suffrage for women ... this Bill proposes to deal, and deal drastically and radically, with the whole electoral basis upon which the Government of this I country rests, both national and local.[34]

She drew attention to certain aspects of Adamson's Bill including the abolition of the business franchise, changes to residence requirements which would give the vote to 'tinkers', and changes to the local government franchise which would give the vote to non-ratepayers. Her opposition was standard Conservative party policy, as such changes would benefit the Labour party. On women, she queried whether women really wanted equal franchise, and was sceptical about women's contribution to public life, citing low numbers in local government.[35] But she was also at pains to point out that she recognised some legitimate grievances (women over 30 without the vote, university women voters under 30, and new widows over the age of 30 removed from the registers when their husbands died), concluding:

> As I have said, I recognise there are many women who have grievances under the present system, and it is on that account that my Amendment does not take the form of asking for the rejection of the Bill.[36]

Her amendment asked for a conference, as before the 1918 Act. Although Atholl was clearly not in favour of equality as advocated by Astor, it should be recognised that her stance in this Parliamentary debate was not simply opposition to equal franchise as such, but comprised a complex range of arguments against a wide-ranging bill. Indeed, had her speech been given by a male politician, it would probably be seen simply as expressing the standard party political position of the average Conservative MP of the period. William W J Knox has argued that Atholl's attempts at improving the position of women and children generally are consistent with a paternal Conservative elitist and imperialist viewpoint,[37] and her take on equal franchise in this debate would support this.

Atholl's amendment was defeated on a division, 288 votes to 72. This was the first occasion that women MPs acted as tellers at the vote (Atholl against the bill and Jewson for). Mabel Philipson, who did not speak in the debates, followed the party line and voted with Atholl against the bill.[38] Astor, of course, voted for the bill, which moved on to pass committee stage over the summer (thanks to much work by Susan Lawrence) and was subsequently adopted by the Labour Government. However the Government fell in October 1924 before the Bill was able to progress any further.[39]

The Women's Unionist Organisation

One result of the progress of the 1924 Bill was that equal franchise was discussed for the first time in the pages of the Conservative women's journal *Home and Politics*, in the report of the 6th Annual Conference of Women Unionists held in London in June 1924.[40] The discussion was 'extremely lively', with a wide range of opinions expressed that give a real insight into the range of opinions of Conservative women across the country for the first time. At one extreme, Miss Lane Poole (Oxford University) argued that that a man was fundamentally politically minded while a woman was not, and swamping the men electors by two million women's votes would not give equality, but injustice—an argument more extreme than Atholl's speech in Parliament.[41] Supporting Astor's position, Dame Helen Gwynne-Vaughan 'spoke vigorously in defence of the girl between 21 and 30', and Mrs Finney (Epsom) urged that factory and shop girls, and other working girls presently unrepresented, should be given the vote.[42] In between, Mrs Clare (St. Helen's), the wife of a Trade Union official, said the government would be better occupied in removing glaring inconsistencies and giving the vote to women of 30 on fairer terms, and Mrs Gower (Pontypool) declared, 'Let them remove all the restrictions on women voters of 30 first'[43]—both opinions which had been expressed by Atholl.

These differing positions show the wide range of views held by Conservatives about femininity and younger women in particular; general support for disenfranchised women voters over 30, but much caution over younger ones. Younger women were seen to be more ignorant and gullible, needing education and life experience to enable them to vote. This was exemplified in *Home and Politics* fictional character 'Betty', the young maid who has never heard of socialism, who has to be educated by 'Mrs Maggs', the respectable middle-aged charlady. As David Jarvis discusses, 'Conservative woman's duty lay in saving Betty from herself and in dispelling her often dangerous illusions,'[44] and this epitomised the broader Conservative perception that young women needed political education. Connected to this was the concern that equal franchise would mean women outnumbering men as electors, following the loss of men in the War—the 1918 Act carefully avoided having a majority of women in any constituency.[45] Astor was not quite alone in her views, but she faced a wide divergence of opinion among her fellow Conservative women, and a lack of support at local party branch level outside Plymouth Sutton. A list in Astor's papers of 83 societies who signed an equal franchise memorial in 1924 includes local branches of Girl Guides, Women's Citizen Associations, Equal Citizenship societies, Women's Co-operative Guilds, six Labour party branches and four Liberal party branches—but no Conservative societies.[46]

Early papers of the national Women's Unionist Organisation (WUO) are lacking from the Conservative Party archives, with no surviving minutes until 1935, but its history has been traced by various historians.[47] Its origins go back to the Women's Unionist Tariff Reform Association (WUTRA), which had support from both sides of the suffrage divide before 1914.[48] David Thackeray has shown how WUTRA's war work helped combat divisive class politics and pacifist propaganda, via civic organisations such as infant welfare centres, girls clubs, soldiers wives clubs, Women's Institutes and the Land Army all helping expand the appeal of Unionist politics.[49] WUTRA effectively became the WUO in 1918, set up 13 regional divisions. and continued to appeal to the housewife and consumer. Chaired successively by Viscountess Bridgeman and Lady Elveden, the WUO claimed to have nearly one million members by 1928.[50] Within the overall National Union, women were represented from 1926 by the Central Women's Advisory Committee, with increased co-operation and clearer demarcation of responsibilities.

Despite an initial 'frosty relationship'[51] with the men's constituency organisations, from 1928 the WUO was brought into the main Conservative party organisation and Marjorie Maxse, the head of the women's department in Central Office, became Deputy Principal Agent. This appointment was seen by Party chair Viscount Bridgeman as a direct reaction to the increased number of women voters; 'I appointed Miss Marjorie Maxse with much wider responsibilities as Deputy Chief Agent to make it quite clear to the Party that the women were to play a very important part in the development of Conservatism in the country.'[52] Maxse had previously been made an area agent in 1921, WUO administrator in 1923, and between 1931 and 1939 she was chief organisation officer, the first woman to occupy such a role in any party.[53] This was a complete turnaround from the situation in 1918, when G. W. Daw wrote in the *Conservative Agents' Journal*, 'There may be a tendency on the part of some Associations to try women as organisers of women. There are doubtless capable women organisers, but to place a woman in authority over her own sex would be courting disaster.'[54] Clearly women voters and women MPs had made a difference to such attitudes; one of Nancy Astor's election agents in 1919 was a woman.[55]

The WUO campaigned on a variety of issues affecting women and children in the early 1920s, including the 1922 Criminal Law Amendment Act on prison for statutory rape, the 1923 Matrimonial Causes Act giving women same right to divorce as men, and the Bastardy Act 1923 on the liability of absent fathers.[56] David Thackeray has written, 'Under the new leadership of Caroline Bridgeman, in 1918 WUTRA welcomed the enfranchisement of women.'[57] However there is no evidence at all after 1918 that the WUO subsequently took any position on equal franchise until 1926.

This possibly reflects interest in the equal franchise issue at local party level. An examination of surviving papers of area Conservative women's organisations in this period, which are very patchy, finds virtually no discussion at all before 1926. These area councils and committees were made up mainly of wives of MPs, peers and local Parliamentary candidates, with some meetings of local organisers, and discussion at all meetings mostly circulates around organisation and fundraising.[58] This fits in with Maguire's observation that women's role and work as members of the Conservative party did not differ significantly from the days of the Primrose League; organising fundraising events, canvassing, and propaganda.[59] Policy was discussed at area conferences, where issues such as seditious teaching in Sunday schools, imperial preference and old age pensions appear, but nothing on equal franchise.[60] There was one resolution on the franchise; in 1924 the Eastern Area Women's Parliamentary Committee conference included a resolution calling on the government to introduce legislation to enable women at the age of 30 to be replaced on the register of Parliamentary voters on the same conditions as men at 21.[61] Although not equal franchise as such, it does echo Atholl's concern in Parliament for the plight of certain disenfranchised women over 30 years old. Meanwhile the *Conservative Agents' Journal* was mainly concerned with topics such as registration of women entitled to the business vote, and circumstances where women lodgers could vote. Issues seen of interest to women included sex equality, but only as part of a long list ('Prohibition campaigns, home welfare, equal opportunities for women in the labour market, sex equality, free school meals for children, permanent communal kitchens, free maternity nursing homes for mothers)'[62] and not the franchise specifically.

The role of Caroline Bridgeman

However the WUO was important to equal franchise in a different way; it was used by successive Conservative leaders, Andrew Bonar Law and Stanley Baldwin, to set out their own long-standing support of equal franchise to Conservative women and women voters generally. This can be seen as part of a long tradition of Conservative leaders supporting women's suffrage against the majority of their party members, from Disraeli onwards.[63] Bonar Law and Baldwin made their positions known via letters to the WUO Chairman, Caroline Bridgeman. Caroline Bridgeman, wife of William Clive Bridgeman (1st Viscount Bridgeman), formed one of first local Conservative women's associations in Owestry in 1904, prior to her husband being elected MP there in 1906. She was leader of the WUTRA and oversaw its transformation into the WUO, which she chaired thereafter. She was admired within the party as an eloquent speaker and a good committee woman.[64]

In 1922, a Conservative election leaflet titled 'Women Should Vote' was published, taking the form of a letter from Bonar Law to Bridgeman:

> You have asked me for an Election Message to women electors and I gladly comply with your request ... I have been a consistent supporter of women's suffrage because I have always believed that women would exercise their votes as citizens looking at the great national questions broadly and fairly. It is in this spirit as full and equal citizens that I ask every woman elector to give her vote on polling day.[65]

Despite its first sentence, it was not actually requested by Bridgeman at all, but a draft sent to her at the last minute. It came with a covering note from Malcolm Fraser of Conservative Central Office, dated 8 November 1922:

> I thought it was essential to get some letter specially for women from Mr Bonar Law. I hope you will forgive me taking your name in vain like this, but I am having this letter used as a leaflet and also sent out to the press.[66]

Bridgeman apparently did not mind; the letter was published without any changes from the draft. This letter did not explicitly mention equal franchise, perhaps an indication that Bonar Law did not think Conservative women believed it to be an important issue. However, altering his message for a different audience, he wrote in another much-publicised letter sent at the same time to the non-party feminist organisation, the National Union of Societies for Equal Citizenship, that 'the discrimination in age between men and women could not be permanent.'[67]

Two years later, Bridgeman again became the recipient of a public letter from the Conservative party leader, but this time it specifically referenced equal franchise. As in 1922, the message was officially sanctioned by the party. Pembroke Wicks from Conservative Central Office wrote to her on 20 October 1924, 'I enclose a draft of the letter which it is proposed that Baldwin should write to you as his message to the Women of Great Britain for the Election. It has been approved by the Principal Agent.'[68] Bridgeman made a few scribbled suggestions on the draft sent to her, but made no changes to the crucial section on equal franchise, where Baldwin declared:

> The Conservative and Unionist Party are in favour of equal political rights for men and women, and desire that the question of an extension of the franchise should be settled by a Conference of all the political parties.

How far did Bridgeman agreed with this pledge? She did not make any pronouncement herself on equal franchise, and it is difficult to discern her attitude. Certainly there was no love lost between her and Astor. She refused to send a message of support to Astor in the 1922 and 1923 election campaigns, leading Lord Astor to write indignantly in 1923 to ask the Prime Minister if it was because of her policy on temperance, 'Or is it that the Women's Unionist Headquarters refuses to support women Conservative candidates because they are women?' Bridgeman wrote back via Baldwin, outlining her position:

> As Chairman of the Women's Unionist Association I refused to send her a message of support last year because I did not consider it to be within my province to send Coupons to candidates—I have refused on the same grounds this year ... I also refused to send her a message in my private capacity as I knew that her views and William's on the drink question did not coincide, and Lord Astor seems to be confusing my answers.[69]

In 1927 after the Cabinet had finally agreed to equal franchise, her husband William wrote that, 'it was the only honourable course after so many foolish pledges had been given.'[70] His wife had had the chance to amend Baldwin's 'foolish' pledge back in 1924, but apparently chose not to.

Caroline Bridgeman gave up the post of Chairman of the WUO when her husband became First Lord of the Admiralty in November 1924, citing pressure of her duties and that it was a good moment for change after the Conservative general election victory, An article in *Home and Politics* declared, 'We owe our very existence to her'.[71] She continued to be a member of the Executive Committee and Vice Chairman of the National Union, and in May 1926 she was elected chair of the central council of the National Union, the first woman to hold such a position in any party. Duncan Sutherland describes that she sought a greater role for women in policy making and in 1927 introduced the requirement that at least one of the four party conference delegates from each constituency was a woman, ensuring a high proportion of women at future party conferences.[72] A woman who regarded herself as her 'husband's adjutant',[73] she retired from politics with him in 1929.

Equal franchise at age 25? Astor changes the discussion, 1925

Following the general election of October 1924, a Conservative government led by Stanley Baldwin took power, and the Duchess of Atholl was made a junior minister.[74] To Astor's dismay, her good friend Margaret Wintringham lost her seat, as did all the former female Labour MPs. Maude Royden exclaimed:

> Great joy to have you back in Parliament, but what losses we have sustained. Mrs Wintringham is the worst of all. And Mrs Philipson survives! Great heavens![75]

The final Private Member's bill on equal franchise to be discussed in Parliament was on Labour MP William Whiteley's bill on 20 February 1925.[76] Although equal franchise had not been in the Conservative manifesto, so was not officially Conservative policy, the situation had been muddied by Baldwin's election pledge to Caroline Bridgeman, which was taken by some as proof that the Conservatives had made a commitment to equal franchise.[77]

At the second reading of Whiteley's bill, the Home Secretary, Sir William Joynson-Hicks (widely known as 'Jix'),[78] put down an amendment to postpone it until later in the Parliament, which would have effectively have killed the bill. During the debate, a crucial exchange took place between Jix and Astor. Jix quoted Baldwin's pledge, declared, 'I am not afraid of young women voters,' and predicted that the government would last until 1929, so there was plenty of time.[79] Joynson-Hicks then said there would be 'Equal votes for men and women', which led to the following exchange:

> Viscountess Astor: ' ... Does the right hon. Gentleman mean equal votes at 21?'
> Sir W Joynson-Hicks: 'It means exactly what it says.' [Hon Members: 'Answer!'] ' ... I will say quite definitely that means that no difference will take place in the ages at which men and women will go to the poll at the next election.'[80]

In a later unpublished autobiographical fragment Jix claimed that every action he took was with the assent of the Prime Minister and colleagues, but this was patently not true in the case of equal franchise and his Cabinet colleagues, and neither is there any evidence that his statement was the result of a pre-discussed plan with Baldwin.[81] Although it took several more years to play out, Astor's intervention and Jix's response to it effectively changed government policy. The fact that Jix's reply was made in the House of Commons, with Baldwin present, meant it came to be seen as a promise by the government to Parliament. Despite much incredulous hostility from other ministers and backbench Conservative MPs,[82] it is clear that when the Cabinet went on to reluctantly approve equal franchise two years later, it was Baldwin's pledge to Caroline Bridgeman and Jix's undertaking to Nancy Astor that swayed many of them. As described by Lord Birkenhead:

> We were nevertheless held to be precluded from voting according to our convictions by a pledge which our light-hearted colleague, the Home Secretary, had given on a Private Member's Bill on Friday, with the Prime Minister sitting beside him ... Against the strong protest of Winston, myself and others, it was decided that we were such honourable men that we could not possibly fall short of a pledge which was delivered without even the pretence of consulting the Cabinet.[83]

Joynson-Hicks's support for equal franchise has been portrayed as happening 'entirely by accident', an action untypical of such a 'stern late Victorian evangelical.'[84] However there is some evidence of sympathy for women's causes. In 1896 William Hicks had added his wife's name, Joynson, to his own on marriage to perpetuate his wife's family name. At his first election campaign in 1908 Constance Markievicz spoke for him as an advocate of the Barmaids Political Defence League (defending them against a Licensing bill), while the women's suffrage movement more generally:

> mobilised a large force of workers and speakers in the division in the interests of Joynson-Hicks, who was reported to have pledged himself to support the extension of the franchise on the same terms as it was granted to men.[85]

Appropriately perhaps given Churchill's continued opposition to equal franchise, Jix beat Winston Churchill in the 1908 election.

It is also perhaps appropriate that it was an intervention by Astor that forced Jix's hand in 1925; there was no love lost between the two of them. In April 1920 Jix found out she was using his corner seat in the House of Commons while he was away in India, and wrote to Lord Astor to complain. Lord Astor replied, stressing her difficulties as the only woman and, 'how extremely unpleasant it would be for my wife if she had to climb over people getting in to and out from an inside seat.' But Jix would not give up, writing to elder statesman Lord Edmund Talbot of her 'preposterous and dishonourable attempt to retain possession of my seat'. Astor had to give up the seat, and Lord Astor wrote stiffly, 'I would have been grateful and my wife would have been relieved had you seen your way to extend to her the same consideration and courtesy as other members.'[86]

The Duchess of Atholl was absent from the 1925 debate, neither speaking nor voting, but as a minister she would have supported the government position. However Mabel Philipson was present, and her opinion can be gleaned from a brief intervention to a speech by A. A. Somerville:[87]

Mr Somerville:	.... Some of us urged the point that the possession of the franchise is a great privilege and that in the exercise of that privilege you should have the best combination of vigour with a sense of responsibility and some experience of life. We consider that 25 is the best age -
Mrs Philipson:	Hear, hear![88]

Philipson was not alone in supporting the idea of equal franchise at the age of 25, rather than 21, which had been suggested in Parliament as far back as 1920.[89] However it grew in currency during the discussions on Adamson's bill in 1924, and was advocated by many Conservatives from 1925 onwards. Whiteley's bill was defeated by the government, the division lost 153 to 220. The only surprise was perhaps that the government vote was not larger given their 419 MPs; as it was, ten Conservatives, including Astor, went into the lobby against them.[90]

The Conservative Women's Reform Association

Astor's vote on Whiteley's bill was a direct party rebellion, and it is clear from letters she sent afterwards to the Chairman and Secretary of the Conservative Women's Reform Association, Lady Trustram Eve and Brenda Bucknill, that it was a big decision for her:

> I felt bound, after some hesitation, to vote against the Government's amendment, which I felt to be an evasion of the undertaking that had been given at the election. I often feel under a great disability when I have to stand up to the party leaders, because on many issues I can produce so little evidence that other women of our party feel as I do ... .[91]

Astor clearly hoped that of all Conservative women, it was the Conservative Women's Reform Association, of which she was a vice-president, who might feel as she did. She asked them to write to the Prime Minister.

The Conservative Women's Reform Association was the successor to the Conservative and Unionist Women's Franchise Association, but campaigned on other reform issues after 1918. It held lectures, drawing room discussions and canvassing classes; passed resolutions, and worked with other organisations including the National Council of Women to lobby the Government. A study of its newsletter *Monthly News* shows its main priorities to be international issues such as Ireland, Empire, and combating Bolshevism and fascism in Europe; and domestic issues such as housing, trade, labour and unemployment. It also supported the election of female councillors and MPs, and many of the equality issues championed by non-party feminist organisations in this period such as widows' pensions, equal pay and equal guardianship. Equal franchise is rarely mentioned however, and furthermore, issues specific to women are not their priority.[92] In July 1921 they reported on progress of bills on overseas trade and safeguarding industries, and made a point of saying these were far more important than lost bills on plumage and marriage to a deceased wife's sister:

> We must learn above all to see things in their right proportion and not let the incidence of our sex recoil upon itself. We should aim at becoming more conscious of our citizenship than our womanhood.[93]

Bucknill and Eve's replies to Astor show how alone Astor really was on equal franchise. Bucknill wrote, 'I am fully in agreement with you', however the Association did not wish to press the issue, so she could not write as their representative, as much as she would like to. Eve replied sympathetically, opining, 'personally I do not see what you could have done except to vote against', but her subsequent letter to Baldwin was sent not as the chairman of the Association but as a private individual. Also, although Eve urged Baldwin not to evade the question of equal franchise, she added that she would prefer votes at 23 to 25 for all.[94]

Equal Franchise on the agenda, 1926–1928

Despite Astor's frustration, the terms of discussion had changed and equal franchise was finally fully on the political agenda. MPs bombarded the government with a steady stream of Parliamentary questions, and private members' bills continued to be introduced.[95] Outside Parliament, non-party feminist groups such as the National Union of Societies for Equal Citizenship, the Women's Freedom League and the Six Point Group rallied to campaign, forming the Equal Rights Political Campaign Committee and holding marches and mass demonstrations.[96] Although other newspapers supported equal franchise, the *Daily Mail* launched a campaign to 'Stop the Flapper Vote Folly', motivated by its proprietor Lord Rothermere fearing its possible effect on the Conservative party.[97]

Astor was fully in support of the non-party campaigns, although treading a careful line between lobbying for the cause and declaring her faith that Baldwin would deliver:

> As a Conservative I cannot claim to represent all elements of my party, but I do for the progressive elements. The Prime Minister is a man of his word, I have no doubt that he means to fulfil his pledge and tackle the suffrage question. Our ultimate victory is assured.[98]

She was clearly worried that pushing too hard would damage the cause. At the suggestion of Lady Rhondda that they raise a fund to bring Mrs Pankhurst back to the UK for the campaign, Astor's reaction was, 'please say No, does not agree. The government are certain to give equal suffrage without this!'[99] She was, however, very polite to Mrs Pankhurst when she duly arrived in London.[100] Emmeline Pankhurst was, by this date, a fellow Conservative woman: as June Purvis has explained, turning to the Conservatives in this period as the party who would uphold the constitution and Empire and oppose communism.[101] She was adopted as Conservative candidate for Whitechapel in 1927, but died before the next election, during the passage of the equal franchise bill in 1928.

In October 1926 a Cabinet Committee was formed to investigate the issue, and this brought a sea-change, as suddenly Conservative women were keen to discuss equal franchise, nationally and locally. On 19 November 1926, Viscountess Elveden, who had replaced Caroline Bridgeman as chair of the WUO (now the Women's Advisory Committee) wrote to tell the government that the Women's Advisory Committee had passed a resolution that unless a conference was set up (to discuss equal franchise), 'Great discontent will ensue among the women of the country with results prejudicial to the interests of the Party at the next General Election.'[102] The South East association general meeting in February 1927 included equal franchise as one of two subjects which they especially wanted the constituencies to consider, with the chair, Mrs Moore-Brabazon, declaring:

> The question of the franchise must be thoroughly gone into so the government's hand can be strengthened in dealing with the situation. It must not be forgotten that there are only two years before the next election to perfect our organisation.[103]

Much of the discussion among Conservative women (and men) was over the age 25 versus age 21 issue. McCrillis records that the WUO passed a resolution in favour of age 25, and there was a mix of reactions locally, with the Glasgow Unionist Association warning that 21 would be a disaster.[104] The Eastern Area women's association conference in February 1927 included resolutions that the franchise for women should be made same as men before the next general election, and that both men and women should have the vote at age 25.[105] Meanwhile, the non-party feminist organisations continued to campaign for age 21. A letter from Eleanor Rathbone to Eva Hubback shows the stress of the situation:

> … Lady Astor is worried because we are pressing for twenty-one; I reassured her it was only on the tactical point. I surmise that possibly the Government has switched to twenty-five … What shall we do about it? My idea is not to protest at the age, but make it perfectly clear that the one thing which concerns us in equal rights … I should get onto Rhondda at once if that happened and try to make her take the same line.[106]

Finally, following a decisive Cabinet meeting on 12 April 1927, the decision was announced in a statement by the Prime Minister in the House of Commons the following day. Baldwin declared that a bill would be introduced during next session for equal franchise at age 21.[107] There would be no cross-party conference, as there had been before the Representation of the People Act 1918 during the First World War.[108]

Pressure continued on the issue throughout the rest of 1927 and early 1928, both inside and outside the Conservative party. Astor continued to balance support for the public rallies with caution, warning at one point that they were in danger of implying the Prime Minister might be tempted to go back on his word: 'I am myself keeping very quiet on this question.'[109] However, now that the government had officially announced their support, the party swung behind. The National Union of Conservative and Unionist Associations passed a motion in October 1927, 'that in the opinion of this Conference the time has come to fulfil Ministerial pledges … there should be Equal Franchise before the next election.'[110] Even Atholl wrote that she would be glad to give her name in support of a mass meeting for equal franchise.[111]

In November 1927 the Conservatives got their fourth female MP, with the election of Gwendolen Guinness, previously Viscountess Elveden but now the Countess of Iveagh and also the Chair of the WUO between 1924 and 1933. Iveagh lent her name to the same equal franchise meeting as Atholl did, although it is clear she had personal doubts both about standing in Southend and also about equal franchise, as she wrote to Baldwin:

> 'I have given way about Southend—in the sure and certain hope that I shall regret it, as I know only too well what it all means … . I am getting more concerned than ever that posterity is going to condemn the vote ever having been given to women—but we can't put back the clock!'[112]

Unbeknownst to Iveagh, her election committee in Southend had asked via Conservative Central Office if Astor could send a supportive election message to Lady Iveagh, but Astor refused, replying, 'Of course it will be excellent to have another woman in the House, and I am delighted about it. But I don't quite see how, holding the views I do about temperance, I can come out and support her.'[113] As with Caroline Bridgeman, temperance was more important to Astor than having a good relationship with other Conservative women.

Passage of the Act

The Government finally introduced the Equal Franchise Bill in 1928, and its second reading took place on 29 March 1928, moved by the Home Secretary, Astor's old adversary, Sir William Joynson-Hicks. The debate went on for more than seven hours.[114] Women MPs from all parties were prominent in the debate, including Ellen Wilkinson and Margaret Bondfield.[115] Nancy Astor's speech included a passionate declaration on the significance of votes for women:

> I had the privilege of being the first woman in the House of Commons, and sometimes I used to doubt whether it was a privilege. When I stood up and asked questions affecting women and children, social and moral questions, I used to be shouted at for five or 10 minutes at a time. That was when they thought that I was rather a freak, a voice crying in the wilderness.[116]

Perhaps more surprisingly, Iveagh also spoke whole-heartedly in support of equal franchise:

> It has been my experience as one connected with the political organisation of women ever since the franchise was granted to them that women have a very great sense of duty and sense of responsibility in the exercise of the franchise, and this applies not less to those who neither asked for the vote nor desired it than to those who worked hard for it. Therefore, I would appeal very earnestly to the House and in particular to those who sit on this side of the House, not to let it be thought that this Measure was granted in any grudging or cavilling spirit by a House of Commons which is overwhelmingly composed of the other sex. This Measure is the outcome of logic and of justice.[117]

The *Morning Post* reported that Lady Iveagh had not contemplated joining in the debate, but was spurred on by the remarks of Brigadier-General Sir George Cockerill.[118] Cockerill had moved to deny the bill its second reading, and his arguments were reminiscent of pre-war attitudes. The main objection he voiced was that women would be put in a permanent majority in constituencies ('Hear hear!' said Astor) and he 'would prefer to see, quite frankly, men put in the supremacy.'[119] However there was no serious threat from Cockerill or anyone else; the bill passed overwhelmingly on division, with 387 Ayes and just 10 Noes. Amongst the Ayes, along with Astor and Iveagh, was Mabel Philipson. Atholl, however, was not present. After the division, 'Lady Astor waved an elated glove; the Women Members smiled at each other benignly.'[120]

Conclusion

Equal franchise was placed onto the Conservative party agenda following Baldwin's pledge in 1924, and then Jix's undertaking in 1925 (the latter extracted thanks to Astor's intervention in the House of Commons). From 1926 the issue came to be at more widely debated, and equal franchise at age 25 seemed a possible compromise for a while, before age 21 was eventually accepted, by the government and by the party, leading to the passage of the Act in 1928.

This analysis demonstrates that equal franchise was a concern for only a minority of Conservative women before 1926, after which it became a matter of mainstream discussion and debate. This is perhaps not too surprising given the political and economic situation after the First World War, with the major concerns even of the Conservative Women's Reform Association being international affairs, housing and industrial unrest. The successive quick general elections in 1922, 1923 and 1924 also played a part in prioritising defeating socialism at home, and Bolshevism abroad. However it is crucial to understand the role of Conservative women before 1926 in order to understand how equal franchise came to be adopted by the government. It was far from inevitable that equal franchise would be passed, given the extreme hostility from cabinet ministers such as

Churchill, and first Bonar Law and then Baldwin used Caroline Bridgeman and the WUO to express their public support for the issue. By 1926 Baldwin's government was sufficiently established for him to move the issue on, and the presence of female MPs (from all parties) in the House of Commons had begun to normalise the presence of women in politics.

The role of Nancy Astor as a constant thorn in the side of the party leadership from 1920 onwards was very important. She enjoyed a very high public profile both in the party and in the country at large. Her strong support for equal franchise as an MP, including cross-party support for Labour and Liberal legislative efforts, and extensive help for non-party feminist organisations campaigning, went a long way to ensuring equal franchise stayed on their agenda. There is a tendency to see Astor's position as the natural one, and Atholl's stance as 'increasingly preposterous'.[121] However the surprising thing is not that Atholl opposed equal franchise in Parliament in 1924; it is that Astor supported it from day one as an MP. Atholl never claimed to be a feminist and was not betraying anyone; she was merely representing the view of her political party, and of the vast majority of its women members at this date—including Mabel Philipson, and, in all likelihood, Caroline Bridgeman. Whereas Astor was supported by many non-party feminists, but by very few women in the Conservative party, not even the Conservative Women's Reform Association. Astor's natural allies in Parliament on equal franchise were Liberals, such as Margaret Wintringham, or Labour, such as Ellen Wilkinson; none of her fellow Conservative women MPs were supportive until after the government announced its support for the issue in 1927. By her own testimony, Astor was the freak, the voice in the wilderness of her party for years: the exception rather than the rule, and she deserves recognition for her principled stance.

Notes

1. For fuller details of what the 1918 Act did and how the 1928 Act came to pass, see: Mari Takayanagi, 'Women and the Vote: The Parliamentary Path to Equal Franchise', *Parliamentary History* 37, no. 1 (February 2018).
2. Ray Strachey, *"The Cause": A Short History of the Women's Movement in Great Britain* (London: Virago, 1928, reprinted 1978), 384.
3. By 1928 the only university not to admit women to degrees was Cambridge, where women had to wait until 1948. Oxford allowed women to take degrees following the Sex Disqualification (Removal) Act 1919.
4. Consequential issues included reducing the maximum scale of election expenses from seven pence to sixpence per voter, and compiling the electoral register in 1929 so as to bring the Act into force as soon as possible.
5. Cheryl Law, *Suffrage and Power: The Women's Movement, 1918–1928* (London: I B Tauris, 1997); Johanna Alberti, 'A Symbol and a Key: The Suffrage Movement in Britain, 1918–1928', in *Votes for Women*, eds. S.S. Holton and J. Purvis (New York: Routledge, 1999).
6. Martin Pugh, *Women and the Women's Movement in Britain, 1914–1999*, 2nd ed. (Basingstoke: Macmillan, 2000), 112–13. Adrian Bingham, '"Stop the Flapper Vote Folly": Lord Rothermere, the Daily Mail, and the Equalization of the Franchise 1927–28', *Twentieth Century British History* 13, no. 1 (2002): 17–37. David Close, 'The Collapse of Resistance to Democracy: Conservatives, Adult Suffrage and Second Chamber Reform, 1911–1928', *Historical Journal* 20, no. 4 (1977): 893–918. Melinda Alison Haunton, '*Conservatism and Society: Aspects of Government Policy 1924–1929*' (PhD, Royal Holloway University of London, 2002).

7. Takayanagi, 'Women and the Vote'; Mari Takayanagi,*Parliament and Women c1900-1945* (PhD, King's College London, 2012) available online via the King's Research Portal, https://kclpure.kcl.ac.uk/portal/. Also see: David Butler, *The Electoral System in Britain Since 1918* (Oxford: Clarendon Press, 1963), 15-38.

8. G.E. Maguire, *Conservative Women: A History of Women and the Conservative Party, 1874-1997* (Palgrave Macmillan, 1998); Stuart Ball, *Portrait of a Party: The Conservative Party in Britain 1918-1945* (Oxford: Oxford University Press, 2013); Neal McCrillis, *The British Conservative Party in the Age of Universal Suffrage* (Ohio State University Press, 1998); David Thackeray, 'Home and Politics: Women and Conservative Activism in Early Twentieth-Century Britain', *Journal of British Studies* 49, no. 4 (2010): 826-48; David Thackeray, *Conservatism for the Democratic Age: Conservative Cultures and the Challenge of Mass Politics in Early Twentieth Century England* (Manchester University Press, 2013); David Jarvis, 'Mrs. Maggs and Betty: The Conservative Appeal to Women Voters', *Twentieth Century British History* 5, no. 2 (1994): 129-52.

9. Mitzi Auchterlonie, *Conservative Suffragists: The Women's Vote and the Tory Party* (London & New York: IB Tauris, 2007); Julia Bush, *Women Against the Vote: Female Anti Suffragist in Britain* (Oxford University Press, 2006); Nicoletta F. Gullace, *The Blood of Our Sons: Men, Women and the Renegotiation of British Citizenship During the Great War* (Palgrave Macmillan, 2002).

10. Pamela Brookes, *Women at Westminster: An Account of Women in the British Parliament, 1918-1966* (Peter Davies, 1967); Elizabeth Vallance, *Women in the House* (Athlone Press, 1979); Brian Harrison, 'Women in a Men's House: The Women MPs 1919-1945', *Historical Journal* 29 (1986): 623-54. Astor still awaits her definitive biography; the most recent, Adrian Fort, *Nancy: The Story of Lady Astor* (Jonathan Cape, 2012), covers equal franchise in two very general paragraphs on pp. 182-183. There is no coverage of equal franchise in S.J. Hetherington, *Katharine Atholl, 1874-1960: Against the Tide* (Aberdeen University Press, 1989).

11. Martin Gilbert and Randolph S. Churchill, eds., *Winston S. Churchill, vol 5, Companion Pt 1, Documents - the Exchequer Years 1922-1929* (1979), memo by Churchill dated 8 March 1927, 963.

12. Apart from the four Conservatives, these were Constance Markievicz (Sinn Fein), who never took her seat in Parliament; Margaret Wintringham, Vera Terrington and Hilda Runciman (Liberal); Margaret Bondfield, Susan Lawrence, Dorothy Jewson and Ellen Wilkinson (Labour). The Liberal and Labour women were all nominally in favour of equal franchise, although Wintringham, Terrington and Jewson lost their seats before 1928 and Runciman was only elected on 6 March 1928, by which time the Equal Franchise Bill had already been introduced.

13. Kenneth Baxter, 'The Advent of a Woman Candidate was Seen … as Outrageous': Women, Party Politics and Elections in Interwar Scotland and England', *Journal of Scottish Historical Studies* 33, no. 2 (2013): 260-83.

14. Equal franchise was previously debated in Parliament in 1919 during the passage of the Women's Emancipation Bill and Sex Disqualification (Removal) Bill, when there were no women MPs to contribute. Thomas Grundy was a former coal miner: many Labour MPs from a coal mining background spoke in favour of equal franchise in this period. For more detail, Takayanagi, *Parliament and Women*, chapter 2.

15. HC Debates, 27 February 1920 vol 125 c2112, Viscountess Astor. Astor was introduced into the Commons on 1 December 1919. Her maiden speech on 24 February 1920 was on one of her pet topics, Liquor Traffic. HC Debates 24 February 1920 vol 125 cc1625-1631.

16. *The Times*, 28 February 1920.

17. *The Vote*, 5 March 1920. Parliamentary Archives, ST/50.

18. HC Debates 27 February 1920 vol 125 c2090, Minister for Health (Christopher Addison).

19. Robert Sanders, a government whip, recorded, 'It was a case of trying to talk the Bill out and I put in a 25-minute speech at very short notice.' John Ramsden, ed., *Real Old Tory Politics:*

The Political Diaries of Sir Robert Sanders, Lord Bayford, 1910-35 (London: Historian's Press, 1984). Entry for 29 February 1920, p. 136.

20. HC Debates 8 March 1922 vol 151, c1289. For more on the passage of this bill, Takayanagi, *Parliament and Women*.

21. Ibid, c1288, Cecil.

22. Cecil represented Gwyneth Bebb in the Court of Appeal in *Bebb v the Law Society* (1913), the unsuccessful test case for women to enter the legal profession: Rosemary Auchmuty, 'Whatever Happened to Miss Bebb? Bebb v The Law Society and Women's Legal History', *Legal Studies: The Journal of the Society of Legal Scholars* 31 (2011): 175–343.

23. The bill was introduced, but got no further. Ten Minute Rule bills are brought to gauge opinion, get publicity and generate debate rather than have any chance of becoming law.

24. Brought by Liberal MP Isaac Foot, HC Debates 25 April 1923 vol 163 c472. Foot stood against Astor in Plymouth Sutton during her by-election in 1919 and they became friends thereafter.

25. University of Reading Special Collections [UoR], Astor papers, MS1416/1/1/614. Astor to Sir John Baird, 14 December 1923.

26. UoR, Astor papers, MS1416/1/2/34. Lady Frances Balfour to Astor, 13 December 1923.

27. Not to be confused with William Adamson (1863–1936) who was Secretary of State for Scotland in this period, William Murdoch Adamson (1881–1945) was MP for Cannock. His wife Jennie became an MP in 1938.

28. Sanders recorded 'The matter is difficult because so many of our people have pledged themselves to the principle.' Ramsden, *Real Old Tory Politics*. Entry for 24 June 1924, p. 215.

29. HC Debates 29 February 1924 vol 170 c859, William M. Adamson.

30. Ibid, c938, Astor.

31. Ibid, c938, Astor.

32. For example Pugh, *Women and the Women's Movement*, 54: 'Mrs Hilton Philipson ... and the Duchess of Atholl ... voted against bills to grant women equal franchise'. Linda McDougall, *Westminster Women* (London: Vintage, 1998), 186: 'In the early years of her parliamentary career she consistently voted against "women's issue" proposals such as the 1924 attempt to lower the age at which women could vote to twenty-one.' Elizabeth Vallance, *Women in the House* (London: Athlone Press, 1979), 121: 'What became clear in this debate was that not only men but some women too were still opposed to the measure.'

33. Atholl's biographer says, 'Kitty would never become a feminist, but she was meeting, mixing and discussing problems on a friendly basis with women who were.' Hetherington, *Katharine Atholl*, 134.

34. HC Debates 29 February 1924 vol 170 c866, Duchess of Atholl.

35. There is no overall study of women in local government in the interwar period comparable to Patricia Hollis, *Ladies Elect: Women in English Local Government, 1865–1914* (Oxford, 1987). However Anne Baldwin's research indicates that Atholl was correct, that many local authorities outside London had a low representation of women. Anne Baldwin, *The Relationship Between Changing Party Politics and the Elected Representation of Women in Local Government, 1919–1939* (MA: University of Huddersfield, 2007).

36. Ibid, c873.

37. William W.J. Knox, *Lives of Scottish Women: Women and Scottish Society 1800–1980* (Edinburgh University Press, 2006), chapter 8: 'Katharine, Duchess of Atholl: The Red Duchess?'

38. See below for Philipson's only view on equal franchise expressed in Parliament, in 1925.

39. More detail in Takayanagi, *Parliament and Women*.

40. Bodleian Library, Conservative Party Archives [CPA], PUB 212/4, 'Home and Politics', 1924. Curiously there was another '6th annual conference' reported in 1925, symptomatic perhaps of unclear early origins of the Conservative women's organisation. CPA, PUB 212/5.

41. It has not been possible to definitely identify Miss Lane-Poole, but presumably she was related to historian Reginald Lane-Poole who was Keeper of the Archives at the University of Oxford at this time.

42. Helen Gwynne-Vaughan served as Controller of the Women's Auxiliary Army Corps and Commandant of the Women's Royal Air Force between 1917 and 1919. She stood as Conservative candidate in Camberwell North in the general elections of 1922, 1923 and 1924, losing by only 254 votes to sitting MP Charles Ammon in 1922.
43. Bodleian Library, CPA, PUB 212/4. 'Home and Politics', 1924.
44. Jarvis, 'Mrs Maggs', 140–42, 133.
45. *Parliamentary and Local Government Electors (United Kingdom)*, HC 138 (1918).
46. UoR, Astor papers, MS1416/1/1/261.
47. Maguire, *Conservative Women*; Thackeray, 'Home and Politics'; Thackeray, *Conservatism for the Democratic Age*; McCrillis, *The British Conservative party*.
48. Thackeray, *Conservatism for the Democratic Age*, 41.
49. Ibid., 110.
50. McCrillis, *The British Conservative Party*, 46.
51. Thackeray, 'Home and Politics', 845.
52. J.C.C. Davidson, *Memoirs of a Conservative: J. C. C. Davidson's Memoirs and Papers*, ed. Robert Rhodes James (Weidenfeld & Nicolson), 266–68.
53. Mark Pottle, 'Maxse, Dame (Sarah Algeria) Marjorie (1891–1975)', *Oxford Dictionary of National Biography* (Oxford University Press, 2004), http://www.oxforddnb.com/view/article/39182 (accessed August 10, 2017).
54. *Conservative Agents' Journal*, no 47, January 1918. Bodleian, CPA, PUB 2/4.
55. Mrs Bessie Le Cras. Parliamentary Archives, LCR.
56. McCrillis, *The British Conservative Party*, 73.
57. Thackeray, 'Home and Politics', 836.
58. Bodleian Library, CPA, ARE 3/11/9 (Lancashire and Cheshire), ARE 7/11/1 (Eastern area), ARE 5/25/1 (East Midlands), ARE 6/11/1 (West Midlands), ARE 9/11/1-2 (South Eastern), ARE 11/11/1-2 (South Western).
59. Maguire, *Conservative Women*, 78–79.
60. Bodleian Library, CPA, ARE 7/11/1 (Eastern area, Annual conference 6 March 1923); ARE 9/11/1 (South Eastern area Women's Parliamentary committee, meeting 13 May 1920); ARE 6/11/1 (West Midlands women's advisory council, 1928).
61. Bodleian Library, CPA. ARE 7/11/1. The Eastern Area included Beds, Bucks, Cambs, Herts, Hunts, Norfolk and Suffolk, and the resolution was proposed by Mrs Lathbury and Mrs Crawley from Luton Division.
62. *Conservative Agents' Journal*, no 47, January 1918. Bodleian, CPA, PUB 2/4.
63. For example, Disraeli declared shortly before John Stuart Mill presented the first mass women's suffrage petition in 1866, 'I have always been of opinion that if there is to be universal suffrage, women have as much right to vote as men.' HC Debates, 27 April 1866, vol 183, c99.
64. Duncan Sutherland, 'Bridgeman, Dame Caroline Beatrix, Viscountess Bridgeman (1873–1961)', *Oxford Dictionary of National Biography {ODNB}* (Oxford University Press, 2004), http://www.oxforddnb.com/view/article/39506 (accessed 28 February 2017).
65. Shropshire Archives, Bridgeman papers, 4929/1/1922/359.
66. Ibid., 4629/2/1922/1-2.
67. Bodleian Library, CPA, PUB 212/1. Letter from Andrew Bonar Law to NUSEC during the 1922 general election, published in *Home and Politics*, December 1922.
68. Shropshire Archives, Bridgeman papers, 4629/1/4/9.
69. Ibid., 4629/2/1923/10-13.
70. Stuart Ball, ed., *Conservative Politics in National and Imperial Crisis: Letters from Britain to the Viceroy of India 1926–1931* (Farnham: Ashgate, 2014). Bridgeman to Irwin, 4 May 1927, p. 138.
71. Shropshire Archives, Bridgeman Papers, 4629/1/4/9. Article from 'Home and Politics', January 1925.
72. Sutherland, *ODNB*, Caroline Bridgeman.
73. McCrillis, *The British Conservative Party*, 48.

74. Atholl became parliamentary secretary to the Board of Education. Eleanor Cecil (wife of Lord Robert Cecil) wrote to Astor, 'I wish you were in the government instead of the good Duchess, who leaves me quite cold. But I suppose one can't spill one's beer and drink it.' UoR, Astor papers, MS1416/1/2/35, Eleanor Cecil to Astor, 13 November 1924.
75. UoR, Astor papers, MS1416/1/2/35. Maude Royden to Astor, 31 October 1924.
76. William Whiteley was another former miner. His bill was supported by a solid slate of Labour MPs including Ellen Wilkinson, at this time the only Labour woman MP.
77. More in Takayanagi, *Women and the Vote*.
78. Jonathon Hopkins, *Paradoxes Personified: Sir William Joynson-Hicks, Viscount Brentford and the Conflict Between Change and Stability in British Society in the 1920s* (MPhil, University of Westminster, 1996); Huw Clayton, 'The Life and Career of Sir William Joynson-Hicks, 1865–1932: A Reassessment', *Journal of Historical Biography* 8 (2010): 1–38. H.A. Taylor, *Jix: Viscount Brentford* (London, Stanley Paul & co, 1933). 'Jix' was his nickname, widely used by his friends earlier in his political career, and also by the wider public and in the press in his later career, as he became more prominent in public life.
79. HC Debates, 20 February 1925, vol 180, c1503 and c1515. Joynson-Hicks. NUSEC feared that 'Delay was dangerous as no political prophet would venture to give even the safest of Governments the three years office necessitated.' LSE Women's Library Collections, 2NSE/C/8, NUSEC annual report 1925. However, Jix's prediction was accurate and there was indeed enough time.
80. HC Debates, cc1500–1503.
81. For more discussion on this, see Takayanagi, *Women and the Vote*.
82. For more reactions to Jix's undertaking see Takayanagi, *Women and the Vote*.
83. Ball, *Conservative Politics in National and Imperial Crisis*. Birkenhead to Irwin, 13 April 1927, p. 132.
84. F.M.L. Thompson, 'Hicks, William Joynson- , First Viscount Brentford (1865–1932)', Oxford Dictionary of National Biography, Oxford University Press, 2004; online edn, September 2010, http://www.oxforddnb.com/view/article/33858 (accessed August 10, 2017).
85. Taylor, *Jix*, 89.
86. Quoted in Hopkins, *Paradoxes*, 103. East Sussex Record Office, Archives of the Joynson-Hicks family, ACC 9851/3/2/8.
87. Annesley Ashworth Somerville was Conservative MP for Windsor 1922–1942.
88. HC Debates 20 February 1925 vol 180 c1532.
89. By Gideon Murray. HC Debates 27 February 1920 vol 125 c2978.
90. The ten rebel Conservatives included Astor, Lord Henry Cavendish-Bentick, Edmund Radford, Colonel H.W. Burton, Sir Robert Newman, Alfred R. Kennedy, A.C.N. Dixey and Lieutenant-Colonel V.L. Henderson. *The Times*, 21 February 1925.
91. UoR, Astor papers, MS1416/1/1/261 Astor letters to Lady Trustram Eve and Mrs Alfred Bucknill, 25 February 1925.
92. British Library, Conservative Women's Reform Association, *Monthly News*, 1919–1924.
93. Ibid, issue 5 July 1921.
94. UoR, Astor papers, MS1416/1/1/261. Bucknill to Astor, 3 March 1925. Eve to Astor, 4 March 1925; Eve to Baldwin, 4 March 1925. Lady Trustram Eve was Fanny Jane Turing. In this period she was chair of the Conservative Women's Reform Association, treasurer of the National Council of Women, and a London County Council councillor.
95. Takayanagi, *Parliament and Women*.
96. Law, *Suffrage and Power*; Alberti, 'A Symbol and a Key'.
97. Bingham, 'Stop the Flapper Vote Folly'.
98. UoR, Astor papers, MS1416/1/1/262. 26 February 1926, speaking notes.
99. UoR, Astor papers, MS1416/1/1/261. Pencilled note on letter from Rhondda, 5 November 1925. Astor's formal reply was more measured: 'I am afraid I don't agree that it would be advisable to enlist Mrs Pankhurst's help for the equal suffrage campaign at this moment, I am certain that the Government are going to give it, and that her intervention really is

not necessary, and might possibly do more harm than good.' UoR, Astor papers, MS1416/1/2/36, 9 November 1925.

100. UoR, Astor papers, MS1416/1/1/914. Astor to Pankhurst, 2 February 1926. 'I am so glad to know you are in London again.'

101. June Purvis, 'Emmeline Pankhurst in the Aftermath of Suffrage', in *The Aftermath of Suffrage: Women, Gender, and Politics in Britain, 1918–1945*, eds. Julie Gottlieb and Richard Toye (Palgrave Macmillan, 2013), 30–31. Purvis also reports that Astor offered to resign her seat in favour of Pankhurst, but Pankhurst politely declined.

102. The National Archives, HO 45/13020.

103. Bodleian Library, CPA, ARE 9/11/2. The South Eastern area included Kent, Sussex and Surrey. Hilda Moore-Brabazon was wife of John Moore-Brabazon, MP for Chatham.

104. McCrillis, *The British Conservative Party*, 180.

105. Bodleian Library, CPA, ARE 7/11/1. Eastern area, 7th annual conference, 23 February 1927.

106. Diana Hopkinson, *Family Inheritance: A Life of Eva Hubback* (Staples Press, 1954), 93.

107. HC Debates 13 April 1927 vol 205 cc358–360.

108. For more on the Cabinet decision, see; Takayanagi, *Votes for Women*.

109. LSE Women's Library collections, 2NSE/D/2. Letter from Astor to NUSEC, 24 November 1927.

110. Cambridge University Library [CUL], Baldwin Papers 48.

111. LSE Women's Library collections, 2NSE/D/2. Atholl to NUSEC, 3 December 1927. The meeting took place on 8 March 1928 at Queen's Hall.

112. CUL, Baldwin Papers, 49. Lady Iveagh to Baldwin, on standing in the Southend-on-Sea by – election, 14 November 1927.

113. UoR, Astor papers, MS1416/1/626. 8 November 1927.

114. HC Debates 29 March 1928 vol 215 cc1359–1482. More detail in Takayanagi, *Votes for Women*.

115. HC Debates 29 March 1928 vol 215 c1403, Wilkinson; c1415, Bondfield.

116. Ibid, cc1452–3, Astor.

117. Ibid, c135, Iveagh.

118. LSE Women's Library collections, 7AMP/D/5/1. *Morning Post*, 30 March 1928.

119. HC Debates 29 March 1928 vol 215 c1379–80

120. LSE Women's Library collections, 7AMP/D/5/1. *Morning Post*, 30 March 1928.

121. Knox, *Lives of Scottish Women*.

Acknowledgements

The author would like to thank Dr Jacqui Turner from the University of Reading for assistance with the Astor papers, and Jeremy McIlwaine from the Bodleian Library, Oxford, for assistance with the Conservative Party Archives.

Disclosure statement

No potential conflict of interest was reported by the author.

ORCID

Mari Takayanagi ⓘ http://orcid.org/0000-0002-3775-1313

The *Elusive* Lady Apsley

Madge Dresser

ABSTRACT

This article proposes to assess the career and political significance of Bristol's first woman M.P., Lady Apsley (1895–1966) who held office between 1943 and 1945. It seeks to do this with reference both to feminist historiography, which questions traditional demarcations between 'women's activities' and mainstream politics, and to the post-colonial scholarship which challenges a strictly metropolitan approach to analysing British political figures.

Introduction

This article proposes to assess the career and political significance of Bristol's first but now largely forgotten woman M.P., Lady Apsley (1895–1966). Lady Apsley won Bristol Central for the Conservatives in 1943 after her husband who had previously held the seat had been killed in an air crash in Malta in 1942.[1]

Given the brevity of her parliamentary career (1943–1945) and the circumstances attending it, it is tempting to dismiss her as a political lightweight of little significance and as a widow who had no distinctive views of her own.

However, although Lady Apsley was in Parliament for less than two years, she was involved in a wide variety of public activities throughout her life, ranging from her work for the Southampton and later Bristol Conservative Women's Associations to her leadership of the women's section of the British Legion during the Second World War. Intrepid and energetic she worked as a Voluntary Aid Detachment (VAD) nurse in the First World War, undertook undercover investigations in the Australian outback, became a qualified pilot and keen amateur motorist and was the mother of two sons. From 1930 she continued an active public life after a hunting accident which left her permanently confined to a wheelchair.[2]

This article will ask what a consideration of Lady Apsley's activities and beliefs can tell us about the role of women in the Conservative Party c. 1920–1950 and of what constituted Tory feminism after full adult suffrage had been achieved. This study sees her as part of what Alan Sykes has characterised as a submerged, disparate but significant strand of radical-right-wing political thinking within the Tory party.[3] It also considers the extent to which she might be a feminist within that context. Building on the pioneering work of Julie Gottlieb' *Guilty Women*, which provides a gendered analysis of women's attitudes to fascism between the wars, this article will seek to fathom the extent to which Lady Apsley's could be a fascist sympathiser in this period and if so how this squared with her subsequent involvement in the war effort and Churchill's endorsement of her in 1943.[4]

Apart from a short *ODNB* entry by G. E. Maguire and brief references to her in studies of women in Parliament, little has been written on Lady Apsley.[5] Researching her has been a challenge given the reported destruction of her papers in the Bathurst family collection at Cirencester Park.[6] This present study takes advantage of the discovery of new primary material held at the Eastnor Castle archives where the family papers of Lady Somers who was Lady Apsley's only sister, are located.[7] This private collection, which at time of writing is only just in the process of being catalogued, contains a typescript memoir by Lady Apsley. But significantly whole chapters of this memoir, namely those which covered her most politically active years, are missing.[8] The remaining material, including letters to her sister between 1926 and 1930, and a journal charting her election defeat in 1945[9] has certainly helped to flesh out the development of her political attitudes, but the memoir's frustratingly incomplete survival makes an interrogation of her political attitudes, especially relating to her attitudes to fascism a more difficult task.

To address this, this study brings together fragmentary evidence from other primary sources including *Hansard*, the local and national press, documents from the Conservative Party Archives including the papers of the Primrose League papers, and other sources. It interrogates such material with an eye to what Julie Gottlieb' calls that 'liminal space between the private and the public sphere,' to reconstruct the social and political networks in which Lady Apsley was embedded.[10] To this end, it considers Lady Apsley's female as well as male relatives, her local associations with properties and the specific local circumstances in which she conducted her public life outside Parliament.[11] It rejects a hard and fast division between her formal political role as MP and her wider public life, and sees her, despite her lack of identification as a feminist, as implicitly part of the wider post-suffrage women's movement.

Her background and family connections

Viola Emily Mildred Meeking was born in London in 1895 to a landed family with military, trade and Oxbridge connections.[12] Official biographical entries note her father Captain Bertram Charles Christopher Spencer Meeking, served with the 10th Hussars in the Boer War and note only that her mother, Violet Charlotte Meeking *nèe* Fletcher, was from Scottish gentry. But by reading surviving sources with an eye to the female line, it emerges that both her mother and maternal grandmother were significant figures in their own right. Bertha Talbot Fletcher, her grandmother and the daughter of 'one of the wealthiest men in Great Britain,' was involved with her sisters in the active management of her own family's extensive estates, sponsored numerous (mainly Anglican) charities and was a founder of the Scottish Mothers 'Union'.[13] Yet, according to Viola's memoirs, the staunchly traditionalist Bertha forbad her daughter Violet, who had enrolled at the Slade School of Art, and was regarded as a 'talented artist,' from completing her course. This was, Viola writes, because it was then considered to be 'on the other side of the social fence for a lady to take up art seriously.'[14] The surviving memoirs make it clear that Viola, revered and respected her mother and regretted her grandmother's action. Yet though both these women exercised their talents, patronage and influence beyond the home and did so with the confident assurance of their class, they still subscribed to traditional patriarchal values. This same contradiction would become evident throughout Lady Apsley's own subsequent public career.

Early life

It is hard to appreciate the development of Viola Meeking's political values without reference to her landed status and family connections. Her early life was spent at the family estate, Richings Park, in Buckinghamshire, (an estate formerly associated with the Apsley and Bathurst families), which had been purchased by her great grandfather, a London department store owner.[15]

When she was 5, her father and his younger brother both died of enteric fever whilst serving in South Africa. Her memoirs state that her mother had gone out to the Cape to nurse him and was devastated by her loss.[16] Viola and her younger sister Finola (1896– 1981) were thus brought up in a female-headed household steeped in the values of empire and sacrifice and beset by relative financial uncertainty. At fifteen, Viola and her mother were shocked to learn that her 'autocratic' barrister grandfather Charles Meeking, (who had since remarried a young French woman), did not make his daughter-in-law his heir. Instead she was left with a cash settlement which was less than what was expected. Richings Park was to go to Viola when she attained adulthood and nothing was bequeathed to her sister Finola.[17] Two years later, after this 'unfair' settlement, her mother married the wealthy stockbroker, sportsman and adventurer Herbert Johnson.[18] Johnson soon moved his new family to live at Marsh Court in Hampshire, the estate which he had purchased some years earlier having commissioned Sir Edwin Lutyens (1869–1944) to rebuild the house and Gertrude Jekyll (1843–1932) to design its gardens there.[19]

In 1914 the Johnsons had donated all or part of Marsh Court for use as a military hospital, The few standard accounts we have of Violet Meeking's life during the Great War simply mention that she worked as a VAD.[20] But significantly it was at Marsh Court Auxiliary Hospital that she served, where it was her mother (whom she venerated) who ran the hospital, presiding there for the next five years as the full time administrator, matron and assistant x-ray operator, later receiving an MBE for her work.[21]

Violet Meeking worked under her mother and alongside her sister at the hospital throughout the war as a full-time volunteer nurse and part-time ambulance driver.[22] It is impossible to assess how her wartime experience may have informed any interest in women's suffrage specifically or in politics more generally as no memoirs survive from this period. However, there is evidence to suggest that her interest in the army policy relating to the welfare of the armed forces stemmed from her conversations with the disillusioned soldiers she treated as a VAD.[23]

The post-war social world of weekend country parties, Hunt balls and London *soirées* into which Viola Meeking was subsequently drawn, also helped to shape her political views. She notes that she and many in her set opposed the Liberal Tory Coalition which was associated with the increased taxation of wealthy landowners. In 1921, the year after her mother's premature death, she was 'grieved' to sell Richings Park, whose sale may have in part been dictated by financial necessity.[24] Interestingly, she also became a member of The Forum women's club in Grosvenor Place, Westminster. This women's residential club 'with all the facilities of a gentlemen's club' had been founded in 1919 by former suffragists to be a 'hub' for those alive to the professional opportunities then opening to women after the passage of the Sex Disqualification (Removal) Act of that year. The club's ethos was described as 'radical but politically unaffiliated 'attracting women from the far right as well as from more liberal circles."[25]

The demarcation between personal and political life in these elite circles was porous, and her intimacy with the Royal Family at Balmoral, and various landed families and prominent industrialists, exposed her to political discussion at the highest levels albeit in a highly-gendered way. 'Described as "one of the prettiest" and most popular girls in Society,' she recollects being asked to most 'though not then perhaps to the smartest political type of party' to meet diplomats and other distinguished people and being expected to 'keep the conversation going.'[26] She recalls diverting Austen Chamberlain by asking him to discourse on the League of Nations and her memoirs show her canny grasp of the various Tory factions then at play.

It was through such networks that she met her future husband. Her marriage in 1924 to Allen Algernon Bathurst aka Lord Apsley, allied her to a family noted for their high Tory and imperial sympathies and love of field sports. Her father-in-law Seymour Henry, seventh Earl Bathurst (1864–1943), a keen hunter and equestrian, was a substantial aristocratic landowner, presiding over some 12,000 acres mainly centred on the family estate at Cirencester Park and a town house in Belgravia.

Her mother-in-law Lilias Margaret Frances, Bathurst [née Borthwick], Countess Bathurst (1871–1965) was an influential figure in Conservative circles, being described by Northcliffe as "the most powerful woman in England without exception-other than the Royalty"[27] The hands-on proprietor of the influential Morning Post, until she sold her interest in 1924, the Countess promoted the Protocols of the Elders of Zion (the forged nineteenth century document purporting Jews were plotting world domination), articulated anti-Irish and anti-alien sentiments and took an uncompromising view against women's suffrage.[28] Her son, who had written for the Morning Post when he first met Violet Meeking, continued on its Board until 1935. Lord and Lady Bathurst had both served as Vice-presidents of the British Empire Union in 1916, a radical right organisation which stood 'for patriotism, social reform, industrial peace, promotion of the Empire and anti-socialism'.[29] The Union was part of a coterie of radical right-wing groups known as the 'Diehards' whose views were promoted by The Morning Post.[30] Circumstantial evidence suggests that Lady Apsley did not agree with her mother-in-law, about women's suffrage.[31] For though she found her 'good to talk to' (both took an active interest in Lord Apsley's political career), she also described Lady Bathurst in a letter to her sister as 'narrow-minded' and 'hard-faced.'[32]

Lady Apsley voiced no such qualms about the views of her new husband, who had been elected as the Unionist MP for Southampton in 1922. Lord Apsley's position on the Morning Post, his earlier pre-war travels to Australia and Iraq and his position on the Council of the Primrose League, sufficiently impressed the 'Diehard' Joynson Hicks, then Under-Secretary of State for the Overseas Trade Department, to appoint him as his Parliamentary Private Secretary.

Lady Apsley: traditional Tory wife or a dedicated Diehard with feminist leanings?

At first glance, the new Lady Apsley looked set to play the traditional role of a society wife. She featured regularly in the social pages of The Tatler and the Times. Portraits of her painted by the society artist Philip de László in 1924 and 1926 respectively portray her in evening dress and a riding habit, the last, affirming the central role which hunting played throughout her life. Those two portraits identify her as part of what some critics would call the 'mink and manure' brigade of sporting Tory women who took advantage of both their entitled social position and the wider freedoms afforded to them after suffrage to live a less constrained life than those of their mothers.[33] An article in *The Sphere* shows her in sporting garb, salmon fishing with a group of other women in Scotland.[34] She herself published the occasional article on hunting and sport for the *Morning Post* and the *British Weekly* attracting the praise of the press baron Lord Beaverbrook.

Throughout her married life, Lady Apsley's values and activities recall that particular brand of 'feminism from the Right' allied to that of Lady Londonderry, Christabel Pankhurst and Mary Allen. This was as Gottlieb observes, a feminism premised not on challenging the notion of 'separate spheres' or class inequality but on allowing women to perform 'their patriotic duties unmolested by antedated sexism.'[35]

An early example of her feminist thinking is evidenced when, a year into their marriage, Lord Apsley was set to leave his wife at home to go to Australia on a mission to investigate complaints about the conditions experienced by poor English migrants there. In the book they subsequently co-authored about their experiences, *The Amateur Settlers*, Lady Apsley archly recounts that the news of her husband's intended departure 'came as a bombshell' and that she refused to be left at home. Instead, she contrived '**with female cunning**' to convince her husband that she would be well placed to enable the investigation to find out about 'the women's side of the question', 'so that the conditions awaiting new settler could be examined from all points of view ... [emphasis mine]'[36]

It is telling that determined though she is not to be excluded from this exclusively masculine project, she does not directly challenge her husband's authority but instead employs 'female cunning' to get her way.

Her subsequent experience in Australia was formative in terms of developing her ideas about gender, race and class. The former Girl Guide, who had done her share of floor scrubbing and bed making as a nurse, now roughed it in a group settlement for poor emigrants. Living in the most primitive conditions under an assumed name, the Apsleys interacted with their neighbours on an ostensibly equal footing. This hands-on experience made Lady Apsley somewhat more empathetic than many of her class to the plight of the white working classes, especially the women:

> Life in Australia is hard for the pioneer woman, but life in England seems to me harder for thousands of women today, drudging hopelessly worn and weary along the over-peopled ways of the working world.[37]

The remedy to poverty as she saw it was not the redistribution of wealth, but imperial expansion under a paternalist regime. As someone used to employing servants, she assumed wealthy white women both in Australia and at home as best placed to train and guide their social inferiors, especially the indigenous people of the Australian outback who are portrayed as racially inferior as well:

> The Aborigines] ... do not have a good reputation as servants' ... but it seemed to me entirely a matter of training. There are few white women in the Bush to teach the black, where there is a patient instructress the childlike minds can be taught to do things.[38]

On the Aspley's' return to Britain in 1925, Lady Apsley combined the management of the family residence in Petty France, Badminton, (near the Bathurst's estate at Cirencester Park) with leadership roles in various political associations, most notably as head of the Women's Unionist Association in her husband's constituency of Southampton. Though the Conservative Women's Association had little say in policy- making, and did not identify as feminist, it was as the 'largest and most active political organisation in interwar Britain' and a crucial force in canvassing and fundraising for the party.[39] As one of the array of women's associations which emerged after suffrage was achieved, it should be seen, as Catriona Beaumont has argued, as part of the wider women's movement in the interwar period.[40]

In 1926, Lady Apsley also founded and was President of the British Empire Union's 'Links of Empire' scheme, (1926–38) with her sister Lady Somers (then the wife of the Governor General of Victoria) as one of its Vice-presidents. The scheme, whose aim was to promote correspondence between women in Australia and the British mainland to cultivate 'the Imperial spirit,' attracted 13,000 members by 1932. Its aims accord with the imperialist, faith-based feminism of Emmeline Pankhurst who also called for cooperation between the classes to achieve (white) women's fuller participation in public life.[41] Apsley's private letters from this time further confirm her embrace of the English nationalism and articulate a racialized protectionist discourse associated with the political values of Diehard Toryism.

> The brown and black people are cutting us out everywhere. USA stand[s] at the X roads all our manufacturers are disheartened by unfair competition and high taxes, all our work people are demoralised with doing less than a day's work and there don't seem the right sort of statesmen to cope with our problems satisfactorily[42]

The election of a minority Labour Government in 1929, which saw the ejection of her husband from his Southampton seat, shows her increasingly suspicious of 'an impossibly large irresponsible democracy electing a Govt with the purpose of bleeding the so-called capitalist' and increasingly anxious about the impact of global competition.[43]

Though keen to see her husband back in Parliament, (her sense of duty made her feel their pleasurable round of flying, hunting and socialising was somewhat 'selfish'), she who had by then had two young sons, was nonetheless anxious about being 'left behind' in the country once her husband got back to Westminster.[44]

However, at the end of 1930 her life was to change forever. Whilst hunting with Lord Bathurst's Hounds, she sustained serious spinal injuries when the horse she was riding stumbled and fell on top of her and she would spend the rest of her life confined to a wheelchair and in chronic pain.

It was shortly after her accident, in 1931, that Lord Apsley returned to Parliament, as the Unionist member for Bristol Central. The *Sketch* featured photographs of the newly elected MP and his family at home putting a brave face on their circumstances. The first features a smiling Lady Apsley in a bath chair alongside her husband, two young sons and a nanny by the duck pond in the grounds of Petty France, the second in her home reading to her children from her wheelchair.[45] These idealised portrayals of domestic life are more poignant knowing that Lady Apsley, had shortly before described her pleasures in life as 'riding a good horse somewhere near hounds, flying, driving a fast car, hitting a golf ball, shooting and catching salmon.'[46] A friend reported she and her husband chose to play 'a heroic game of let's pretend' by ignoring her disability. Though she continued to be featured as a decorative adjunct to her husband in society magazines, such portrayals belied the fact that she was not deterred by her disability from an active political life.[47]

Soon after his election, Lady Apsley also became the Chairman of the Bristol Women's Conservative Association, whose membership she increased over eightfold by 1937 to nearly 8000.[48] Aside from opening bazaars for local unionist associations and worthy charities,[49] Lady Apsley spoke at various local meetings to the party faithful and though the records are unforthcoming about the specific tactics she employed, she clearly had a flair for political organisation. Her suspicion of organised labour outweighed her earlier empathy with the poor for though she elsewhere advocated economic protectionism to preserve British jobs, her utterances now revealed a complacent attitude to the plight of the unemployed. Like many Conservative women in this era, she focused on the post-war shortage of domestic servants, even complaining in one letter to the press that the unemployed in Durham were ignoring domestic jobs in large houses which were there for the taking.[50]

By mid-decade Lady Apsley, who had obtained her pilot's licence just before her accident, had joined the Board of Western Airways of which her husband was Chairman, travelled with her husband to Australia and co-authored two books one on hunting and riding for women and the other on the history of rural pursuits.[51] She had a specially designed car to accommodate her 'invalid's chair,' and though it is not clear whether she continued to drive herself or had a driver, she went on a motoring tour to the continent in 1936.[52]

Soft on Fascism? Lady Apsley and appeasement

It was on this latter trip that she wrote to *the Times* from Germany *en route* from Hungary, praising the Labour Camps of Hitler's Germany, something omitted from her *ODNB* entry. Her letter was a response to a previous feature by the *Times's* special correspondent called 'the Nazi way' which described the effective but dictatorial way the German population was managed. The article depicted the compulsory deployment of unemployed young men in Labour camps where they were compelled to sing Nazi anthems and endure harsh working conditions.

Apsley took issue with the feature, stating she was far more favourably impressed by the two Labour camps she visited. Describing the young men there, as happy to work (unlike the British unemployed 'most of whom would' 'prefer to do nothing and draw the dole'), she was most taken by these 'bronzed Norse gods' and clearly thrilled to 'hear them playing guitars and singing (Nazi?) songs' which she called 'an unforgettable experience'. Hitler's suppression of the German trade unions did not affect her favourable impression, She warned against 'judging other nations by our own standards.'[53] One Bristolian responded by accusing her with some justice her of 'half holding up Hitler and the Nazis as an example for the British worker'.[54]

But Apsley was not unrepresentative in her seeming unconcern about the oppressive nature of the Nazi regime. She was one of a spate of tourist commentators who were dazzled by the aesthetically pleasing vision of national harmony that they encountered.[55] Her silence about Hitler's persecution of the Jews, which by 1936 was well known in

Britain,[56] is not surprising. Anti-Semitism was an intrinsic part of aristocratic British culture, particularly in Diehard circles in which she and her husband's family had been involved. The Apsley's close family friend, Rudyard Kipling was part of an actively Anti-Semitic network in the 1920 and *The Morning Post* continued its long-standing anti-Jewish agenda in the 1930s when Lord Apsley was still on its board. Lady Apsley herself makes references to moneyed Jews, 'Jewesses', profiteers, and 'Jew boys' in both her unpublished and published work.[57]

Nor was she perturbed by Hitler's suppression of the Communists. For Tories of her set, their hatred of Bolshevism overshadowed any concerns about the conduct of fascist regimes. As Julie Gottlieb, has pointed out, 'their anti-Bolshevism ... meant that Conservative women approached fascism from a very different starting point than others for whom—as feminists, as Liberals or as Leftists—anti-fascism was instinctive and visceral'.[58]

In sum, the radically right-wing strand in Tory thinking to which Lady Apsley subscribed overlapped in important respects with fascist values given its 'belief in the organic holism of the nation, and [a conviction] ... that the individual's rights are subordinate to the duties the citizen owed to the British nation/state.'[59] And though not ideologically consistent, it accepted the need for the state to plan and manage the economy and society and to 'exert social control' to this end.[60]

During the mid 1930s, British aviators such as Lord Apsley were actively courted by the Nazi envoy Joachim von Ribbentrop on his mission to Britain build up support for German rearmament.[61] Lady Apsley was closely associated as a founder member of the Forum Club's women's flight group, with a coterie of women aviators (such as Lady Londonderry and Mavis Tate) who as Gottlieb notes were sympathetic to fascism. Mary Allen, a member of the British Union of Fascists was also a Forum Club member.[62]

It's not known if Lord Apsley accompanied his wife on her visit to Germany, or how she got access to visiting the Labour camps, but it is significant that Lord Apsley had joined the Anglo-German Friendship Society that same year. Only a few months after the publication of his wife's letter to the *Times,* Lord Apsley had been a guest of honour at a Nuremburg rally having been personally introduced to Hitler at a dinner the night before.[63]

Yet it must be conceded that Appeasement was a widely popular policy with a war-weary public for much of the 1930s, and the Anglo-German Friendship Society had initially attracted a wide array of members. As Gottlieb points out, it was the prevailing Conservative Party strategy to make a gendered appeal to the pro-peace inclinations of its women voters.[64] Certainly, Lady Apsley played the peace card but she also shied away from any public condemnation of Hitler or Mussolini, advising her fellow female Unionists to focus on family and domestic concerns rather than 'bother so much about ... Mussolini or Hitler ... .'[65] The implication was that Germany's and Italy's domestic policies were their own business and not the appropriate target for outsider criticism and this was as Griffiths points out, a characteristic ploy of fellow travellers of the right. In April 1938, she played a leading role organising a pro-appeasement rally at Bristol's Colston Hall which featured Lord Halifax as the main speaker and a platform of supporters including Lord Apsley and such overtly pro-fascist figures as Mavis Tate and Tom Culverwell.[66]

G. C. Webber, Alan Sykes and Richard Griffiths point to the increasingly confused and disparate reaction of the far-right as Hitler's expansionist aggression became impossible to ignore. Despite their sympathy with many fascist ideals, most became increasingly uneasy about Hitler's intentions and methods.[67] Yet the Apsleys, along with many on the radical right actively continued to support Chamberlain and promoted appeasement even after Kristallnacht in October 1938 and Germany's annexation of Moravia and Bohemia in March 1939.[68] Lady Apsley's appointment as county commandant for the ATS for Gloucestershire in 1938 did not initially dampen her enthusiasm for Chamberlain or appeasement. At the AGM of the Bristol Women's Unionist Association in Bristol in February 1939 which she chaired, her husband told the audience that 'Hitler [whom he now acknowledged as a dictator] was a clever man and a wise one ... ' who 'realised that' 'the German people did not want to fight England.'[69] The following month, Lady Apsley again advised Women Unionists before a pro-appeasement demonstration in Yeovil not to 'bother so much about what Mussolini or Hitler is thinking or doing' but 'concern ourselves with home politics. that matter to us to our families, to our children ... and civilisation as a whole.'[70]

Lady Apsley's views were however were tempered by a practical eclecticism at odds with political purism of card-carrying British fascists[71] and by a profound sense of English patriotism. Once war was declared, if not shortly before, both she and her husband rallied against the Axis.

Lady Apsley at war

Lady Apsley was, like so many women, separated from her immediate family at the outset of war. Lord Apsley had left England in 1939 to serve first with the Royal Hussars and then with the Arab Legion in the Middle East.[72] Her sons (aged 11 and 13 in 1940) were sent to Canada around the same time. Bristol was heavily blitzed throughout the war with 5 major raids between 1940 and 1941. Much of the devastation occurred in Lord Apsley's constituency of Bristol Central during which time Lady Apsley took over her husband's constituency duties.[73]

The bald reportage of Lord Apsley's death on the 17 December 1942 fails to convey the particularly devastating circumstances in which Lady Apsley learned of his fate. For her sons, had just made the

> perilous journey [back to Britain] through waters infested by submarines' to meet both their parents for a Christmas family reunion and '[T]he joy of their safe arrival was shrouded the next day by the news of their father's death in an aeroplane accident in [Malta] ... .[74]

Lady Apsley had already thrown herself into the war effort as Senior Commandant of the Gloucestershire ATS. Aside from making broadcasts, she had to devise systems ('literally from nothing') for recruiting women for war work. She also served as the ATS welfare officer for the county from 1940 to 1943[75], chaired the Conservative and Unionist Women's Association and served on the Sodbury Rural District Council 1941–3.[76]

Amid this all, she had been elected the head of the Women's Section of the British Legion and was installed at the Annual Conference at Westminster Hall early in 1943. The importance of British Legion's Women's Section, along with that of the ATS and the Women's Voluntary Service (WVS) though often discussed under the wider question of women's role in the war effort, confirms Lady Apsley's role as a woman of increasing public importance.[77] Such roles, as Hinton points out, were dominated by women of the upper classes. (Lady Reading, who established the WVS, had long socialised in the same circles as Lady Apsley).[78] The image of jam making and knitting belies the size, complexity and reach of these organisations which performed work essential to the reproduction of the State. As Caitriona Beaumont argues, such associations gave housewives and mothers 'the opportunity to contribute in a very active and public way to the war effort.'[79] The administrative challenges posed by running the British Legion's women's section further confirm the significance of Lady Apsley's public role. Apsley widened the brief of the women's section to include looking after the welfare of servicemen's and ex-servicemen's dependents and serving the wider public -which in war-time took on a special significance. She is credited with professionalising the management of the women's section whose activities ranged from supplying additional pensions, deploying women for part-time war work, distributing clothing to bombed-out civilians, providing clubs, hostels and canteen facilities for the forces, and rest homes and an orphanage as well as preserving fresh produce for government Preservation centres.[80] The British Legion alone had no fewer than 2284 women's branches and 164,000 members by 1945, 'thanks to Lady Apsley's leadership.'[81] It is hard to deny that the chairmanship of such organisations had a manifestly political dimension.

It was amid executing her various duties that Lady Apsley, was chosen to succeed her deceased husband as Conservative candidate for Bristol Central. A wartime electoral truce between the parties meant that no official Labour candidate was allowed to stand against her, but there were three independents, including the charismatic socialist campaigner and wife of the popular Aneurin Bevan, Jennie Lee. Lady Apsley ran as a champion of Churchill and national unity blandly purporting (much to Jenny Lee's disdain) "to represent ... all classes and all interests' [and to] 'stand for British ideals, faith, freedom and fair play ... "[82] Such were the confused cross currents of this contested election that the local Communists reportedly issued a pamphlet in support of Apsley.[83] As the New Statesman correspondent Lionel Fielden noted, though Jenny Lee attracted 2000 people at a local cinema dwarfing the paltry numbers her opponents could command, Lee's acolytes were young and from outside the ward so their support did not translate into hard votes.[84]

Bombs and war had meant only a rump of older voters were still resident in the contested constituency.[85] Some of those eligible to vote were reportedly suspicious of Jennie Lee who didn't wear a wedding ring or take her husband's name. Lady Apsley by contrast was someone, Fielden opined, whom locals knew and trusted and whose 'gallantry' won over an apathetic and ill-informed electorate.[86] Nonetheless, Apsley had to deal with hecklers at often rumbustious meetings at which she was accompanied by male Tory minders[87].

The very fact that Lady Apsley overcame her disability and testing family circumstances to become the city's first woman's M.P., that she rallied Conservative women's support across the city to work on her behalf and that she had already acted as caretaker for her husband's constituency, as well as taking on war work seemed to be overwhelmed by her identity as his disabled widow.[88] Fielden, who admits to feeling discomfited at seeing Lady Apsley wince with pain as she attempted to rise from her chair to speak at a meeting, portrays her as a 'gallant' 'cripple':

> For the pen of a Balzac to describe the reverent rising of the 18 when the cripple's chair was wheeled in. Nobody could dislike Lady Apsley; few could fail to sympathise with her bereavement and her gallantry; but what has that to do with politics?[89]

Despite her good showing in the election, an unnamed correspondent for *The Spectator* was also uncomfortable with 'the gallant' Lady Apsley's political role:

> ... the number of women who have succeeded their husbands in the House of Commons is getting so considerable as to inspire the hope that the thing will not become a habit. To be, or to have been, someone's wife is not sufficient reason for selection as a candidate or election as a member.[90]

In fact, Lady Apsley was only the fourth such widow to have followed in her husband's stead and in the first instance Conservative Central office reportedly had doubts about selecting her, so his unease about widows dominating selection procedures seems over-stated, signifying perhaps, a deeper unease about female politicians.[91]

Whilst the 1943 campaign in Bristol Central proved the importance of the Bristol Women's Conservative and Unionist Association in getting out the vote, it also helped to precipitate a hardening of party divisions amongst women political activists. The cross-party group Women for Westminster which had lobbied on issues affecting women's welfare and status, and was initially chaired by the Tory MP Lady Davidson, lost much of its Tory backing and failed to establish a Bristol branch largely because of its partisan championing of Jennie Lee over Lady Apsley in the 1943 election.[92]

Her career in the commons

On the 25th of February 1943, Lady Apsley dressed in full mourning, made her debut in the Commons to the cheers of backbenchers as she entered in her 'self-propelled' wheel-chair.[93] But this chivalric reception belied the fact that the House was an overwhelmingly male one which marginalised the priorities and concerns of its newly enfranchised female electorate and sometimes regarded the 15 female MPs then serving with patronising disdain.[94] Sir Cuthbert Morley Headlam characterised Lady Apsley as " ... a charming woman and I admire her pluck tremendously but she is rather too earnest a parliamentarian for me, I found her a bit boring after a bit."[95]

Just how earnest a parliamentarian she was compared to other female and male members is hard to determine precisely in the absence of a quantitative comparison of her contributions in relation to her counterparts in the House.[96] But, despite being one of the few women MPs who never served on a standing committee,[97] she was certainly an engaged one. Her first recorded contribution was on March 18 1943 where she by all accounts impressed the Commons by her maiden speech in which she talked about the treatment of disabled servicemen.[98] By the end of her term she is reported to have made no fewer than 187 contributions in the form of speeches, questions and contributions to debates.[99] Her energies were mainly but not exclusively focused on what we would now call 'quality of life' issues which tended to be identified as the proper concern of female M.Ps. and as less central to the 'hard' masculine core of proper politics, namely foreign and economic policy. Her traditionalist Tory views were on occasion tempered by her personal experience as a disabled person, as a woman, and as someone exposed first hand to the needs of the poor through her constituency and wider welfare work with the ATS.

She and other Tory women MPs (who included Mary Astor, Thelma Cazalet-Keir and Frances Viscountess Davidson) would occasionally ally with Labour and independent women MPs such as Ellen Wilkinson, Dr. Edith Summerskill, and Eleanor Rathbone on issues affecting the welfare of women[100] Lady Apsley joined a cross-party deputation of women MPs to lobby Attlee (then Deputy Prime Minister) for more female representation on various government committees concerned with post-war reconstruction.[101]

Eloquently exalting the importance of the housewife 'as the bedrock of the nation,' Lady Apsley saw women first and foremost as wives and mothers. Though her intention was not to rule out women's wider professional development, her advocacy of a separate curriculum for girls stressing domestic science and her failure to answer Edith Summerskill's and Eleanor Rathbone's point that unpaid housework consigned women to 'a form of serfdom'[102] played into the hands of her more reactionary male colleagues.[103] Apsley's contrarian insistence to preserve respect for patriarchy was counterbalanced to some extent by her fierceness in bearding male colleagues when she felt women's interests were being side-lined as in the case of Lord Profumo's patronising dismissal of British servicewomen's wish to continue in paid employment after the war[104] or Herbert Morrison's failure to consider appointing a woman assistant inspector of constabulary at the Home Office to advise chief constables on the selection and training of women police.[105]

When the issue of Family Allowances was raised in 1945, women MPs united in protest the Government decision to pay the Allowance directly to fathers. Where did Lady Apsley stand on what Brookes characterised as the women members' 'last great feminist battle of the war'?[106] It transpires that Lady Apsley did eventually support them, but only after she was assured that paying the Allowance to the mother (which she conceded was more practically convenient) would not be contravening the authority of the father. In this she still stood by a patriarchal model of family authority.[107]

In her insistence on preserving patriarchal family structures, she explicitly reviled the idea of 'matriarchy' associating it with the 'stone age' 'aboriginal tribes' she had encountered in Australia and asserting it to be

> 'an extremely primitive type of civilisation alien to the English tradition and one to which I, for one, hope we shall not return.'[108]

But Apsley's concern about preserving the authority of the father, grounded though it was in a crude social Darwinism, must also be understood in the light of her own experience as a constituency MP and ATS welfare officer. She personally knew the Bristol Tory Magistrate Lady Inskip who pioneered national reforms in the treatment of juvenile offenders in this era[109] and attributed the rising rates of criminal offences amongst the young in Bristol as 'largely due' to the absence of fathers because of their long hours at work or war-time service. So, Apsley's reluctance to undermine the status of the father was not simply reactionary but raised a question with which we are still grappling, namely the importance of fathers to the socialisation of their children.

Lady Apsley did occasionally take a stand on less identifiably 'feminine' issues. Her personal passion for rural pursuits and her upbringing in historic country houses underpins her consistent concern for the conservation of Britain's countryside and built heritage.[110] Her anti-Bolshevism led her to vote against her government when she felt they were ceding too much of Polish territory to Soviet control and she also spoke up on behalf of Albanian refugees at the war's end. She was all for fostering enterprise particularly for small businesses and in the civil aviation industry and her experiences in Australia had early on alerted her to appreciate the propaganda potential of film. She contributed to the public discussion both inside and out of Parliament about how film could best serve the national interest.[111]

The 1945 election and life after parliament

Lady Apsley lost her seat in the 1945 election which saw Churchill and the Tories generally swept from power.[112] Loyal to Churchill and the National Government, her campaign made general promises to restore 'peace, progress and prosperity' to Bristol and urged national unity.[113]

She repeatedly stressed her opposition to the nationalisation plans proposed by Labour which she implied were the plans of 'cranks and sectional interests'[114]

> Did they [the electorate] think that nationalisation of the banks, land. fuel power and transport and the removal of free enterprise was the quickest, cheapest and soundest way to attain the food, work and houses for the returned soldiers, sailors and airmen after they had finished the Job?[115]

Such a policy, she averred, would be disastrous for both the city and the nation.[116]

The chance survival of one of Lady Apsley's notebooks from 1945 in the Somers Collection affords a uniquely frank account of her political attitudes and of how she saw herself treated by the Conservative party machine.

Railing against Churchill and Eden's decision to hold a July election, she accuses them of having 'no idea of the depth of anti-Conservative feeling engendered by the Labour opposition, Fellow travellers, pacifists, Communists etc.[117] 'It was a blow to us all,' she recounts and clearly a particular shock to her for she had been oblivious to the fears many Bristolians had about a return to the high unemployment of the interwar period if Labour were defeated.[118]

Three days before the election she took the initiative to sit hidden in a car bedecked with party colours and her posters to gauge the reactions of the passing public:

> Till then I had thought the trend was with me. As I watched people passing—a cross section of Bristol, I saw them note the car and practically all looked away. They were not going to vote for me. This was shattering. -not to me but to what I believed would happen to the Country.[119]

She blames the then Home Secretary Herbert Morrison who pushed through changes in the voter registration as well as broader demographic changes in the constituency for the loss of many of her votes.[120] Her bemoaning of the loss of double voting is telling with regard to her take on democratic representation. She resentfully contrasts the lack of support she had from her own Party, 'very few men came to help me … I had to do most 'things' single handed,'[121] with the deployment by the Labour Party of 'full time trade union paid officials,' many of whom she was convinced, had, been exempted from conscription been in order 'to get Ernest Bevin's full cooperation during the war … .'[122]

Her contempt for her Labour rival, the anti-imperialist campaigner Stan Awbery (who won 63% of the vote to her 36%,)[123] reveal an inherent snobbery which if known couldn't have gone down well with an electorate reportedly ready to vote for 'the end of the Squirearchy.'[124]

> … I knew that the Labour candidates were quite incapable of doing or understanding what England and the British Empire required to put her on her feet and would go immediately for cutting up the remains of the cake with disastrous results. I felt being defeated by someone

not worthy to black my boots—a conchy of the [Great]? war, a trade union official, a Welsh-man from Newport, a poor speaker with nothing to recommend him but a life spent forward-ing Labour and Labour people and interests,'[125]

After three years as a well-known member of Parliament, Lady Apsley recalls, 'it was a bit of a come down to fold up my tents and return to Cirencester.' There was talk of her being pro-posed as Conservative and Liberal Parliamentary Candidate for Bristol North in 1948 but it was not until 1950 that she stood as a National Liberal candidate for Bristol Northeast. Her tone seemed increasingly reactionary and out of touch (she opposed the creation of the NHS)[126] and her consequent defeat led that year to her withdrawal from formal politics.[127]

The end of her Parliamentary career had not immediately meant the end of her political involvement or public influence. She served alongside Sir Alex Korda and J.A. Rank as one of only 2 women among the 20 members of the British Cinematograph Films Council in 1945–1946. She remained the chair of the British Legion's Women's Section, the BBC broadcasting her last address from the Albert Hall in 1948. But though she was credited for professionalising the women's service, and later deemed an 'outstanding' leader, she resigned soon afterwards, partly out of frustration with the British Legion's stubborn refusal to admit women to its National Executive Council.[128] She continued until 1952 as president of the Bristol Women's Conservative Association which boasted a member-ship of some 12,000. Increasingly though, her remaining energies were devoted to hunting, field sports and conservation though oral testimony suggests she continued to take an interest in the welfare of the disabled.[129]

Conclusion

Lady Apsley's political values and actions are difficult to evaluate using the contemporary categories of 'feminist' or progressive politics. She is undeniably part of the 'submerged tradition' of radical right-wing Conservatism whose imperialist, racist and Anti-Semitic values along with a hatred of Bolshevism locate her as a reactionary. Yet, the constellation of values to which she subscribed also encompassed critiques of free market capitalism and an attachment to the preservation of the nation's historic and natural heritage not entirely divorced from the concerns of contemporary progressive politics. Her emphasis on dom-esticity as the primary female domain, grounded as it was in racial and biological essenti-alism, was in many ways at odds with her own energetic participation in public affairs. In this she is typical of the type of right-wing feminism described by Gottlieb and Maguire, a feminism which limited her effectiveness in combatting sexual discrimination and fore-grounding women's interests in the formal political sphere. Nonetheless, she made the attempt to integrate a consideration of women's interests in the formulation of public policy both inside and outside Parliament, and the questions she raised about the nature of sexual difference and about how the state should consider parenting and women's unpaid work in the home were important ones which to this day remain unresolved.

Notes

1. See Madge Dresser, ed., *Women and the City: Bristol 1373–2000* (Bristol: Redcliffe Press, 2016), 174–5.

2. For a full list of Lady Apsley's public roles see Carnegie Mellon University http://tera-3.ul.cs.cmu.edu/NASD/d23d381a-642a-4cb1-bd42-5373f518ed1d/lemur/4001.sgml (accessed April 7, 2017).

3. R. Thurlow, (review of Alan Sykes, *The Radical Right in Britain: Social Imperialism to the BNP* (Basingstoke: Palgrave Macmillan, 2005), in *The English Historical Review, Vol. 122, No. 495 (Feb., 2007)*, 283–4; Alan Sykes, *The Radical Right in Britain, The Radical Right in Britain: Social Imperialism to the BNP* (Basingstoke: Palgrave Macmillan, 2005), 1–0.

4. Julie V. Gottlieb, *Guilty Women: Foreign Policy and Appeasement in Inter-War Britain* (Basingstoke, Hampshire: Palgrave, 2015), 9.

5. G. E. Maguire, 'Bathurst, Violet Emily Mildred, Lady Apsley (1895–1966)', in *Oxford Dictionary of National Biography*, ed. H. C. G. Matthew and Brian Harrison (Oxford: OUP, 2004); online ed., ed. David Cannadine, October 2008, http://www.oxforddnb.com/view/article/58675 (accessed March 16, 2017) (henceforth Maguire, Lady Apsley, *ODNB)*; Pamela Brookes, *Women at Westminster: An Account of Women in the British Parliament 1918–1966* (London: Peter Davies, 1967), 134, 151, 228: She is also mentioned in Julia Swindells, 'Coming Home to Heaven: Manpower and Myth in 1944 Britain', *Women's History Review* 4, no. 2 (1995): 223–34; in G. Maguire, *Conservative Women A History of Women and the Conservative Party, 1874–1997* (London: Palgrave Macmillan, 1998) and there is an entry on her in John Barnes, Historian website, http://barneshistorian.com/vm-apsley.php, (accessed April 1, 2017).

6. Email from the Countess of Bathurst, 26 February 2015.

7. Finola Meeking (1896–1981) married Lieutenant Colonel Arthur Herbert Tennyson Somers-Cocks, 6th Baron Somers (1887–14 July 1944), in 1921, her papers are contained within the wider collection of the Somers family papers housed at Eastnor Castle, Herefordshire, now the estate of James Hervey-Bathurst who is the grandson of Arthur, Lord Somers and Finola Meeking. Their only child and daughter, Elizabeth, was his mother, from whom James Hervey-Bathurst inherited Eastnor Castle. http://eastnorcastle.com/eastnor-castle-archvies/ (accessed August 29, 2017).

8. Eastnor Castle Archives [henceforth ECA], Meeking and Fletcher box, Lady Apsley, Type-script memoir.

9. ECA, Meeking and Fletcher box, notebook 1 of 2; ECA, Suitcase, Lady Somers and Lady Apsley Correspondence c. 1926–1930.

10. Gottlieb, 'Guilty Women,' 236; see also Kevin. J. Behony 'Lady Astor's Campaign for Nursery Schools in Britain, 1930–1939: Attempting to Valorize Cultural Capital in a Male-Dominated Political Field', *History of Education Quarterly* 49, no. 2 (May 2009):196.

11. For the importance of locally focused studies see Karen Hunt and June Hannam, 'Towards an Archaeology of Interwar Women's Politics', in *The Aftermath of Suffrage: Women, Gender, and Politics in Britain, 1918-1945*, ed. Julie V. Gottlieb and Richard Toye (Houndmill, Basingstoke, Hampshire, 2013), 125–126 and 137.

12. For the purposes of clarity, Lady Apsley is referred to here as 'Viola, (a variant of her birth name Violet), until she formally takes on the title Lady Apsley on her marriage. According to her great nephew James Hervey-Bathurst, her mother, Violet Fletcher of Saltoun, was known in the family as Violet and her daughter as Viola. Email James Hervey-Bathurst to author, 10 October 2017. Viola Meeking's' paternal great-grandfather, the London draper Charles Meeking, probably purchased Richings Park in 1855. The Meeking's coat of arms seems to have been acquired by her barrister grandfather, also called Charles Meeking ,who died in 1912. Viola's father was educated at Eton and Cambridge before dying aged 36 at Bloemfon-tein., *the Times*, 21 March 1913 http://www.ebooksread.com/authors-eng/arthur-charles-fox-davies/armorial-families--a-directory-of-gentlemen-of-coat-armour-hci/page-222-armorial-families--a-directory-of-gentlemen-of-coat-armour-hci.shtml, (accessed April 9, 2017)]' Richard Ive 'Richings Park', *Understanding Historic Parks & Gardens in Buckingham-shire*, The Buckinghamshire Gardens Trust Research & Recording Project (29 March 2016), http://www.bucksgardenstrust.org.uk/wp-content/uploads/2015/03/Richings.pdf (accessed April 2, 2017); 'Parishes: Iver', in *A History of the County of Buckingham: Volume* 3, ed.

William Page (London, 1925), 286–294. British History Online http://www.british-history.ac. uk/vch/bucks/vol3/pp286-294 (accessed April 1, 2017).

13. Bertha Talbot, one of three daughters of one of the wealthiest men in Great Britain, the M.P. C. R. M. Talbot of Margam Abbey and Penrice Castle, Glam, married John Fletcher, Saltoun Hall, Haddingtonshire, Scotland. See Talbot family in *Dictionary of Welsh Biography* http://yba.llgc.org.uk/en/s-TALB-MAR-1700.html; 'Death of Olivia Talbot,' *Edinburgh Evening News*, 8 October 1894; email from James Hervey-Bathurst to author 10 October 2017; for her role in the Scottish Mothers' Union, see ECA, Lady Apsley, Typescript memoir c 1950s-1966, Part I, 37.

14. ECA, Lady Apsley, Typescript memoir c 1950s–1966, Part I, 41ff.

15. Richings Park was famed for its associations with Alexander Pope and other literary figures.

16. http://www.angloboerwar.com/forum/17-memorials-and-monuments/26272-meeking-2-brothers (accessed April 9, 2017).

17. ECA, Lady Apsley, Typescript memoir, Part III, 3–4. EAC, Lady Apsley, Typescript memoir, Part I, 51. Richings Court had reverted to her barrister grandfather until Violet came of age. There seems to have been some controversy over the circumstances of her grandfather's death and by implication, the settlement, as her grandfather's body was exhumed a year later, The Times, Friday, Mar 21, 1913; 6; Issue 40165.

18. ECA, Lady Apsley, Typescript Memoir, Part III, 23–24.

19. 'Marsh Court,' https://historicengland.org.uk/listing/the-list/list-entry/1000149; http://www. lutyenstrust.org.uk/portfolio-item/new-book-marsh-court-missing-chapters-francis-james/ (accessed April 11, 2017); Dan Cruickshank, *The Country House Revealed: A Secret History of the British Ancestral Home* (London: BBC Books Random House, 2012), 234–72.

20. For more on VADs-members of the Voluntary Aid Detachment see http://www.redcross.org. uk/About-us/Who-we-are/History-and-origin/First-World-War/Volunteers-during-WW1 (accessed April 7, 2017)

21. Violet Johnson was listed as a donor and organiser of Marshfield Auxiliary Hospital and her health which had been affected by her 'solicitude for the wounded' men she nursed reportedly hastened her 'untimely' death from flu after the war. For her central role in the hospital see http://www.redcross.org.uk/About-us/Who-we-are/History-and-origin/First-World-War/ Card?fname=violet&sname=johnson&id=120196; (accessed April 7, untimely 2017); https:// infogalactic.com/info/1919_New_Year_Honours#Civil_Division_10 (accessed September 9, 2017). photo of Violet Charlotte Johnson's memorial can be found on https://www. findagrave.com/cgi-bin/fg.cgi?page=gr&GRid=80171674; https://www.findagrave.com/cgi-bin/fg.cgi?page=gr&GRid=80171674 (accessed April 7, 2017); https://historicengland.org. uk/listing/the-list/list-entry/1392554 (accessed April 7, 2017)

22. Lady Apsley recalls in a letter to the press that 'during the Great War I scrubbed ... floors and made beds for two years before I became a VAD staff nurse at a military hospital ... .', *Gloucestershire Echo*, January 16, 1943.

23. See her letter about the 'debacle' of the March retreat of 1918 in *The Daily Telegraph*, March 28, 1938.

24. Quotation from *The Sketch*, December 5, 1923; Described as the Chatelaine of Ritchings Parks in *The Sketch*, October 31, 1917 the sale is evidenced in ECA, Lady Apsley, Typescript Memoir, Part III, 70, though it is contended that she was still wealthy in her own right, see email from James Hervey-Bathurst to author, 10 October 2017.

25. 'Women's Air Club,' *The Daily Mail*, September 7, 1929. *Bristol Evening Post [henceforth BEP]*, January 20, 1966; Lady Apsley owned a De Havilland Dragon G-ACAO, thanks to Terry Mace http://afleetingpeace.org/wingsofpeace/ for this information. For more on the Forum Club see Elizabeth Crawford, *The Women's Suffrage Movement - A Reference Guide 1866-1928* (London: UCL Press, 1999), 120 and *'Alice Williams', Dictionary of Welsh Biography* (National Library of Wales) http://yba.llgc.org.uk/en/s10-WILL-ALE-1863.html. Amy Johnson was one of its members as was the women's rights activist Maria Sophia Allen.

26. Quotation from The Sketch 5 December 1923; EAC, Meekng and Fletcher box Typescriptt memoir typescript, Part III, 1–4.

27. Cited in Keith Wilson, ed., *The Rasp of War: The Letters of H.A. Gwynne to the Countess Bathurst 1914–1918* (London: Sidgwick and Jackson, 1988), 2.

28. Ibid., 6–12, ff. The Countess retained close links with *The Morning Post* editor J.A. Gwyne who continued as editor right up to its amalgamation with the *Daily Telegraph* in 1937 cited in 'Bathurst, Lilias Margaret Frances, Countess Bathurst (1871–1965), Colin Seymour-Ure', *ODNB*, (accessed March 18, 2017).

29. Quotation is from *The Register* (Adelaide), May 29, 1928; http://trove.nla.gov.au/newspaper/article/56624838 (accessed April 7, 2017). Mike Hughes, *Spies at Work*, (privately published revised edition 2008), 4, 25–9; Arthur McIvor '"A Crusade for Capitalism": The Economic League, 1919–39', *Journal of Contemporary History* 23, no. 4 (1988, October), 633.

30. Mike Hughes, Spies at Work, 4, 25–9; Arthur McIvor '"A Crusade for Capitalism": The Economic League, 1919–39', *Journal of Contemporary History* 23, no. 4 (1988, October), 633; G. C. Webber, *The Ideology of the British Right* (London and Sydney: Croom Helm, 1986), 21–6, 39–40; Panikos Panayi, 'The British Empire Union in the First World War', in Tony Kushner and Kenneth Lunn, eds. *The Politics of Marginality: Race the Radical Right and Minorities in Twentieth Century Britain* (London: Frank Cass, 1990), 113–30.

31. Her war work, her membership of the Forum club and her comments about her mother suggest she supported women's suffrage.

32. ECA, Letters to Finola Somers from Lady Apsley,

33. Email correspondence with the Hon. Mrs. Sandra de Laszlo, 13 March 2017; The Catalogue Raisonné of Works by Philip de László (1869–1937), http://www.delaszlocatalogueraisonne.com/de-laszlo; (accessed April 10, 2017), The Tatler, August 13, 1927; WDP 30 July 1924; Jeremy Crang, "The Women's Auxiliary Service in the Late 1930s', *Historical Research* 83, no. 220 (2010): 352.

34. 'Salmon Fishing in the Highlands,' *The Sphere*, September 27, 1924.

35. Julia Gottlieb, *Guilty Women*, 105–6; The Marchioness of Londonderry, *Retrospect*, (London: Frederick Muller, Ltd., 1938), 144–7.

36. Lord and Lady Apsley (ND but 1926), *The Amateur Settlers* (London: Hodder and Stoughton), 63–4.

37. Apsley, *Amateur Settlers*, (London, Hodder and Stoughton, 1926), 190.

38. Ibid., 109 and 189.

39. Julie V. Gottlieb, *Guilty Women: Foreign Policy and Appeasement in Inter-War Britain* (Basingstoke, Hampshire: Palgrave, 2015), 101.

40. Caitriona Beaumont, 'Citizens Not Feminists: The Boundary Negotiated between Citizenship and Feminism by Mainstream Women's Organisations in England, 1928–39', *Women's History Review* 9, no. 2 (2000): 411–29.

41. June Purvis, 'Emmeline Parkhurst in the Aftermath of Suffrage', in *The Aftermath of Suffrage*, eds. Julie V. Gottlieb and Richard Toye, 24 and 34.

42. ECA, Marsh Court Hospital Box 6.June 1929?

43. ECA, Marsh Court Hospital Box 6. 19 July 1930.

44. ECA, Letters to Lady Finola Somers, Tuesday 10 Dec 1929; 6 April 1930.

45. 'Familiar Family Studies: Lord Apsley with his Wife and Sons', *The Sketch*, December 2, 1931.

46. 'Women's Brave Spirit, Lady Apsley's Example', Northern Star (Lismore, NSW), August 18, 1936. http://trove.nla.gov.au/ndp/del/article/94656876#pstart9655176

47. Ibid, she is listed as taking a flying lesson in 1936.

48. *WDP*, 2 17 February 1934, 15 April 1937.

49. See for example, *WDP*, 2 August 1934, 14 November 1935

50. *WDP* 13 April 1933; Viola Apsley letter to the editor, *The Times*, July 16, 1936.

51. Lady Apsley and Diana Shedden, *To Whom the Goddess* (London: Hutchinson and Co., 1932); Lady Apsley, *Bridleways Through History: A History of Hunting from Prehistoric Times*, (London: Hutchinson and Co., 1936); McGuire, Lady Apsley, *ODNB*.

52. *BEP*, January 20, 1966.

53. *The Times*, April 8, 1936; Richard Griffiths, *Fellow Travellers of the Right: British Enthusiasts for Nazi Germany 1933–1939* (Oxford: Oxford University Press, 1983), 208.
54. R.D. Calvert Letter to the Editor, 8 April 1936.
55. Angela Schwartz, 'British Visitors to National Socialist Germany', *Journal of Contemporary History* 28, no. 3 (July 1993): 487–509, esp. 503–5.
56. Tony Kushner, 'Beyond the Pale? British Reactions to Nazi Anti-Semitism, 1933–39', in *The Politics of Marginality*, 143–6, 150–2.
57. *Amateur Settlers*, 142; EAC, Memoirs, Part 1, Chapter 1, 3–5.
58. Julie V. Gottlieb, *Guilty Women*, 17.
59. R. Thurlow, (review of Alan Sykes, *The Radical Right in Britain*, in *The English Historical Review* (2005), 283.
60. Ibid.; *Gloucestershire Echo* 16 January 1943.
61. Ribbentrop became Hitler's foreign minister in 1938' Harrison, *Fellow Travellers*, 137–41.
62. Julie Gottlieb, *Guilty Women*, 105; *Daily Mail*, September 7, 1929.
63. Nick Crowson, *Facing Fascism: The Conservative Party and The European Dictators 1935–1940* (London: Routledge, 1997), 22; Mike Hughes, *Spies at* Work, 11; Harrison, *Fellow Travellers*, 225.
64. Julie V. Gottlieb, '"We Were Done the Moment We Gave Women the Vote": The Female Franchise Factor and the Munich By-elections 1938–1939', in *The Aftermath of Suffrage*, eds. Gottlieb and Toye, 173.
65. *WDP*, March 28, 1938.
66. *The Western Daily Press and Bristol Mirror*, April 6, 1938.
67. G. C. Webber, *The Ideology of the British Right*, 46–8; Richard Griffiths, *Fellow Travellers of the Right*, 1939.
68. *BEP*, April 13, 1939. G. C. Webber, *The Ideology of the British Right*, 46–7.
69. *BEP*, February 23, 1939.
70. *WDP*, March 28, 1939; *Exeter and Plymouth Gazette*, March 17, 1939.
71. Apsley's own lack of ideological consistency stems in part from a long-standing Tory distrust of abstract rationalism but also from the fact that typically of women of her class, she never had a formal education and was somewhat contemptuous of academic rigour. Lady Apsley, *Bridleways Through History* (London: Hutchinson, 1936), 13; G. C. Webber, *The Ideology of the British Right*, 46–7,125–9. For her views on immigration to Australia see her Letter to the Editor, the *Times*, January 7, 1938.
72. http://www.chch.ox.ac.uk/fallen-alumni/major-lord-allen-algernon-bathurst-apsley; http://www.bristolblitzed.org/?page_id=63; *Gloucestershire Echo,* January 16, 1943.
73. Yet she was described only as his 'staunch helper' in the press, *WDP*, December 22, 1942.
74. *Gloucestershire Echo*, January 16, 1943.
75. She was appointed in October 1938 whilst still supporting appeasement *Gloucestershire* Echo, October 21, 1938. See her letter to *The Daily* Telegraph, December 14, 1938; For the increasingly wide range of traditional men's jobs ATS were taking on, see Women in National Service, esp. Dr. Edith Summerskill (Fulham, West), HC Deb August 3, 1943 vol 391 cc2111-201 2111; Jeremy Crang, Women's Auxiliary Services, *Historical Research*, 351.
76. http://barneshistorian.com/vm-apsley.php (accessed April 9, 2017).
77. See for example, Harold L. Smith, 'The Womanpower Problem in Britain during the Second World War', *The Historical Journal* 27, no. 4 (1984, December), 925–45.
78. James Hinton, 'Introduction,' in *Women, Social Leadership, and the Second World War: Continuities of Class* (Oxford University Press, 2002-11-21). Accessed August 26, 2017) http://www.oxfordscholarship.com/view/10.1093/acprof:oso/9780199243297.001.0001/acprof-9780199243297-chapter-1; ECA, Lady Apsley, Typescript Memoir, Part III, p.3. For the increasingly wide range of traditional men's jobs ATS were taking on, see Women in National Service, esp. Dr. Edith Summerskill (Fulham, West), *Hansard,* HC Deb 3 August 1943 vol 391 cc2111-201.
  The ATS was absorbed into the Women's Royal Army Corps in 1949, (which itself was not fully integrated into the British army until 1992).; MacGuire, Lady Apsley, *ODNB;*

http://www.nationalarchives.gov.uk/womeninuniform/wwii_intro.htm (accessed September 26, 2017).

79. Catriona Beaumont, *Housewives and Citizens: Domesticity and the Women's Movement in England, 1928-1960* (Hounmills, Basingstoke: Macmillan) cited in Madge Dresser and June Hannam, *Women and the City*, 147–8.

80. *Gloucester Citizen*, November 22, 1943; Brian Harding *Keeping Faith: The History of the Royal British Legion* (Barnsley So. Yorkshire: Leo Cooper, 2001), 186–7.

81. Graham Wootton, *The Official History of the British Legion* (London: MacDonald and Evans Ltd., 1956), 276–2, 278; *Eastbourne Herald*, June 16, 1945.

82. *WDP*, January 12, 1943, but see Jenny Lee's response to such assertions in *WDP* February 13, 1943.

83. *Birmingham Daily Post*, February 16, 1943.

84. Lionel Fielden, Bristol After Thoughts, *The New Statesman and Nation*, February 27, 1943, 136–7.

85. Ibid.

86. Ibid.

87. Ibid. 'England Votes', *Life* [Magazine], April 5, 1943; Lionel Fielden, Bristol After Thoughts, Feb 27, 1943, 136–7.

88. Fielden, Bristol After Thoughts, *New Statesman*, Feb 27, 1943, 104; for Unionist Women's support see BRO, Records of Bristol Conservative Association, Bristol West Women's branch, 38036/BW/6d (1943).

89. Lionel Fielden, Bristol After Thoughts, *New Statesman*, Feb 27, 1943, 136–7.

90. Anon., 'A Spectator's Notebook', *The Spectator*, Feb 26, 1943 http://archive.spectator.co.uk/article/26th-february-1943/4/a-spectators-notebook February 25, 1943 (accessed September 9, 2017); Lionel Fielden 'Bristol After Thoughts', *New Stateman and Nation* Feb 27, 1943, 136–7.

91. Lady Apsley was the fourth widow to succeed her deceased husband into Parliament, the first being Margaret Wintringham in 1921; Hilda Runciman (1928) and Agnes Hardie (1937) succeeded her. UK vote100: celebrating 100 years of the vote in 2018 in the UK Parliament,' https://ukvote100.org/2016/06/06/widow-,.mps/ (accessed September 9, 2017). For reservations about her selection see Anon, A London Diary, *The New Statesman and Nation*, February 13, 1943, 105.

92. Laura Beers, 'Women for Westminster,' Feminism and the Limits of Non-Partisan Associational Culture', in *The Aftermath of Suffrage: Women, Gender, and Politics in Britain, 1918–1945*, ed. Julie V. Gottlieb and Richard Toye (Basingstoke: Palgrave Macmillan, 2013), 227–32.

93. The *Times*, February 26, 1943; WDP 20 February 1943; Newcastle Journal 26 February 1943; Pamela Brookes, *Women at Westminster: An Account of Women in the British Parliament 1918–1966* (London: Peter Davies, 1967), 134; *The Times*, February 26, 1943.

94. Richard Kelley Women Members of Parliament: House of Commons Background Paper (14 October 2014) in *Women in Parliament: A Guide to the History of Women's Participation in Parliament and Their Representation in the Historical Collections* (London: Houses of Parliament, 2015), 73; Brian Harrison, 'Women in a Men's House the Women M.P.s, 1919–1945', *The Historical Journal* 29 no. 3 (1986, September), 623–54 Published by: Cambridge University Press Stable URL: http://www.jstor.org/stable/2639051 (accessed March 10, 2107).

95. Sir Cuthbert Headlam (Author), Stuart Ball, ed., *Parliament and Politics in the Age of Baldwin and Macdonald: The Diaries of Sir Cuthbert Headlam* (Cambridge: Cambridge University Press, 1999), 11 July 1944, 412.Thanks to John R. Stevens for this reference.

96. *Women in Parliament*,73 Brian Harrison, 'Women in a Men's House the Women M.P.s, 1919–1945', *The Historical Journal* 29, no. 3 (Sep., 1986): 623–54 Published by: Cambridge University Press Stable URL: http://www.jstor.org/stable/2639051 (accessed March 10, 2017) 19:25 UTC; Julia Swindells, 'Coming Home to Heaven: Manpower and Myth in 1944 Britain', *Women's History Review* 4, no. 2 (1995): 223–34.

97. https://kclpure.kcl.ac.uk/portal/files/30807371/2012_Takayanagi_Mari_1069335_ethesis.pdf (accessed April 7, 2017).

98. *The Daily* Telegraph, 24 1943 called her maiden speech 'one of the two most moving speeches the House of Commons has listened to for a long time … '; The *Lancet*, 1943, 214,442–44.

99. *Hansard* 1803–2005, People (A), Viscountess Apsley. http://hansard.millbanksystems.com/people/viscountess-apsley/ (accessed April 7, 2017), Her first contribution was to urge that small gardens be included in plans for post-war housing provision, her last recorded entry was on June 14, 1945 concerning Old Age Pensions.

100. Harrison, 624; *WDP*, August 6, 1943.

101. *Daily Telegraph*, March 3, 1943. The deputation headed by Dame Irene Ward included Conservatives Mary Astor, Thelma Cazalet-Keir and Mavis Tate as well as Labour MP Dr. Edith Summerskill.

102. Maguire (1998) *Conservative* Women, 85–5; Hansard, 'Women in National Service' 3 August 1943, Volume 391, 2125–6 and 2129, http://parlipapers.proquest.com/parlipapers/docview/t71.d76.cds5cv0391p0-0013?accountid=14785 (accessed April 5, 2017).

103. See for example, *Hansard*, 'Family Allowances Bill,' 8 March 1945, 408, 2259.

104. Julia Swindells,'Coming Home to Heaven: Manpower and Myth in 1944 Britain', *Women's History Review* 4, no. 2 (1995), 223–34.

105. *Hansard,* 'National War Effort, Women Police', March 25, 1944, 910–1. http://parlipapers.proquest.com/parlipapers/docview/t71.d76.cds5cv0407p0-0011?accountid=14785 http://gateway.proquest.com/openurl?url_ver=Z39.88-2004&res_dat=xri:hcpp&rft_dat=xri:hcpp:hansard:CDS5CV0400P0-0007 (accessed April 7, 2017).

106. Pamela Brookes, *Women at Westminster*, 141.

107. *Hansard,* HC Deb 08 March 1945 vol 408 cc2324-2325

108. Ibid.

109. Dresser (2016), *Women and the City,* 161–2. http://freepages.military.rootsweb.ancestry.com/~memoirs/docs/announcement.htm (accessed April 8, 2017).

110. Re bridleways, HC Deb, *Hansard,* February 2, 1944 vol 396 cc1265–62 , http://hansard.millbanksystems.com/people/viscountess-apsley/1944 (accessed April 9, 2017); re sewerage in rivers *Hansard*, HC Deb June 8, 1944 vol 400 cc1550-1551, HC Deb July 13, 1944 vol 401 cc1897; Written Answers (Commons) April 12, 1945 vol 409; re open spaces, parks and reforestation see Feb 13, 1945, May 4, 1945; re playing fields Feb 15, 1944, March 22, 1944; re fertilizers, July 27, 1944 and February 1, 1945, 1627–8 http://hansard.millbanksystems.com/people/viscountess-apsley/1944/1945 (accessed April 9, 2017). For her imperialist vision of a renovated House of Commons, see *The Times*, November 21, 1944.

111. *The Amateur Settlers,* 143–4; (HC Deb) *Hansard*, December 20,1944 vol 406 cc1834-1835;28 November 1944 vol 404 cc2426.

112. Thelma Cazalet-Keir also lost her seat and the election was seen by some in the press as a backlash against Conservative women MPs.

113. She identified 'five great tasks ahead: —The prosecution of the war against Japan, demobilisation and the re-shaping of the forces required for the Far East, getting industry restarted on civilian necessities of life, re-building our export trade, carrying out the far-reaching proposals of the Four Years Plan for food. work, and homes. For the successful solution, national unity on as wide basis possible was essential.' *WDP*, June 23, 1945.

114. http://www.conservativemanifesto.com/1945/1945-conservative-manifesto.shtml [accessed 15 November 2017].

115. *WDP*, June 20 and June 11, 1945.

116. Ibid.

117. ECA, Fletcher Family Box, Notebook titled 'Cirencester'.

118. Ibid., See for example the letter to the editor from L.M. Atkinson, *WDP*, December 10, 1945.

119. ECA, Fletcher Family Box, Notebook titled 'Cirencester'.

120. Ibid.

121. Ibid.

122. Ibid.

123. Ibid.; Election statistics from http://www.politicsresources.net/area/uk/ge45/i04.htm (accessed September 1, 2017).

124. Atkinson letter, *WDP*, December 10, 1945.
125. ECA, Cirencester Notebook.
126. *WDP*, November 26, 1949.
127. *WDP*, May 27, 1946, *Daily Mail*, January 23, 1950; *Daily Telegraph*, February 11, 1950; *Sheffield Telegraph*, February 11, 1950; *Daily Mail*, January 23, 1950; *Daily Telegraph*, February 11, 1950; *Sheffield Telegraph*, February 11, 1950.
128. Brian Harding, *Keeping Faith*, 295 and 298; Graham Wootton, *The Official History of the British Legion*, 295.
129. Interview with Keith and Mary Rogers by Madge Dresser, 19 March 2016. Keith Rogers was Deputy Parliamentary agent for Bristol Northeast from 1949 and he and his wife had been active in the Young Conservatives.; Thanks too to Bristol Cllr Nicola Bowden-Jones for sharing her family's recollections in conversation with Madge Dresser, 16 June 2016.

Acknowledgments

This article grew out of a paper presented to the 'Rethinking Right Wing Women conference' organised by Julie Gottlieb Clarisse Berthezène and Jeremey McIllwaine at the Bodleian Library in 29-20 June 2015. The author would like to thank the organisers, as well as Melanie Unwin and Mari Takayanagi of the Parliamentary archives, Michael Hughes, Senior Archivist, Bodleian Library and Helen Langley as well as to Christine Williams, Jim Brennan and Jennifer Bank for their encouragement and advice. Particular thanks go to Carol Dyhouse, June Hannam, Moira Martin and Glyn Stone for reading and commenting on drafts of this article.

I am grateful too to James Hervey-Bathurst for allowing me access to his family's archives at Eastnor Castle, Herefordshire and express my appreciation for the able assistance of the archivists Hazel Hill and Stephen Price who are cataloguing the collection.

Disclosure statement

No potential conflict of interest was reported by the author.

Women in the organisation of the Conservative Party in Wales, 1945–1979

Sam Blaxland

ABSTRACT

Despite being hidden from view and side-lined by history, women were a key and active part of the Conservative Party's success in Wales in this period. Although rarely candidates or Agents, a number of Conservative women were forceful and brave political campaigners. Whilst they were often the defenders of social conservatism and rigid gender norms their actions and discourse sometimes owed more to the kind of 'progressive' politics they were resisting than they seemed to realise. On a wider scale, many middle-class women members in Wales, as in Britain on the whole, provided the Party with financial and electoral support, but their membership of branches and associations was often part of a broader patchwork of respectability, social activity, conservatism and resistance of societal change. As a result, these groups offered women an opportunity to exercise a form of social and organisational leadership.

Introduction

Despite popular perceptions and consequent misunderstandings, the Conservative Party, and right-wing politics, have always had firm bedrocks of support in Wales. Although the Labour Party dominated, electorally, in prominent industrial regions, support for Conservatism in places like Cardiff, Monmouthshire, Pembrokeshire, significant sections of the North Wales coast, and the large rural counties that border England has been substantial. For the vast majority of the post-Second World War period, the Party has been Wales' second strongest political force both in terms of parliamentary seats won, as well as the share of the vote gained at election times. Of (roughly, depending on boundary changes) 36 Parliamentary seats in Wales the Conservative Party held between three at its worst performance in 1966, and eleven at its best in 1979. In 1983 it won fourteen.[1] The share of the vote the Party won was at its highest in 1959 and 1979 at 32%, whilst its lowest was 24% in October 1974. The Welsh share of the vote tended to be ten percentage points lower than the equivalent figure for England.[2] The Party, therefore, whilst weaker overall in Wales than in other parts of Britain, was the nation's 'second party' in this period, providing a threat and a challenge to Labour in some of the nation's most marginal seats.

Conservatism relied heavily on various peoples and groups to bolster or to reinforce these significant but often precarious foundations. The fact that many seats outside of the industrial heartlands were marginal demonstrates that there were tangible rewards for working in the Party's name. It is in this context that Party activists, and women in particular, were key cogs in the political machine. Although a myriad of factors determined how the electorate chose to vote, historians have concluded that grass-roots activist support undoubtedly helped advertise, raise funds for, and provide a voting base for the Party.[3] The women in these ranks continually outnumbered their male counterparts by a considerable margin, including in Wales. Indeed, more women were members of the Conservative Party in post-war Britain than any other political movement, forming the backbone of local Conservative politics as a result.[4] Although many women were members of the Labour Party in this era as well, the proportion of women members was lower, deterred, perhaps, by the Party's more general 'cloth-cap' and masculine image.[5] Although there are no precise surviving figures, what evidence there is suggests that there were twice as many female as male members of the Conservative Party in Wales in the post-War period.[6] In comparison, women made up 40% of the total membership figure for the Labour Party in 1949, for example.[7] Some of these Tory women were more than just members, becoming active and vociferous public campaigners. Despite this central role, their presence in the broader picture of this period—particularly in Wales—has thus far been underrepresented.

To redress this imbalance, this article focuses on the activities and the rhetoric of local female activists and associations in Wales from 1945 to 1979. In a break from most political history scholarship on this period, it utilises less conventional archival and printed sources, many of which are from the perspective of women themselves, like secret constituency reports, petitions, letters, committee minutes and newspaper reports. The latter is of particular value because it was through the local press (and the generally conservative *Western Mail* in particular) that women activists were occasionally given a platform to articulate opinions that tended to be a blend of their Party's, and their own, views on politics and society. This article addresses two different aspects of women's involvement in local Conservative politics. It discusses the campaigning work of a handful of senior activists, and the language used as part of that. It then focuses more broadly on the role played by wider women's associations. Few women filled the role of parliamentary candidate, but a significant number were influential campaigners in public at election time, deconstructing any notion that all were passive or subservient cogs in a patriarchal machine. Whilst women performed many of the typical gendered roles ascribed to them, such as organising tea parties and stuffing envelopes, this forum gave prominent figures in their ranks a platform to exercise a form of organisational and social leadership that often had much more to do with attempts to buttress a more traditional version of their world view whilst resisting the rapid social and cultural changes of the era, than it did with pure politics. In both cases women actively shunned the emerging language and actions of second-wave feminism and 'liberation'. However, because these political women were much more three-dimensional than is often presumed, their actions and language often meant they more closely mirrored these movements than they would have admitted or recognised, or that stereotypes allow for. This therefore poses wider questions about the persistence, in some quarters, of conservatism in this period, but it also sheds light on the similarities and the differences between those women who identified as 'left' and 'right' wing.

In addressing this issue, the article makes a contribution to several historiographical fields. Welsh women's history is a relatively new area of study and scholarship is still developing. It was not until 1981 that Deidre Beddoe mused upon what an alien, newly arrived on Earth, would think if she read the entire cannon of Welsh history. Beddoe suggested that the alien would be confused about how the Welsh procreated, so absent were women from the narrative and the analysis.[8] Since then, Beddoe has been at the forefront of redressing what was a clear imbalance, along with fellow historians like Angela V. John, and Ursula Masson. Their work offered strong pieces of social history that filled yawning chasms in the historiography.[9] When these authors mentioned politics, however, there were curious absences. For example, when Beddoe gave the Welsh Political Archive lecture in 2004 with the promising title 'Women and Politics in Twentieth Century Wales', the legions of Welsh Conservative, or right-wing, women were absent from the discussion.[10] This was in-keeping with more general historiographical trends. Although Beddoe had no call to say it in 1981, what the same alien would have noticed, had she been inclined to look, was that the Conservative Party was also wildly under-represented in an unfortunately small corpus of Welsh political history that was dominated by Liberalism or the politics of Labour and unionism.[11] Even since 1981, only a handful of pieces of scholarship have attempted to engage with either women or Conservatives in any great depth or detail.[12]

Wales, therefore, is not the first natural port of call for anyone studying either Conservative or women's history, let alone a fusion of the two. But it is not just the Welshness of the historiography that impedes this; so does the politics of gender history. This historiography has long emphasised the links between (big and small 'l') Labour and women. Although sources on working women are often less conventional and regularly more difficult to obtain—like oral testimonies—the context of growth in the field of social history and feminism from the 1960s onwards meant that historical research tended to lean towards areas such as working mothers and women's life in working-class areas or neighbourhoods.[13] Hence, the popular image of the politicised woman from modern Wales takes the form of the miner's wife, heroically joining the world of picket lines, strikes, and nation-wide travel tours—in many cases for the first time—during the infamous 1984/85 strike.[14] The former MP for Swansea East, Sian James, perhaps typified this; even more so after she featured as a central character in the 2014 film *Pride*, which was based on that period. Labour history has tended to shun Conservatism for obvious reasons, whilst a strong nationalistic strain in Wales has dismissed it for the way in which is emphasises Britishness and continuity, not separateness and difference.[15]

When thinking about Conservative women in British history more broadly, there is, most obviously, the burgeoning corpus of work on Margaret Thatcher. This presents her as an individual who made remarkable symbolic strides for women in British politics, who rhetorically espoused many feminine qualities, and who 'displayed little interest in helping other women advance, made anti-feminist statements and distanced herself from the women's movement'.[16] For Green, Thatcher was someone whose hostility to ideas like working women grew as she herself became more successful, although she was 'clearly aware that her femininity could be politically useful'.[17] She was a middle-class 'domestic feminist'.[18] Jackson and Saunders argued that Thatcher had to 'create her own model of female leadership', whilst for Laura Beers Thatcher worked to 'valorise housewives' but was 'unsupportive' of equal rights and did 'little to encourage' women's participation in the workplace.[19] For her latest biographer Charles Moore, she made much of 'housewifely virtues', whilst having a resolute belief in the notion that 'she alone' through her actions and her policies had 'rescued Britain from its post-1945 years of semi-Socialist decline'.[20]

At the other end of the scale, when focusing on 'ordinary' Conservative women, historians have tended to concentrate on them as voters, analysing their natural social conservatism, the overtly masculine image of Labour, and the effective rhetoric the Party deployed around household budgets and family life.[21] Much less attention has been paid to women in their capacity as vigorous and politically conscious activists, or to the nature of Women's Associations across the country, and how they shed light on the nature of middle-class culture after the Second World War. Some work has discussed the nature of women's activities as rank-and-file members and the importance of local associations, groups and committees, but this kind of female conservatism, as Cowman argued, is presented by such authors as 'a problem that required investigation' or as 'something unexpected and perplexing'.[22] Campbell, for example, presented Conservative women largely as 'powerless' and 'subordinate' actors in a 'highly conformist' organisation.[23] Few have questioned the extent to which women exercised a significant degree of political independence and agency in the form of social leadership as part of, or through, these forums, often commanding and marshalling larger groups of peers more effectively than their male counterparts. There has also been little attention paid to the role key female activists played in disseminating the Party's policy and—crucially—their own personal messages to a wider electorate. Examples from Wales as explored in this article demonstrate both that Tory women wielded a form of quiet but forceful influence in and around their spheres, and that they were sometimes, in their own right, brave and vociferous independent political campaigners.

The period 1945-1979 has been selected for a number of key reasons. It was after the General Election defeat of 1945 that Women's Associations were formally incorporated into the Party structure and a deliberate recruitment drive under the guise of Lord Woolton's scheme spiked their numbers, albeit temporarily.[24] The 1940s is also a useful point to begin the discussion because it has been suggested that women born before 1945 were inherently more conservative than those raised after it under the welfare state. As the increasingly older membership of the Conservatives between 1945 and 1979 would have tended to have fallen into this bracket, this period allows for an exploration of the social attitudes of such groups.[25] Although the character and the timbre of local political societies had changed markedly by 1979—the year a Conservative woman was elected Prime Minister—the vehicle and the mechanisms had not crumbled to ruins or rusted as they would do by the beginning of the twenty first century. Tory women activists still performed many, although not all, of their traditional functions, so a further sense of continuity within this time-frame can be established. On the other hand, however, the wider nature of societal change between 1945 and 1979 adds a different dimension. The period witnessed a sea change in British political culture and social life almost unrivalled in the modern era, one that encompassed rising affluence, and dramatic social change with the arrival of second-wave feminism, radical left-wing politics, and the dawn of a distinct and unbridled youth culture.[26] In the specific realm of politics, this was the era of rapid changes in the field of electioneering, conducted more on the television as time passed and less through the public meeting or on the doorstep.[27] The latter had always been a crucial part of the local activist's raison d'être in a less technologically advanced Britain. As such things impacted particularly on women, this makes charting the changes, continuities, and the reactions within their associations all the more fruitful and intriguing. A greater body of work exists on this topic from pre-Second World War years, and the inter-war period.[28] This article's analysis of the post-war period allows comparisons with that better understood era to be teased out. Although Conservative women and their culture changed significantly after the Second World War, in many respects there are significant parallels to draw between the post- and the inter-war periods.

Grass-roots activists and their ideologies

It is easy for the historian to miss the level of influence Conservative women had in Wales because they so rarely occupied prominent positions or ones associated with power like prospective parliamentary candidate or Agent—the figure who was trained by the central Party and employed to organise and run Associations.[29] When women were chosen for such roles it was because the results were foregone conclusions or inconsequential, or because, in the case of an Agent, they possessed the feminine 'gift ... of administration'.[30] Almost all Agents in this period were young, unmarried, and working in unwinnable seats.[31] Between 1945 and 1979, only nine women stood as Conservative candidates throughout Wales' 36 constituencies[32]—none of which were marginal, let alone winnable. That averaged out at less than one per General Election.[33] Many of the barriers that willing women ran up against were local selection panels, where Association chairmen regularly side-lined women.[34] Even though she was labelled an experienced and good campaigner, Pamela Thomas was struck off the interview list for the seat of Newport in the run up to the 1964 election purely because of her sex.[35] Women, as Maguire noted, were often complicit in the drive to stop other women becoming candidates on the grounds of their natural conservatism, or jealousy.[36] The sources sometimes reinforce many of the more obvious interpretations and stereotypes of Tory women as rather politically naive and interested only in the superficial. A visit by David Gibson-Watt MP to speak to the Barry constituency's women in 1970, for example, was reported as having gone 'down a treat' because of his 'lofty charm' which the women thought was 'nice'.[37] It is in this context that much of the analysis about women's relative lack of prominence in the higher echelons of local Conservative politics has been conducted.

The context of Welsh political culture in this period is also vital to our understanding of Conservative women, their backgrounds, their activities and the pattern of their dispersal across Wales. Labour dominance—both politically and culturally, with a small and large 'l'—in Wales was one key factor that determined why, in some seats, despite reasonable numbers of Conservative votes, very few people, including women, were willing to declare themselves as outright Conservatives, or to work for the Party.[38] One woman in Rhondda was reported to have shooed the Conservative candidate, Francis Pym, away from her door in 1959 even though she was going to vote for him, because of her concern at 'what the neighbours would say' if she saw them talking.[39] Jonathan Evans, a future Conservative politician, growing up in the Ebbw Vale seat in the 1960s described how he perceived there to be a system of political nepotism that abounded in Labour-dominated regions, particularly the public sector. He sensed that promotion would go to teachers, for example, who were generally supportive of Labourism, and this added to people's reluctance to declare a Conservative affiliation.[40] It was said, only half-jokingly, that to put up a Conservative poster in many parts of industrial Wales was to invite a 'half brick through the living room window'[41], or a 'whiz-bang' through the letterbox.[42] Even by the end of this period, reporters in the Valleys still commented on the strength of such feelings and attitudes. People with long memories spoke critically of Churchill's supposed sending of troops to Tonypandy, whilst children declared they would vote Labour, when they were old enough to, like their parents.[43] Although the Party was strong in many parts of Wales this overarching attitude had the potential to colour broader perceptions of it.

Despite this, however, the case of Wales in this period opens up an opportunity to re-evaluate the wider role played by women across Britain, the most noticeable of whom tended to be senior figures in a local association, often heading up the women's branch, or playing an active role in it. When one studies local files, and the reports in the middle pages of newspapers, however, it is possible to offer a much more nuanced picture of women's public involvement, and in assembling a small collective biography of such figures, other different themes emerge. Although backroom work was an essential task of most willing Conservative women, they sometimes took themselves, and their party's message, out on the stump, demonstrating in the process a flare, an independence of mind, and an autonomous political identity. These women were often (although not always) the wives of prospective candidates, or association chairmen: supposedly 'his staunchest supporter, his most enthusiastic worker, his permanent organiser'.[44] A typical image that appeared in campaigning material, and particularly in the press throughout this period, was the candidate standing over his spouse as she stuffed envelopes full of electioneering material.[45] But their organisational role sometimes extended beyond merely being a 'staunch supporter' of a husband, something that had undoubtedly been a strong feature of inter-war local Conservatism. Another of the features of that period had been the Primrose League which had the tendency to 'look back' whilst still making a 'contribution to the modernisation of right-wing politics', and it was this mix of characteristics that tended to define some key Welsh Conservative activists after 1945.[46]

In assessing particular individuals is it possible to re-examine the role of Conservative women, and draw attention to the fact that they were far from a homogenous group. An important example of such a woman was Hilda Protheroe-Beynon, the leading female activist in the Carmarthen seat in the late 1950s and 1960s. As the wife of the Association's Chairman she was, in her own words, 'virtually press-ganged into being a candidate' for the 1964 General Election. On the surface, 'Mrs P-B' (as she was known locally) was an archetypical Tory woman: a self-declared 'ordinary housewife'—despite being a farming businesswoman—who organised and gave speeches strictly between 'the housework and the meals'.[47] But observers sent to report on the campaign in Carmarthen noted that she delivered such speeches in a manner that demonstrated she 'did not give a rap for highfaultin' political cross-talk', speaking her mind 'bluntly, militantly, and without fear or favour'. Concentrating primarily on pensions and agricultural issues she injected notable life into the election 'with robust platform speeches ... which [were] always off the cuff'. Although praise was understandably forthcoming from the supportive *Western Mail*, reporters took special care to note how Mrs P-B supplied 'the sparkle' and 'the fireworks of the hustings' attracting much attention for the Conservatives 'by her personality'. Local Conservatives were reported to be pleased that, whatever the outcome of the election in Carmarthen, the case for Conservatism had been put forward 'in no ineffective manner' by their candidate.[48]

It is noteworthy that her rustic and almost eccentric campaign tactics stood in such contrast to the methods of the incumbent Labour member for the seat, Megan Lloyd George, who was one of two female Labour MPs in Wales at the time.[49] Lady Megan was as far from a typical Labour woman as could be imagined—and unusual even for a politician, given her elite background and 'family tradition of political service'.[50] She was part of what the *Western Mail* called 'a deadpan exercise in the earnestness of political aspirations'.[51] 'Mrs P-B' was fighting a hopeless campaign and therefore had nothing to lose, but it still remains significant that in a contest against another woman, and a Lloyd George in particular, it was she who provided the 'sparkle' that resulted in newspaper stories being about her and not Lady Megan. Such a positive interpretation is reinforced by a memo from Conservative Central Office which noted that she was 'extremely well known' because of her 'colourful and ebullient' character'.[52] In her style and her tactics she was forthright and unlike the typical image of a Conservative women, or the wife of a senior figure. Even though she claimed to be reluctant about campaigning, there is more than just a faint echo of Margaret Thatcher in 'Mrs P-B', who, despite cultivating her own image as a housewife, had said in 1959 that she would 'vegetate if I were left at the kitchen sink'.[53]

This blend of conservatism with strident campaigning tactics was to be found in other women in Wales in this period. Some, like Kathleen Smith, who was an activist in Caernarfon in the 1960s, also introduced a greater sense of ideology into proceedings, making a forceful argument about her personal views on the place of women in politics and society. In 1966 she penned an article for the *Western Mail* that demonstrated a curious mix of the kind of progressive language associated with the decade, and a much longer-standing social conservatism. Under the eye-catching headline 'Why not put more women in power?', Smith argued that women should be Members of Parliament in equal ratios to men, and perhaps in even greater ratios considering their stronger abilities to budget, form good relationships, and represent broader interests. Again, there were similarities between this piece and one of Thatcher's earliest (and most feminist) forays into public discussions on the matter, when, in 1952, she had written 'Why not a woman Chancellor or Foreign Secretary?'[54] It also echoed rhetoric from the wider Women's Movement in this period—the fulcrum of which was the emergence of the Women's Liberation Movement in 1968—which had recognised that 'public life and the workplace were primarily male spaces'.[55] Smith set out feminine political qualities of 'persuasion' and 'selflessness' contrasting these with the masculine traits of 'belligerence, grab and exploitation'.[56] Her 'overriding reason' for arguing that Britain needed women politicians, however, was because of the 'moral contributions' they could make. She wrote that 'now the Church sits on the fence' it was up to women to articulate 'guidance' on 'crime, affluence, contraception and abortion ... or any other serious problems of modern life ... .always, women have set the moral standards through their influence in the home, but now that the Church has lost its grip on life, it is vital that women should publically exert their influence on moral issues'.[57]

Although she did not explicitly say it, Smith was offering an outright disavowal of the kind of progressive and feminist ideas and rhetoric that were quickly becoming a feature of political discourse in Britain in the mid-1960s.[58] For all the generalisations that have been made about that decade, it was one in which, through many areas of life—be it music, urban redevelopment, social legislation or political movements—'modernity [was] made visible, tangible', causing high levels of excitement, anxiety and disapproval.[59] Conservative reactions to modernity were not new. Inter-war Conservative women had constantly disassociated themselves from feminism in its (very different) 'first wave' form on the grounds that it was too aggressive and controlling. Clear parallels, however, exist between Conservative critiques of both first and second wave versions of feminist ideas.[60] Smith's argument was not anti-women, but it was grounded in a traditional understanding of feminine qualities. In taking aim at the failures of the Church she bound up many of the concerns about moral decline with the role women specifically could play to fill that vacuum. What she seemed less conscious of was the fact that parts of her argument, and certainly the headline of the piece itself, owed something to this relatively new discourse that she was trying to distance herself from. Whilst her language displayed many continuities with statements from the earlier inter-war period, Smith's explicit call for women to take up positions of power was a very post-war type of rallying cry: it appeared the same year as Juliet Mitchell's 'ground breaking' essay on women and 'the Longest Revolution' did in New Left Review.[61] Although Mitchell and Smith would surely have balked at the idea that they shared a vaguely similar position, elements of their rhetoric were indeed familiar. Crucially, Smith's article was also indicative of the drawing of battle lines between Labour and the Conservatives in Wales. As Evans and Jones have noted, the steady decline in the strength of Labour associations since the war was given a shot in the arm and a new impetus in the lead up to the emergence of second wave feminism, and with that came renewed and fresh associational activity.[62] The context of 1966 is key too. Harold Wilson had been in power for two years and his Labour government would go on to enact sweeping liberal reforms in areas like contraception and abortion that Smith was so concerned about.[63]

Despite these very significant changes, and the ways in which the grass-roots of other political parties were changing, a sense of continuity still remained a central theme in Conservative circles, unsurprisingly so considering the socially and culturally conservative worlds of Tory women's societies. In 1970, Wales' 'top Tory' activist, Mrs Irene Everest, was still exhibiting a remarkable blend of those characteristics that had defined some of her counterparts like 'Mrs P-B' and Kathleen Smith. She ran a large association in Barry, where the 'bachelor' candidate Raymond Gower was supposedly accorded 'hero' status (he had defeated a rare female Labour MP, Dorothy Rees, to win the seat in 1951) and whose 2,000 members took on the 'feminine election tasks of addressing envelopes'.[64] Everest herself admitted that she only had so much time to devote to politics because her husband's business 'keeps him working late'. She spoke from platforms about 'prices, cost of living, and housewifely election issues'.[65] Again, however, initial appearances provide a telescoped view. Buried deeper in the report on Mrs Everest's activities are the revelations that she was a forceful and independently minded campaigner, deliberately travelling to Labour Party stronghold areas, 'preferably alone' and unaccompanied.[66] These were places where a vigorous political street culture had long set the tone of debate, and the deliberate decision to travel to such places was indicative of a certain kind of independence of thought and action.[67] Although she was quoted as saying that this wasn't 'a bit brave', the reality would have been slightly different. She had been warned that in places like Caerphilly 'I would probably have my car turned over'.[68]

Whilst this was obviously an example of exaggeration for effect, such places had large communities that were certainly hostile to Conservatism. Mrs Everest's decision to 'go into non-Conservative areas' because she found the 'hostile looks' from other women 'exhilarating' speaks volumes about the attitudes of these women canvassers.[69] Such vignettes should encourage a re-evaluation of Campbell's suggestion that Conservative activists were 'coy'.[70] It emphasises the importance of studying individuals and not thinking about groups of political women as homogenous, and it demonstrates that those who took on leadership or campaigning roles could be quite the opposite of coy.

A note of caution should be sounded here, however. Whilst some prominent Conservative women in this period were demonstrating an unusual degree of autonomy, it is still possible to note subtle but important differences when they were compared with activists from other political parties. Two Conservative women from Wales in 1959 and 1966 went on to the record to argue that it was 'male prejudice' that kept women away from front-line politics and stymied their ambitions, but in Labour ranks similar activists argued that 'prejudice' was 'dying' and on the wane in local Labour associations.[71] One commented that she had been 'welcomed as a candidate and as a woman', signifying a subtle but significant difference between the two main political parties in Wales in this period.[72] Labour wives like Mrs Llewellyn Williams were far more likely to talk of the need to go out to work during her husband's 1959 campaign. In contrast, when the Conservative camp were asked the same questions, Mrs Anthony Arnold replied that she provided her spouse with 'a pair of comfortable flat shoes'.[73] It was Labour, a party that in theory had been committed to sexual equality from its beginnings[74], which adopted and supported Eirene White as the MP for Flint East from 1950 to 1970 whilst the Conservative Association in the seat argued that their representative had to be a man because the industrial nature of the constituency was 'unsuitable' for a woman.[75] In terms of campaigning strategies and public profiles, Conservative women—including the fiery and independent ones—still adopted more traditional methods in this period, as they were expected to. (Mrs Everest raised eyebrows in 1970 for not wearing a hat whilst campaigning).[76] It would have been unthinkable, for example, for a wife of a Conservative candidate in 1970 to be pictured, dressed informally, and perched on her doorstep hugging her 13 stone Pyrenean mountain dog as a means of gaining attention. This was Plaid Cymru's tactic.[77] Four years later, young Plaid Cymru female activists were pictured, lined up and holding each other by the waste—physical symbols that their (often older) Conservative counterparts would never have engaged with.[78]

Like the women whose footsteps she followed in, Irene Everest helps complicate the historical construction of a 'typical' Conservative woman. Most women did not go so forthrightly into the political arena, or make such bold statements. The fact that these women did, however, is of great importance. They help convey a subtler and more complex idea of the Conservative grass-roots woman in this period. In some ways, and particularly in regards to their value systems, they were representative of the wider cohort of women. In public, they remained, into the 1970s, symbols and exponents of a certain brand of gendered politics, and of social and cultural conservatism. On the other hand, however, these senior activists were transgressive and less representative in their openly political nature, their willingness to parade their politics, and their campaigning techniques. In behaving as they did, and in making some of the statements they made, they certainly demonstrated that sections of the Conservative Party had moved on considerably from the turn of the century when the Primrose League was 'instrumental in keeping [women's] activities in the background'.[79] There is also evidence that some of the persuasive new ideas regarding gender that were entering British politics had not passed such women by unnoticed. The language of liberation could indirectly be found in some of their pronouncements, and their independence of thought and activity demonstrated a further sense of change from the inter-war period, even if such women were relatively rare. Such attributes reflect, in many ways, John Campbell's portrayal of the most famous Conservative woman of all, Margaret Thatcher: she was 'the archetypal Tory lady in a hat … quintessentially … suburban', but also highly unusual; someone with deep convictions and a zeal for the political, who vociferously demonstrated 'exceptional single-mindedness'.[80]

Associations, class and leadership

Despite being some of the most active and more unconventional women, key figures like Protheroe-Beynon, Smith and Everest were part of a much more densely populated world, where very large groups of women met in various circumstances to work for the Party or socialise under its auspices. At the end of the 1940s, the Conservative Party was still something that people joined in earnest—and in many seats in Wales they did so in greater numbers than those who joined Labour. In 1949, Swansea West's Association had 2,450 female members (and 350 male).[81] The equivalent figures for the Labour Party were 279 and 417 respectively.[82] The Barry seat boasted an 'astonishing' 6,000 Conservative women members alone in the same period, when Labour's total membership figure was 1, 111 (564 men and 547 women).[83] Even seats like the notoriously radical Merthyr Tydfil had 300 women members in its Association during this time.[84] Strikingly, this was the same number of women members as the Labour Party had in the seat. The only seats in which Labour women outnumbered men in the post-war period were those in urban (and suburban) Cardiff, and Newport.[85] Conservative figures were certainly healthy, although they never reached some of the towering figures in other parts of Britain in this early period, such as the 20,000 members in Bradford.[86] Though Conservative numbers declined notably in this period, by the 1970s many of the women's branches in those Welsh seats where Conservativism had fertile ground were still strong. Barry for example still had 2,000 women members in 1970.[87] As many historians have noted, women were vital as Party workers, ensuring that the local political machine continued to tick.[88] But their wider activities, their political consciousness, and their social make-up demonstrates that these larger groups of Conservative women were key actors in local politics, and the associations they gathered in offered opportunities for a form of political and social engagement and leadership.

The typical image of a Conservative woman at election time was a volunteer 'busily addressing envelopes at long trestle tables', and this was indeed commonplace in most Welsh constituencies too.[89] They were also door-knockers and leaflet-deliverers.[90] This kind of campaign tactic may already have been on the wane by the 1940s—Labour in particular had developed 'remarkably' in its ability to communicate with voters over the airwaves in the 1930s—but pavement politics was not suddenly displaced.[91] In the early post-war period the two were part of a tactical mix. For example, the likes of Peter Thorneycroft went out of his way to address crowds made up exclusively of women and offer sincere thanks for helping to elect him as the MP for Monmouth in 1945.[92] Even after the television relegated the local activist's importance for spreading the word, they did not diminish completely, and they still played a part in that process.[93] The television, after all, did not enter every home, and even when electricity finally came to all houses in all remote areas of Wales, fears of cost or modernity meant some traditional canvassing methods would have been appreciated.[94] Women also raised enormous amounts of money for the Party, an activity which took on a different tone after the 1949 Maxwell Fyfe Report ruling that limits had to be put on individual donations to single constituencies.[95] This cash went into oiling the mechanisms of the local Party, paying, if possible, for Agents, cars, posters, and election expenses.[96] A proportion of it was also sent to Central Office in the form of a quota scheme, calculated on a sliding scale formula.[97] Annual fetes, balls, and cocktail parties, as well as other general events, often raised enormous sums.[98] As with political campaigning, fundraising gave women a profile and an importance at the grass-roots that was recognised and acknowledged across the board. As Donald Walters, an association chairman for much of this period, noted in 1974 'we could not operate a viable Conservative Association in Cardiff North West' without 'the women'.[99] Many years later he maintained that women members had been 'everything' to the local Party.[100] As such, this activity should be characterised as more than just peripheral gendered work. As so many seats in Wales were marginal, and very few were ever in rude financial health, women's work sustained the Party, ensuring it could operate 'on the ground' in many parts of Wales.

Women therefore were undoubtedly the Party's 'strongest organisational assets'.[101] However, although money and activity helped fund and advertise Conservatism, the extent to which their activities were politically advantageous to the party is less obvious to pin down. Money in this period still came from other sources, like business and donations.[102] They certainly created conditions for the Party to advertise itself more effectively and more loudly, but it is impossible to know what degree of success it would have achieved without such volunteer help.[103] Bale is correct to argue that 'there is no straightforward correlation between strength of organisation and constituency success'.[104] It is reasonable to suggest, however, as Johnson has done, that at least in terms of making the Party's presence felt, making it appear more mainstream, and for persuading some key people to vote, women were an important aspect of the local Conservative machinery.[105] It is also widely accepted that similar kinds of Labour activity in Wales helped draw favourable 'general attention' to the Party.[106]

On the other hand, some forms of political influence that Welsh Conservative women wielded were less positive in the eyes of the Party. Two examples from the early 1950s demonstrate this. After a defeat in the Conway constituency in 1950, the local Association dispensed with its candidate, Colonel Price-White, and instead chose another local man, Peter Thomas, to represent the Party instead.[107] The Bangor Ladies' Branch took great umbrage at this, however, writing to the Party Chairman, Lord Woolton, to dissociate itself from the Association.[108] They wrote letters to the local press and collected a 600-name strong petition calling for Price-White to be reinstated as a candidate.[109] At the same time an argument was unfolding in Swansea West, where the Mumbles Ladies' Branch disassociated itself from the Association over a dispute about how much money should be directed to social rather than political ends.[110] The disagreement left the Association without a women's Chairman, and the 'rebel' women were threatened with disciplinary action from the Central and Regional Offices if they did not 'fall into line'.[111] When the marginal Swansea West seat was not won by the Conservatives at the following election, the fractious nature of the Association, which very much included the women, was blamed.[112] Both incidents demonstrate, however, that forceful and principled members of Ladies' branches in Wales were not always cast from the mould of conformist and loyal foot soldiers. They were capable of operating, en masse and independently within the Party, in a manner not in keeping with their image as passive pawns in a patriarchal Party system.

Political non-conformity and attempts to disrupt the workings of an Association were possible from women's sections, but this was certainly not common. The most significant and noteworthy aspect of their activity was when the political realm met the social one. Conservative women had long been characterised (if only tongue in cheek) as a 'pack of savage matrons in mink baying for blood and flogging and capital punishment'.[113] Without doubt, Associations in Wales were shot through with a staunch social conservatism (as demonstrated by their chief campaigners). Pledges to maintain, and then to re-introduce, capital punishment were regularly met by cheers from Tory women.[114] They were often the barrier to other women achieving senior positions, and groups across Wales were reported as being 'resolutely anti-feminist'.[115] Yet, simultaneously, such organisations were a place where women could exercise a form of social leadership that often had very little to do with politics. Hinton argued that during the Second World War middle-class women, through their voluntary work, upheld the continuities of class rather than broke these barriers down. Organisations like the Women's Voluntary Service provided opportunities for 'housewives to assert themselves in the public sphere, but to do so in ways that did not threaten the overarching' class and gendered norms of the era.[116] For these women, an ethos of public service contrasted with the more 'individualistic sensibilities characteristic of the emerging consumer culture'.[117] The case of Conservative grass-roots women demonstrates a continuity with this kind of behaviour, even if their strength and numbers dwindled as the decades past. Hinton argued that, by the 1950s and 1960s, with the proper arrival of consumer culture and social movements, the 'death knell' was sounded for such organisations: explicitly feminist groups should not be seen as continuity organisations, because their aims and ideological underpinnings were so starkly different.[118] Those wartime-style organisations that did continue to exist seemed 'old fashioned'.[119] This is correct, but this study of Wales suggests that these kinds of institutions did not necessarily die, even if they were weakened and even if they did indeed become more about fighting against the 'tide of the times'.[120] If one kind of group symbolised continuities with the kinds of social groups and the kind of work that Hinton identified, then it was these types of socially and culturally conservative, 'resolutely anti-feminist' women's associations.

There are several layers of evidence for this, one of the most striking features of which is how such organisations remained staunchly and rigidly middle-class well into the post-war decades. This interpretation stands in contrast to many of the conclusions that are drawn about this era. Firstly, this period encompassed the so-called 'de-alignment' of class politics, with the breakdown of economic structures supposedly resulting in 1974 being the final year when definable class-based voting took place.[121] Secondly, scholarship also indicates that across Britain during this period, Conservatism attracted significant levels of working-class supporters and voters as it had done since the nineteenth century.[122] Similarly, the Labour Party had always had a distinct middle-class dimension to it.[123] Undoubtedly, Conservatism garnered support in Wales from outside its middle-class base. If it had not, it would not have won some of its more marginal seats in the period. But activists and voters remained two very separate constituencies, and many of the long standing features of Welsh political and social life meant that to express public support for Conservatism still unfavourably marked one out in an area of Britain where the roots of class, tradition and community were buried deep. Class, as Ina Zweiniger-Bargielowska has argued, was centred on self-perception, self-identification and collective identity as well as more material and wealth-orientated factors.[124]

Social surveys from the 1960s highlighted that people actively associated moving to the more leafy and suburban Western fringes of Swansea, for example, with going 'up a step', with some of them joining the Conservative women's society as a result.[125] When Charlotte Bennett, a former Organising Secretary and later Agent in Wales during the 1970s and 80s, was asked who Conservative activists were in Wales she replied: 'I think of posh ladies!'.[126] A Labour Agent in the same period admitted that she had long received 'jibes' about her 'Conservative-type' hyphenated surname.[127] It is telling that one Valleys activist had to launch a defence of her fellows in 1972 by saying that 'we are not snobs, not wealthy, not grinding the faces of the poor'.[128] Dividing lines of class and perceptions, were therefore drawn between the two parties, artificially exaggerating the divide between them, their supporters and their activists. It was in this context that women exercised a similar kind of organisational agency as identified by Hinton, based on political voluntary work and social activities, or a fusion of both, that was bound up with their social class. Luncheon clubs, which were a staple of middle-class activity, were organised with vigour and rigour by Conservative women—'arrive at 1pm prompt on the first Friday of every month'[129]—the cost and culture of which would have been off-putting to many working-class women.[130] Pictures from such events, held in places like Swansea's Dragon Hotel, show formal, and often older, women gathered in pleasant and relatively plush surroundings.[131] Cocktail parties and cheese and wine evenings, both of which carried strong middle-class connotations, were organised so regularly (often in stately homes, or places like Cardiff Castle) that on some occasions, like in 1964, separate associations found that they had booked the same venue for the same kind of, but separate, event.[132]

It was within this sphere that middle-class women performed leadership and organisational duties, marshalling and co-ordinating events that had a much wider social impact. What becomes clear is that, whilst events were held broadly under the umbrella of politics, this was much more an expression of a wider social, rather than political, identity. Politically, many of these grass-roots women seems to express an apathy about politics that may have been a driving factor for some of their more senior members, like Irene Everest, to transgress, perhaps feeling forced to take their message to the public sphere. Conservative women on the whole, however, tended to be far less like their Labour counterparts, who had a long history of being much more politically motivated, listening to lectures and speeches on a more regular basis.[133] The unusually high proportions of Labour women (and the general strength in numbers) in seats that were marginal, like those in Cardiff, might well be explained by their explicitly more politicised ethos.[134] Again, the Conservative contrast echoes Hinton's analysis of those wartime middle-class groups. He argues that because 'class had a life beyond politics it can supply a richer and more fruitful conceptual framework' than politics alone.[135] In such light, the behaviour of certain

Conservative women at political meetings takes on a fresh character. Take, for example, the report from a bemused Regional Area Agent in 1957, who, whilst attending a meeting in Pontypool, watched 'an influx of about 20 women members' into the meeting 'who were actually attending a whist drive in the room upstairs. They were all members of the Association [but] to my amazement they all took a ballot paper and after handing [it] in they trooped back to the whist drive'. He added, 'it is typical of the unorthodox energies displayed by the women's organisation'.[136] For such women, the Conservative Association was not their first priority, but it was undoubtedly part of a patchwork of respectability, and of socialising with like-minded individuals, in whose world politics lent an air of grandeur, but was not their primary concern. (Anecdotal evidence suggests the same was true of many people—mainly men—who drank in Conservative Clubs).

This notion of community respectability and voluntary work was not just confined to political activity. Carmarthen's Hilda Protheroe–Beynon, for example, whose husband was a JP and had an OBE, was an active member of the farming union, the Girl Guides, the Church, and 'other' wider, generally middle-class, groups.[137] Social studies of football clubs in rural Wales in this period reveal that women exercised very similar organisational roles within those bodies, essentially ensuring that a long-standing feature of the local community could continue to function, even if they had very little interest in football itself.[138] To understand the rationale behind women joining and staying in Conservative Associations we need, therefore, to look beyond the boundaries of the political, whilst keeping it firmly in our sights. We also need to understand the changing nature of society, and the way in which some women were resitting this. Conservative associations had once been a conduit for middle-class housewives to do something, but in a world of more freely available entertainment and leisure pursuits, this was less of a driving force. The country was quickly changing from a time when 'acceptable behaviour was more circumscribed, conventions more rigidly adhered to, and choices in lifestyle and leisure more limited, localised, and repetitive'.[139]

But upholding some sense of tradition and maintaining continuity was clearly still a motive for many women, especially in an era that was increasingly marked out by the blooming of radical, feminist politics. Declining and tired Labour associations had been given a shot in the arm, and had some new life breathed into them, by fresh ideas.[140] Into the 1970s and beyond the increasingly older membership[141] of these associations in Wales became largely subconscious resisters of such change, buttressing traditional notions of gender and politics whilst setting their political activity into a wider social context.[142] Despite the ageing profile of the women and the more fatigued nature of grass-roots politics at the end of this period in general, dozens still volunteered, for example, to make trifles for prominent social functions, or sandwiches for branch meetings (whilst the men put away the chairs) in the stronger associations.[143] They became the last bastions of an associational and voluntary culture that was a much greater feature of the pre-war and war years, but one that continued to relate to conservatism and the Conservative Party. Hinton was correct to argue that such activities appeared old-fashioned, but that was a reflection of the Party's membership and activists, of which there was still—unlike now—a significant rump.[144]

Conclusion

Our greatest understanding of a Conservative woman is what we know about former Prime Minister Margaret Thatcher, and yet legions of less visible women were part of the Party's structure across the country, contributing to the tone and the nature of the wider organisation. In some respects, what we know about Thatcher can be transposed onto these more 'normal' and conventional Tory women in this case study of Wales. Like her, some of the more senior and prominent activists were independently-minded, forceful and vociferous political campaigners, different in many respects to the more common image of hard-working women who ultimately played a back-stage and subservient role in local politics. Like Thatcher, also, they were the proponents of a form of social conservatism, advertising and making speeches about their housewifely virtues and concerns. What is so noticeable, however, is that they slot much more neatly into a feminist discourse than they would have admitted, or perhaps would have realised. In arguing, for example, that women should be as equally represented in parliament as men were, their language owed much to the rhetoric of the times, even if their reasoning and explanations for such attitudes certainly did not. In this sense, such women from this period represented a paradox. The values they wished to express to a broader public were rooted in a social conservatism and a permissiveness that often had to be departed from in order for them to make their arguments.

More broadly, women's branches and associations in Wales retained their conservative and traditional character in a much more typical fashion—an avenue of analysis in itself which has remained unexplored in Welsh historiography. These Associations were also vehicles for women to explore and exercise a form of influence. Although the extent to which they did so is difficult to pin down, it is certainly the case that through their voluntary and fund-raising work, women helped advertise the Conservative Party to the Welsh electorate. As most Welsh seats held by Conservatives were marginal, and because there was a streak of suspicion about Conservatism running through the Welsh electorate, the significance and the importance of such work cannot be dismissed, even if the electorate tended to vote based on other, broader, national issues; the information for which they received more and more from the radio and, increasingly, the television. For such activists, however, politics was not always the primary motive for their engagement with political organisations. The Conservative Party in this era remained one of the final organisations through which members could express a sense of sympathy with pre-1960s society and culture. Through this associational and voluntary work, these middle-class, and increasingly older, women contributed to buttressing the traditional perceptions of class and gendered political hierarchies. Hence, despite the supposed 'de-alignment' of class politics in this period, there was still a staunch and identifiably middle-class tone to Conservative activists by the 1970s—evidenced by their behaviour, the continuation of luncheon clubs, and their increasing average age. In an era often loosely defined by radicalism, and in a part of Britain often loosely defined as left-wing, it is important to note the significance, and the longevity of such women and their organisations.

Notes

1. For an overview of results and electoral statistics, see Denis Balsom and Martin Burch, *A Political and Electoral Handbook for Wales* (Farnborough: Gower Press, 1980); and Arnold J. James and John E. Thomas, *Wales at Westminster: A History of the Parliamentary Representation of Wales 1800–1979* (Llandysul: Gomer Press, 1981).
2. Lukas Audickas, Oliver Hawkins and Richard Cracknell, House of Commons Briefing Paper: UK Election Statistics, 1918–2016, 7 July 2016, 18–9.
3. See for example, John Ramsden, *The Age of Churchill and Eden, 1940–1957* (London: Longman, 1995), 115; Stuart Ball 'Local Conservatism and the Evolution of the Party Organisation', in *Conservative Century: The Conservative Party Since 1900*, eds. Anthony Seldon and Stuart Ball (Oxford: Oxford University Press, 1994), 274.
4. Joni Lovenduski, Pippa Norris and Catriona Burness, 'The Party and Women', in *Conservative Century: The Conservative Party Since 1900*, eds. Anthony Seldon and Stuart Ball (Oxford: Oxford University Press, 1994), 611.
5. Joni Lovenduski, 'Sex, Gender and British Politics', in *Women in Politics*, eds. Joni Lovenduski and Pippa Norris (Oxford: Oxford University Press, 1996), 14.
6. See, for example: Swansea West Basic Report, 1949, CPA, CCO 1/7/521; Cardiff West Basic Report, 1949, CPA, CCO 1/7/521; Basic Report Barry, CPA, CCO 1/8/528, 21 February 1951; '1,000 women Conservatives at open-air meeting', *Western Mail*, July 3, 1953.
7. Duncan Tanner, Chris Williams and Deian Hopkin, eds., *The Labour Party in Wales, 1900–2000* (Cardiff: University of Wales Press, 2000), 306.
8. Deidre Beddoe, 'Towards a Welsh Women's History', *Llafur* 3, no. 2 (1981): 32.
9. See, for example, Deirdre Beddoe, *Out of the Shadows: A History of Women in Twentieth-Century Wales* (Cardiff: University of Wales Press, 2000); Angela V. John, ed., *Our Mothers' Land: Chapters in Welsh Women's History, 1830–1939* (Cardiff: University of Wales Press, 1991); Ursula Masson, *'For Women, for Wales and for Liberalism': Women in Liberal Politics in Wales, 1880–1914* (Cardiff: University of Wales Press, 2010).
10. Deidre Beddoe, 'Women and Politics in Twentieth Century Wales', *National Library of Wales Journal* 33, no. 3 (2004): 333–47.
11. That year, for example, Kenneth O. Morgan published his ground-breaking book *Re-birth of a Nation*, which paid very little attention to Conservative politics. See Kenneth O. Morgan, *Re-Birth of a Nation: Wales, 1880–1980* (Cardiff: University of Wales Press, 1981).
12. Exceptions are Felix Aubel, 'The Conservatives in Wales, 1880–1935', in *The Conservatives and British Society, 1880–1990*, eds. Martin Francis and Ina Zweiniger-Bargielowska (Cardiff: University of Wales Press, 1996); Sam Blaxland, 'A Swinging Party?: The Need for a History of the Conservatives in Wales', *North American Journal of Welsh Studies* 9 (2014); Matthew Cragoe, *An Anglican Aristocracy: The Moral Economy of the Landed Estate in Carmarthenshire, 1832–1895* (Oxford: Clarendon Press, 1996); Matthew Cragoe, 'Defending the Constitution: The Conservative Party and the Idea of Devolution, 1945–74', in *The Art of the Possible: Politics and Governance in Modern British History, 1885–1997: Essays in Memory of Duncan Tanner*, eds. Chris Williams and Andrew Edwards (Manchester: Manchester University Press, 2015); Andrew Edwards, *Labour's Crisis: Plaid Cymru, the Conservatives, and the Decline of the Labour Party in North-West Wales, 1960–74* (Cardiff: University of Wales Press, 2011); Geraint Thomas, 'The Conservative Party and Welsh Politics in the Inter-War Years', *English Historical Review* 533, no. 128 (2013); sections in Martin Johnes, *Wales Since 1939* (Manchester: Manchester University Press, 2012).
13. Anna Davin, 'Redressing the Balance or Transforming the Art? The British Experience', in *Retrieving Women's History: Changing Perceptions of the Role of Women in Politics and Society*, eds. S. Jay Kleinberg (Oxford: Berg, 1998), 63–4.
14. For examples of Welsh history that stress the importance and the prominence of labour, see the iconic expression of the tradition: Hywel Francis and David Smith, *The Fed: The South Wales Miners in the Twentieth Century* (London: Lawrence and Wishart, 1980). See also

David Smith, ed., *A People and a Proletariat* (London: Pluto Press, 1980); and Gwyn A. Williams, *The Merthyr Rising* (London: Croom Helm, 1978).

15. For a discussion of this see see Martin Johnes, 'For Class and Nation: Dominant Trends in the Historiography of Twentieth Century Wales', *History Compass* 8, no. 11 (2010): 1257–74. See also Andy Croll 'People's Remembrancers' in a Post-Modern Age: Contemplating the Non-Crisis of Welsh Labour History', *Llafur* 8, no. 1 (2000), 6.

16. Harold L. Smith, 'The Women's Movement, Politics and Citizenship, 1960s–2000', in *Women in Twentieth Century Britain*, ed. Ina Zweiniger-Bargielowska (Harlow: Pearson, 2001), 285.

17. E.H.H. Green, *Thatcher* (London: Hodder Arnold, 2006), 15

18. Green, *Thatcher*, 15.

19. Ben Jackson and Robert Saunders, *Introduction, in Their Making Thatcher's Britain* (Cambridge: Cambridge University Press, 2012), 11; Laura Beers, 'Thatcher and the Women's Vote', in *Making Thatcher's Britain* eds. Ben Jackson and Robert Saunders (Cambridge: Cambridge University Press, 2012), 118.

20. Charles Moore, *Margaret Thatcher, The Authorised Biography: Volume One* (London: Penguin, 2013), xiv, xv.

21. See Ina Zweiniger-Bargielowska, 'Explaining the Gender Gap: The Conservative Party and the Women's Vote, 1945–1964', in *The Conservatives and British Society, 1880–1990*, eds. Martin Francis and Ina Zweiniger-Bargielowska (Cardiff: University of Wales Press, 1996), 196; Butler and Stokes quoted in Zweiniger-Bargielowska, 'Explaining the Gender Gap', 202; Joni Lovenduski, 'Sex, Gender and British Politics', in *Women in Politics*, eds. Joni Lovenduski and Pippa Norris (Oxford: Oxford University Press, 1996), 14; Pippa Norris and Joni Lovenduski, 'Gender and Party Politics in Britain', in their *Gender and Party Politics* (London: Sage Publications, 1993), 40–1; Lovenduski, Norris and Burness, The Party and Women, 611; and G. E. Maguire, *Conservative Women: A History of Women and the Conservative Party, 1874–1997* (Basingstoke: Macmillan, 1998), 119.

22. Krista Cowman, *Women in British Politics, c.1689–1979* (Basingstoke: Macmillan, 2010), 89.

23. Beatrix Campbell, *The Iron Ladies: Why Do Women Vote Tory?* (London: Virago, 1987), 265, 269, 275; See also Martin Pugh, *Women and the Women's Movement in Britain, 1914–1959* (London: Macmillan, 1992), 310; David Jarvis, The Conservative Party and the Politics of Gender, 1900–1939', in *The Conservatives and British Society, 1880–1990*, eds. Martin Francis and Ina Zweiniger-Bargielowska (Cardiff: University of Wales Press, 1996), 188; Susan Kingsley Kent, *Gender and Power in Britain: 1640–1990* (London: Routledge, 1996), 335, 350.

24. Andrew Thorpe, *Parties at War: Political Organisation in Second World War Britain* (Oxford: Oxford University Press, 2009), 149.

25. Beers, *Thatcher*, 116.

26. Mark Donnelly, *Sixties Britain: Culture, Society and Politics* (Harlow: Pearson, 2005), xiii, 3, 11.

27. David Butler and Richard Rose, *The British General Election of 1959* (London: Macmillan, 1960), 75.

28. See for example Martin Pugh, *The Tories and the People 1880–1935* (Oxford: Oxford University Press, 1985); David Jarvis, 'Mrs Maggs and Betty: The Conservative Appeal to Women Voters in the 1920s', *Twentieth Century British History* 5 (1994): 129–52.

29. Ball, *Local Conservatism*, 284.

30. Conway Basic Report, 1 August 1956, Conservative Party Archive (CPA), Conservative Central Office (CCO) 1/11/515.

31. 'Women as Party Agents', *Western Mail*, February 22, 1950. In 1950 the seats that had women Agents were Cardiff South East (Miss Midgley), Pontypool (Miss Lewis), Aberavon (Miss Wilson), Abertillery (Miss Lewis), Pontypridd (Miss Hiley), Gower (Miss Maitland), and Anglesey (Miss Browning).

32. Again, roughly 36 depending on boundary changes.

33. Figures compiled by the current author from candidate biographies in Ivor Thomas Rees, *Welsh Hustings 1885–2004* (Llandybie: Dinefwr Press, 2005).
34. For example, East Flint members were regularly clear on the fact that a woman was unsuitable for the seat because of its industrial profile. A Labour woman ended up holding it for twenty years from 1950 to 1970. G. Summers to J.P.L. Thomas, 19 October 1948, CPA, CCO 1/7/516.
35. Howard Davies to Paul Bryan, 3 January 1962, CPA, CCO 1/14/540.
36. Maguire, *Conservative Women,* 168.
37. 'Women Found 'Nice' Tory Worth Wait', *Western Mail,* June 17, 1970.
38. 4000 people voted Conservative in Rhondda West in 1966 – a seat and an election that were notoriously unfavourable for the Tories. See Johnes, *Wales,* 272. Yet there was no organisation to speak of in the constituency.
39. 'The Steelworker Who Will Vote for a Conservative', *Western Mail,* October 6, 1959.
40. Interview, Jonathan Evans, 21 November 2014.
41. 'A busload of hope for Tryer Tuck', *Western Mail,* May 1, 1979.
42. This was the way Kingsley Amis chose to describe an unusual Conservative-supporting neighbour of his protagonist in the novel *That Uncertain Feeling,* which is set in a fictional south Wales town not unlike Swansea. See Kingsley Amis, *That Uncertain Feeling* (St Albans: Panther Books, 1975), 59–60.
43. 'Tory Braves the Streets of Bevan Land', *Western Mail,* February 18, 1974.
44. 'When they fight, their womenfolk are with them – shoulder to shoulder', *Western Mail,* September 29, 1959.
45. See, for example, Hugh Rees, former MP and then candidate for Swansea West, standing over his wife, pictured in *Western Mail,* March 24, 1966.
46. Zweiniger-Bargielowska, 'Explaining the Gender Gap', 206; Cowman, *Women,* 91.
47. 'Mrs P-B supplies the sparkle', *Western Mail,* October 8, 1964.
48. Ibid.
49. The other was Irene White for East Flint.
50. 'It's 'Male prejudice' that keeps so many out of Parliament', *Western Mail,* September 25, 1959.
51. 'Mrs P-B supplies the sparkle', *Western Mail,* October 8, 1964.
52. Howard Davies to Paul Bryan, 6 September 1962, CPA, CCO 1/14/517/1.
53. John Campbell, *Margaret Thatcher, Volume One: The Grocer's Daughter* (London: Jonathan Cape, 2000), 101.
54. Green, *Thatcher,* 14.
55. Donnelly, *Sixties Britain,* 158.
56. 'Why Not Put More Women in Power?', *Western Mail,* April 1, 1966.
57. Ibid.
58. Smith, 'The Women's Movement', 279.
59. Trevor Harris and Monia O'Brien Castro, 'Conclusion', in their *Preserving the Sixties: Britain and the Decade of Protest* (Basingstoke: Palgrave Macmillan, 2014), 192–3, 4.
60. Stuart Ball, *Portrait of a Party: The Conservative Party in Britain 1918–1945* (Oxford: Oxford University Press, 2013), 169.
61. Donnelly, *Sixties Britain,* 159.
62. Neil Evans and Dot Jones, 'To Help Forward the Great Work of Humanity': Women in the Labour Party in Wales, in *The Labour Party in Wales, 1900–2000,* eds. Duncan Tanner, Chris Williams and Deian Hopkin (Cardiff: University of Wales Press, 2000), 238.
63. Mark Donnelly, 'Sixties Britain: The Cultural Politics of Historiography', in *Preserving the Sixties: Britain and the Decade of Protest,* eds. Trevor Harris and Monia O'Brien Castro (Basingstoke: Palgrave Macmillan, 2014), 10–11.
64. 'Women Found "Nice" Tory Worth Wait', *Western Mail,* June 17, 1970.
65. 'A Day in the Life of a Top Tory', *Western Mail,* June 12, 1970.
66. Ibid.

67. Evans and Jones, 'To Help Forward', 230; 'A Day in the Life of a Top Tory', *Western Mail*, June 12, 1970.
68. 'A Day in the Life of a Top Tory', *Western Mail*, June 12, 1970.
69. Ibid.
70. Campbell, *The Iron Ladies*, 298.
71. 'It's "Male Prejudice' that Keeps so Many out of Parliament", *Western Mail*, September 25, 1959; 'Why Not Put More Women in Power?', *Western Mail*, April 1, 1966.
72. Ibid.
73. 'When They Fight, Their Women Folk are with Them – Shoulder to Shoulder', *Western Mail*, September 29, 1959.
74. Cowman, *Women*, 122–3.
75. G. Summers to J.P.L. Thomas, 19 October 1948, CPA, CCO1/7/516.
76. 'A Day in the Life of a Top Tory', *Western Mail*, June 12, 1970.
77. 'Cardiff North', *Western Mail*, June 17, 1970.
78. 'Kilbrandon will be Principal Plank in Plaid Platform', *Western Mail*, February 11, 1974.
79. Lovenduski, Norris and Burness, *The Party and Women*, 617.
80. Campbell, *Margaret Thatcher*, 1, 3.
81. Cardiff West Basic Report, 1949, CPA, CCO 1/7/521.
82. Tanner, Williams and Hopkin, *The Labour Party*, 306.
83. Barry Basic Report, 21 February 1951, CPA, CCO 1/8/528; Ramsden, *The Age of Churchill*, 112; Tanner, Williams and Hopkin, *The Labour Party*, 306.
84. Ebbw Vale Basic Report, July 1949, CPA, CCO 1/7/538; Merthyr Tydfil Basic Report, undated, CPA, CCO 1/7/522. On the Chairman of East Flint claiming the seat was unsuitable for a woman, remarkably similar words were used in 1950 about the Dartford seat by its Chair. 23 year old Margaret Roberts (as Mrs Thatcher was then) ended up being selected for the seat nonetheless. See Moore, *Margaret Thatcher*, 76.
85. Tanner, Williams and Hopkin, *The Labour Party*, 306.
86. Ramsden, *The Age of Churchill*, 112.
87. 'A day in the life of a top Tory', *Western Mail*, June 12, 1970.
88. Maguire, *Conservative Women*, 141.
89. R.B. McCallum and Alison Readman, *The British General Election of 1945* (London: Oxford University Press, 1947), 80.
90. Maguire, *Conservative Women*, 141.
91. Laura Beers, *Your Britain: Media and the Making of the Labour Party* (Massachusetts: Harvard University Press, 2010), 196.
92. 'Capt. Thorneycroft Increases Majority', *Abergavenny Chronicle*, November 2, 1945. This was after a by-election, the previous Conservative candidate for the seat, Leslie Pym, having died during the 1945 campaign. He was announced as the winner at the declaration, however, with his Labour opponent having to congratulate a dead man. See Gerard Charmley, 'Parliamentary Representation', in *The Gwent County History, Volume 5: The Twentieth Century*, eds. Chris Williams and Andy Croll (Cardiff: University of Wales Press, 2013), 306.
93. 'Elections in the TV Age', *Western Mail*, June 17, 1970.
94. Johnes, *Wales*, 73.
95. Stuart Ball, *The Conservative Party and British Politics 1902–1951* (Essex: Longman, 1995), 112.
96. Ramsden, *The Age of Churchill*, 136.
97. Ball, The *Conservative Party and British Politics*, 112–113; David Butler and Michael Pinto-Duschinsky, 'The Conservative Elite, 1918–1978: Does Unrepresentativeness Matter?', in *Conservative Party Politics*, eds. Zig Layton-Henry (London: Macmillan, 1980), 189.
98. Finance Sheet 31 May 1950, CPA, COO 1/8/510. For example, In 1949 the Conway Association's women raised £525 from their Ball, £609 from the Conway Castle Fair, and £691 from the Christmas Fair – equivalent, in total, to roughly £41,200 in 2017 money.
99. Cardiff North West Conservative Association Minute Book, 1974 Annual Report, undated, National Library of Wales (NLW), Welsh Political Archive (WPA), GB0210 CARCON.

100. Interview, Sir Donald Walters, 19 January 2015.
101. Ball, 'Local Conservatism and the Evolution of the Party Organisation', 284.
102. John Ramsden, *The Winds of Change: Macmillan to Heath, 1957–1975* (Essex: Longman, 1996), 75; Tim Bale, *The Conservatives since 1945: The Drivers of Party Change* (Oxford: Oxford University Press, 2016), 20.
103. Ball, 'Local Conservatism', 308–309.
104. Bale, *The Conservatives*, 20–21.
105. Janet Johnson, 'Did Organization Really Matter? Party Organisation and Conservative Electoral Recovery, 1945–59', *Twentieth Century British History* 14 no. 4 (2003): 412; Ramsden, *The Age of Churchill*, 115.
106. Evans and Jones, 'To Help Forward', 223.
107. 'Socialists Hold 25 out of 36 Welsh Seats', *Western Mail*, July 27, 1945
108. Mrs Macmillan to Lord Woolton, 3 August 1950, CPA, CCO 1/8/510.
109. Petition, c. October 1950, CPA, CCO 1/8/510.
110. Unsigned report re Swansea West women, c. 1950, CPA, CCO 1/8/526.
111. Unsigned report re Swansea West women, c. 1950, CPA, CCO 1/8/526.
112. Swansea West Basic Report 20 September 1950, CPA, CCO 1/8/526.
113. 'Prisons and Punishment', *The Daily Telegraph*, April 21, 1961.
114. 'Box pledge on hanging lauded', *Western Mail*, March 10, 1966.
115. 'Women on the Tory front', *Western Mail*, 2 June 1970.
116. James Hinton, *Women, Social Leadership, and the Second World War* (Oxford: Oxford University Press, 2002), 2.
117. Hinton, *Women*, 9.
118. Hinton, *Women*, 236, 238.
119. Hinton, *Women*, 238–239.
120. Hinton, *Women*, 239.
121. See in particular Bo Sarlvik and Ivor Crewe, *Decade of Dealignment: The Conservative victory of 1979 and electoral trends in the 1970s* (Cambridge: Cambridge University Press, 1983) which argues that whilst class-based politics and voting behavior did not disappear in the 1970s, it was seriously weakened. Also see David Denver, *Elections and Voters in Britain* (Basingstoke: Palgrave Macmillan, 2007) for a similar analysis. Also see Patrick Joyce, 'Introduction', in his *Class* (Oxford: Oxford University Press, 1995), 3.
122. Eric A. Nordlinger, *The Working Class Tories: Authority, Deference and Stable Democracy* (London: Macgibbon and Kee, 1967); Robert T. McKenzie, *Angels in Marble: Working Class Conservatives in Urban England* (London: Heinemann, 1968); Jon Lawrence, *Speaking for the People: Party, Language and Popular Politics in England, 1867–1914,* (Cambridge: Cambridge University Press, 1998).
123. Evans and Jones, 'To Help Forward', 224.
124. Zweiniger-Bargielowska, 'Explaining the Gender Gap', 195.
125. Colin Rosser and Christopher Harries, *The Family and Social Change: A Study of Family and Kinship in a South Wales Town* (London: Routledge and K. Paul, 1965), 83.
126. Interview, Charlotte Bennett, 28 October 2015.
127. *Western Mail*, February 14, 1974.
128. Rhondda Conservative and Unionist Association records, speech by Mrs J. Lysaught, 1 November 1972, NLW, WPA, GB0210 RHOCON.
129. Swansea West Luncheon Club Minute Book, 5 July 1968, West Glamorgan Archives (WGA), D/D CMLC 1.
130. Ball, *Portrait*, 163; Hinton, *Women*, 12.
131. Swansea West Luncheon Club Minute Book, 5 July 1968, WGA, D/D CMLC 1.
132. 'Air blue over Tory drinks', *South Wales Echo*, 17 September 1964.
133. Evans and Jones, 'To Help Forward', 223–4.
134. Evans and Jones, 'To Help Forward', 221.
135. Hinton, *Women*, 12–13.
136. S.B.H. Oliver to CCO, 28 March 1957, CPA, CCO 1/12/545.

137. Howard Davies to Paul Bryan, 6 September 1962, CPA, CCO, 1/14/517/1; See her profile in Ivor Thomas Rees, *Welsh Hustings 1885–2004* (Llandybie: Dinefwr Press, 2005), 239–40.
138. Ronald Frankenberg, *Village on the Border: A Social Study of Religion, Politics and Football in a North Wales Community* (London: Cohen and West, 1957), 104.
139. Ball, *Portrait,* 169.
140. Evans and Jones, 'To Help Forward', 238.
141. See, for an illustration of this (despite being slightly outside this time period) a picture from Julian Lewis' 1983 campaign in Swansea West, where he was pictures with 'loyal party workers', all of whom were very elderly women stuffing envelopes. Dr Lewis is now the MP for New Forest East. 'Special Focus: Swansea West', *Western Mail,* June 2, 1983.
142. Beers, *Thatcher,* 113.
143. Abergavenny Minute Book 2 October 1973, NLW, WPA, GB0210 MONION, file 25; Monmouth Conservative Association Minute Book, 13 April 1973, NLW, WPA, GB0210 MONION, file 24.
144. One only need look at half empty conference halls during keynote speeches at Conservative Party conferences, or read the words of former minister Sir Eric Pickles about the dwindling numbers of party members in the country at large. See 'Tories urgently need more volunteers, says Sir Eric Pickles', *BBC News,* October 1, 2017.

Acknowledgements

I would like to thank Dr Martin Johnes, Dr Teresa Phipps, and Dr Daryl Leeworthy who all provided comments on earlier drafts of this article.

Disclosure statement

No potential conflict of interest was reported by the authors.

Diana Spearman's role within the post-war Conservative Party and in the 'battle of ideas' (1945–1965)

Stéphane Porion

ABSTRACT

Diana Spearman's role and influence within the post-war Conservative Party have been overlooked, as the major studies on this party, but a few, mention her name. Yet, after graduating from the LSE, she contested two general elections in Labour strongholds, she worked in the male-dominated Conservative Research Department (CRD) after the war for quite a long time, was among the very few female members of the international Mont-Pélerin Society, founded and chaired a short-lived group comprising only male free-market economists or Conservatives in 1965, and was a regular contributor to the *Salisbury Review* in the 1980s. She exerted a tremendous influence on Enoch Powell and Richard Law in the late 1940s, as the latter published *Return from Utopia* in 1950—a digest of Sperman's and Hayek's ideas. According to Powell, she was 'an outstanding and tireless philosopher of Conservatism'.

In *Sex, Gender and the Conservative Party: From Iron Lady to Kitten Heels*, Sarah Childs and Paul Webb recall the commonly held gendered view of the Conservative Party's history in the twentieth century: 'For large parts of the twentieth century, the Conservatives were the political party most hospitable to women. (…) In respect of women voters, Conservative support from women is long recognized as significant for Conservative electoral success'.[1] They add that 'these observations are now, however, under challenge or, at least, subject to qualification',[2] as one may indeed question the actual extent of women's integration within the Conservative Party regarding, for instance, the party's paucity of women in its higher echelons from 1945 to 1970, reflected by the very low number of female Conservative MPs at the time.[3] For example, Conservative MP Evelyn Emmet remembered in 1961 that 'men were reluctant to see a woman fill any place which might be theirs'.[4] Conservative women found it hard to navigate the party after the Second World War, since it was still a male-dominated party. G. E. Maguire also notes in her 1998 landmark analysis of Conservative women that 'in spite of the immediate post-war rejuvenation, the Conservative Party increasingly found it difficult to recruit younger women',[5] so as to revamp the image of a party which was no longer prioritizing its upper-class and male membership.

From a political perspective, if women were ambitious, willing to climb the ladder of the Conservative Party's hierarchy, they had to cope with 'the conservative sexual politics of the mid-1940s and 1950s'.[6] This was the case of the young Margaret Thatcher, who was only selected for a winnable seat in Finchley in the late 1950s, because she was seen by Conservative Central Office as 'a woman of immense personality and charm with a brain clearly above the average'.[7] Therefore, for Conservative women to overcome the 'anti-woman complex' or the 'misogynistic attitude of some male Conservative counter-parts' distrusting their presence outside the private sphere of home, they had to embody beauty and intelligence in order to dazzle the audience in public political debates.[8]

There is still a limited number of gendered analyses of the post-war Conservatives based on a political historical approach. G. E. Maguire wrote an extensive study of Conservative women's history (1998), spanning more than a century, with only three chapters on the period 1945–1970. As for Beatrix Campbell's *Iron Ladies* (1987), it mainly focuses on the Thatcher era. In *Conservative Century* (1994), Joni Lovenduski, Pippa Norris and Catriona Burness explore changes in the role of women in the party and those in party policy on women.[9] When Joni Lovenduski and Pippa Norris published their book *Women in Politics* in 1996, they regretted that their study had 'no contribution on the Conservative Party (an omission) for women as actors in British politics, but only one on the Labour Party'.[10] As for *Women's History: Britain 1850–1945* edited by June Purvis in 2000, it does not address the issues of Conservative women's history and role after 1945. Martin Pugh's significant analyses mainly deal with 'popular Conservatism' or the women's movement in Britain since 1914, but do not exclusively concentrate on Conservative women in the post-war years.[11] Krista Cowman's 2010 book provides useful, but scanty, information on Conservative women after 1945, but as the author acknowledges, 'taking a longer view uncovers a narrative which is much patchier than studies concentrating on later periods might suggest'.[12]

Sarah Childs and Paul Webb's book (2012) addresses the Cameron years to discuss 'the importance of feminization to the Cameron project'.[13] Three other recent stimulating analyses of Conservative women in post-war Britain should be mentioned as they started to fill a gap in the historiography. In 2010, Katie Haessly wrote a PhD thesis on British Conservative MPs and 'Women's Issues', 1950–1979, focusing on the role of Conservative women MPS who pursued a feminist agenda in the House of Commons.[14] Clarisse Berthezène offers fresh insight into the main question of feminist Conservatism on the period 1928–1964 and reviews the current historiography of studies of Conservative women.[15] She points out that there is much more research in political science on gender and British Conservatism in the late twentieth and early twenty-first centuries.[16] Finally, in tandem with Julie Gottlieb, Clarisse Berthezène edited a collective book entitled *Rethinking Right-wing Women* in 2018, 'casting attention to Conservative women, women leaders and the changing features of institutionalization of the party's attitudes to gender issues and sexual equality'.[17]

Diana Spearman (1905–1991) is a rather little known figure in the historiography of the post-war Conservative Party, for if one looks up her name in the secondary literature, one is likely to come across very few or even no references to her name at all.[18] Yet, there were actually two Dianas named Spearman, as Alexander Cadwallader Mainwaring Spearman, —a Conservative MP from 1941 to 1966 and a champion of free market ideas—married twice, and his second wife was also named Diana. He married Diana Violet Constance Edith Doyle in 1928, but divorced her in 1951 at a time when the Conservatives were back in power. She was the daughter of Colonel Sir Arthur Havelock James Doyle, 4th Bt. and Joyce Ethelreda Howard.[19] She was born in India in 1905 and raised in a wealthy and educated family. Her father was in the Indian army; her family was 'military to the core' and 'had produced six generals between 1756 and 1856'.[20] In addition, her mother was a grand-daughter of the 17th Earl of Suffolk and 10th Earl of Berkshire. Diana Spearman studied at the London School of Economics from 1925 to 1931, getting the Social Science Certificate with distinction in 1927 and the Academic Diploma in Psychology in 1931, while being engaged in private research in Sociology.[21] She also completed one year of a B Sc (Economics) degree in 1927–1928 and attended a seminar on economic theory in 1929–1930.[22] She was then the first ever female researcher to be appointed at the Conservative Research Department from 1934 to 1939 and then again from 1949 to 1965. She also managed to get through the selection process within the Conservative Party and thus contested two general elections in Labour safe seats unsuccessfully—the first one in Poplar South in 1935 and the second one in Hull Central in 1945.[23]

In early April 1947,

> thirty-six scholars, mostly economists, with some historians and philosophers, were invited by Professor Friedrich Hayek to meet at Mont Pelerin in Switzerland, to discuss the state and the possible fate of liberalism (in its classical sense) in thinking and practice and in the hope of strengthening the principles and practice of a free society and to study the workings, virtues, and defects of market-oriented economic systems.[24]

R. M. Hartwell depicts the creation of the Mont-Pèlerin Society (MPS) as 'a true academy of intellectuals' and 'an international association of scholars' 'to educate the intellectuals and to lay the intellectual foundation of a liberal society and economy'.[25] After her unsuccessful electoral experiences, Diana Spearman officially accepted Hayek's invitation to join the MPS on 3 December 1948.[26] They are thought to have first met in 1931 when Hayek gave a special series of lectures at the LSE, or she was first possibly introduced to him through her husband's connections before 1948. However, she was not officially incorporated as 'one of the 64 original members of the Mont-Pèlerin Society[27] in 1947' as Richard Cockett or Geoffrey Foote claim,[28] but as 'one of the oldest members of the society, not quite an original member, but very nearly' in Hayek's own words.[29] She was thus acquainted with very influential free market male thinkers, including F. V. Hayek, Lionel Robbins, Dennis Robertson and M. Oakeshott. She had the honour to address the MPS platform during the 1959 Oxford meeting.[30] Interested in high politics and concerned with the rise of Fascism and Nazism before 1939, and then by that of Communism in a Cold War context, she published *Modern Dictatorship* (1939) and *Democracy in England* (1957).[31]

More generally, in the post-war decades, she became active in the free market campaigns of the Institute of Economic Affairs.[32] In February 1965, she also, from her house in Lord North Street, set up a short-lived group of free-market champions called the 'Longbow Group', which only comprised men. In the late 1970s, she helped to organize the Salisbury Group with Roger Scruton and Michael Oakeshott, giving life and inspiration to the *Salisbury Review*,[33] which she founded with Roger Scruton in 1982.[34] Enoch Powell,—one of her dear friends and former colleagues[35]—summed her up thus: 'She was an outstanding and tireless philosopher of conservatism (…) [upholding] rigorously in books and articles the economic and social implications of High Tory beliefs and principles'.[36] In addition, Powell claimed elsewhere that she seemed most at home with the leading figures in the politics of an earlier generation. (…) For many years Diana hosted a soirée of up-and-coming politicians whom she introduced to leading personalities in the Conservative Party and subjected to the stimulus of her well-stored and vigorous mind.[37]

In *The Iron Ladies*, Beatrix Campbell attempted to sketch out a portrait of Conservative women in the twentieth century with special emphasis on its second half and on the Thatcher years. She put forward the view that the Conservative woman is 'a remarkably unstudied political animal' and that 'there is no stereotype of the Conservative women', and concluded: 'Women are everywhere in a weak position and yet are not weak. Women are subordinate and yet are strong. That describes the Tory woman'.[38] Hence the following question: what sort of Conservative woman was then Diana Spearman? In one of her obituaries, she is presented as a mix of different types of women, raising even more the question of political categorization of Conservative women:

> [Diana Spearman] was a remarkable amalgam of two distinct types—the practical, no-nonsense Tory woman, capable of running two farms while actively campaigning for a Parliamentary seat, and the political hostess, whose delight in argument was complemented by an erudition that made her more than a match for any professor.[39]

According to Sarah Childs and Paul Webb, there would be 'two distinct, and arguably, conflicting types of Conservative women: first, the traditional woman member infamous for making sandwiches and stuffing envelopes, and secondly, the career woman, that is the Conservative woman who was seeking political office'.[40] Diana Spearman would belong to this second category to a certain extent, which 'comprised few in number as those seeking selection found it difficult to be selected for the party's vacant held and winnable seats, the most efficient route to Parliament'. The same political scientists also highlight the Conservative woman candidate's disinclination to see herself as a representative of women, or even as a gendered being who feminized her agenda[41]—that was exactly the case for Diana Spearman.

Furthermore, the history of British Conservatism is still largely dependent on the narrative set out by W. H. Greenleaf that identified a 'twin heritage' within the British Conservative Party—a paternalist branch and a free market liberal one.[42] Commenting upon this particular view, Clarisse Berthezène argues that 'fitting women into these categories, which refer to policies, and are themselves defined along gender lines, leads most of the time to legitimize the marginal status of women in politics and immure them in a lesser role'.[43] She adds:

> Writing British Conservative women's history can be done without questioning these categories and the methodology of traditional political history. The study of women's involvement within the Conservative Party would tend to show that Conservatism, instead of being articulated as a particular stance towards the role of the State, as Greenleaf contends, mainly depends on the efficacy and the role of civil society as E. H. H. Green suggested at the end of his book *Ideologies of Conservatism* (2002) without explicitly mentioning women.[44]

This paper will show instead, through the study of Diana Spearman's role within the Conservative Party, that she could fit into the free-market liberal category, while at the same time playing a great part in reshaping the ideology of the party in a pre-Thatcherite vein before the 1970s. She intended to be a Hayekian prophet, who would spread the gospel of the spontaneous and competitive order of market forces. As Diana

Spearman convincingly explained in the 1980s, when Thatcher was implementing a free and monetarist economy:

> Hayek gave an intellectually satisfying explanation of why economic planning is never successful, and usually makes things worse, in his exposition of the limits of human knowledge. If it is impossible even for a government with a whole crop of statisticians or for the administration of a large public company to have sufficient knowledge of the innumerable decisions which make up the web of the economic system, to make accurate forecasts about the effects of their own actions, the basis of a planned economy is destroyed.[45]

To make a case study of Diana Spearman's role and ideas, a biographical approach is a necessary start to analyse the wide range of primary material (from the LSE, the Bodleian Library, the Hoover Institution, the Churchill College Archives Centre and Diana Spearman's writings),—although it is worth mentioning that there are no personal papers in the LSE Women's Library. The methodology should then be two-fold. Firstly, Conservative historians have widely based their recent studies on E. H. H. Green's *Ideologies of Conservatism* (2002), which offers an intellectual history of the party.[46] Their historical project is to explain how the Conservatives won 'the battle of ideas' in the post-war period, when the thesis of the post-war consensus and the neglect of ideologies long obscured the study of the revamping of Conservative ideology shifting to free-market ideas before 1979. Following suit and to fill a gap in the literature, this article will try to map Diana Spearman's role and Hayekian influence within the Conservative machine and her participation in the advent of Thatcherism.

Furthermore, by adopting a gendered historical approach to the study of Diana Spearman, it is possible to highlight interesting points related to feminist and women's politics. In terms of visibility, Diana Spearman played a 'behind-the-scene role' as she never became an MP, but instead, worked in an almost exclusively male organization of the Conservative Party (the Conservative Research Department).[47] She had no difficulty fitting into a gendered paradigm, especially by becoming one of Rab Butler's 'backroom boys', as she was intelligent and educated. Moreover, her experience as a Conservative female candidate is definitely a good instance of gendered prejudice, as regards to the selection process and the type of constituencies given to women candidates. Spearman's case exemplifies a gender gap in the representation of women in the House of Commons, or more particularly in Conservative Cabinets in the post-war period. For example, women constituted only 4% of the British Parliament in 1969. Last but not least, Spearman's ideas on women's issues did not embody a feminist agenda. Conversely, she adopted a Whig historical approach to women's citizenship.

Diana Spearman: never an MP due to a political gender bias

Diana Spearman showed an early Conservative leaning as she was already canvassing for the Conservatives at the age of 18 at Oswestry[48]—where her home was located in the 1920s.[49] In the 1923 general election, Unionist and Conservative candidate William Bridgeman was returned to Parliament with 46.6% of the share of vote in this constituency.[50] In 1935, she decided to contest the general election, but was only selected for a Labour safe seat. She epitomized the 'Margaret Thatcher' type of good candidate, full of qualities perceived to be indispensable to male candidates at the time; she offered 'a plat-form oratory, full of fire and vigour'.[51] As Katie Haessly notes,

> this long, sometimes arduous process of selection was not an easy one for a qualified man to navigate and was often more difficult for a woman, (…) it is easy to see that any woman who did make it through the process successfully had to prove herself to be exceptional, not just more qualified, compared to her opponents.[52]

Even though Diana Spearman made a convincing campaign, trimming down Labour's share of vote, she did not manage to win a seat. She had particularly tried to appeal to the young and to women 'to return a young Candidate (…) and to send a woman back to Parliament to work for peace and prosperity'.[53] In 1935, there were 19 Conservative women candidates, but only 6 won a seat, while the Conservative majority was reduced by 83.[54] As a journalist highlights, 'although unsuccessful, [Diana Spearman] polled almost twice as many votes as any previous Conservative in that constituency'. Despite 'her energy, courage and determination (…) she faced down the prevailing prejudice against women'.[55]

Joni Lovenduski, Pippa Norris and Catriona Burness have underscored the significant step of selection for candidates to get a 'safe seat'.[56] In the case of Conservative women candidates, their number gradually rose from 1 to 19 between 1918 and 1935, but most of them were 'chosen for hopeless or near hopeless constituencies'[57] because of the party's prejudice against them.[58] Diana Spearman is one typical example among many illustrating this trend, despite all her personal qualities and high level of education for the time. Yet, 'studies suggest that women candidates' chances did not differ significantly between parties [in the interwar years]'.[59]

Yet, Diana Spearman did not suffer from 'economic factors that worked against women', since she came from a wealthy background. As Krista Cowman puts it, 'before the Second World War, Conservative candidates were expected to foot the bill themselves. This disadvantaged women candidates, who had lower levels of affluence or economic independence'.[60] Diana Spearman was also lucky as her husband was a stockbroker and could support her. Generally speaking, at constituency level, selectors were often looking for a team: implicitly or explicitly, they wanted their candidate to be married and have a partner who could be involved.[61] Moreover, and more importantly, there were prejudices against woman candidates in the constituencies about proper gender roles: a woman could be excluded from selection if she had a young child, as her main role should be that of a mother taking care of children in the private sphere at home. Spearman had no children at the time and could thus escape discrimination over questions about her family life during the interview stage.[62]

In 1945, Diana Spearman was again offered selection in a Labour safe seat. Her husband had been elected MP in the Scarborough and Whitby constituency, with 60.8% of the share of vote, a few years before in a 1941 by-election, when he was only opposed by an 'independent Democrat' (W. R. Hipwell), for wartime practice meant that the parties which were part of the coalition government should not contest it.[63] Elizabeth Vallance argues that '[women candidates'] husbands had, as it were, legitimized their political aspirations and this "halo effect" of male acceptability was perhaps at the time essential'.[64] Diana Spearman undoubtedly benefited from her husband's becoming a Conservative MP during the war.[65] Despite an active campaign mainly centred on the issues of 'free enterprise', 'liberties' and 'the small business',[66]—'[Diana Spearman's] dynamism in canvassing Central Hull earned her the sobriquet of "the Mighty Atom"'[67]—she did not manage to change the anticipated outcome. In 1945, there were 14 Conservative women candidates, only Lady Davidson was returned to Parliament in the context of a Labour landslide victory.[68]

Diana Spearman's candidate's file unveils the fact that after 1945 she suffered from a political gender bias on different grounds. Firstly, Mr. Thomas, who interviewed her in 1946, wrote in his Note of Interview that 'she appears to have a rather nervous personality which might not be impressive in front of a selection committee most of whom would—as usual—be hostile to the idea of a woman candidate'.[69] Secondly, being divorced in 1951 became a main hurdle to her candidacy, as Mr Hare reported in his Note of Interview in 1954: 'Intelligent as she is, I do rather doubt whether her personality would impress a Selection Committee in a good seat. The fact that she is divorced is also against her'.[70] More generally, being a woman candidate was the main reason for selection committees to turn down their candidacy as noted by Mr Thomas in 1946:

> Incidentally, I am growing somewhat depressed by the lack of enthusiasm everywhere for women candidates. (...) I feel this unwillingness to take women is probably a reflection on our female ex-M.P.s the majority of whom did scant justification to their sex in the House of Commons.[71]

Diana Spearman renewed her attempts to become an MP in 1953, but eventually gave up by 1959.[72]

At the end of her life, she wrote some political fiction about a former Conservative Foreign secretary who was again in the limelight in the 1960s, after having been out of office for 30 years. There are many echoes to Diana Spearman's own life. She wished she had been a candidate in a safe constituency, as was the case for the main character in her novel, who is interviewed by a journalist about his very quick ascension to political office: 'You were twenty-three when you went into Parliament—rather lucky to get a safe seat so early, but I suppose with your connections it was easy'.[73] Even if she never became an MP, she was to achieve so much more by working at the Conservative Research Department exerting a 'behind-the-scenes power', as was the case for some other influential women members of the Conservative Party.[74]

Diana Spearman's stance on women's issues

There was a significant number of Conservative women who were not interested at all in addressing 'women's issues' in post-war Britain, which are defined as 'those issues which gave women more rights in regard to their bodies, their families and encouraged equality within society' (including education and pricing)'.[75] Another problem that Sarah Childs and Paul Webb stress is that 'what constitutes women's "interests", "issues", "concerns" and "perspectives", is widely contested. Different women (from varying socio-economic, cultural, or political backgrounds and experiences) might well hold different views about what counts as a "women's issue"'. They also add that 'feminist, less- or non- feminist women, and left and right wing women, will likely have different views of what constitutes women's interests even if they agree on what constitutes women's issues'.[76] Another conundrum was the label 'feminist' in post-war Britain, which had a negative meaning and was likely to have a devastating impact on the career of Conservative women. When Joni Lovenduski attempted to define 'feminism' in relation to British politics, she was aware that she was defining a main hurdle for women who were taking a political career and pointed out 'the social stigma and/or political penalty attached to the word'.[77] However, Katie Haessly acknowledges that 'while no female Conservative MP at this time identified herself as a feminist, there were of course some who did have feminist leanings, albeit in many cases very slight leanings'.[78]

Diana Spearman would fit into the paradigm of Conservative women who were not concerned with women's issues. Indeed, in most of her writings, she did not tackle them. In 1948, when she rejected any form of managed economy as stifling profits and incentives, she only talked of 'women' as customers, like men, who should 'go back to profit incentives' and spend freely in an economic system of free enterprise.[79] She might have had in mind the British Housewives' League which was unhappy with Labour economic controls being detrimental to women that were concerned with the price of the shopping basket. By the same token, when Diana Spearman analysed the scourges plaguing British society in the 1960s, she only identified the issues of 'the barriers of class and the difficulties of overcoming them', as well as 'men's careers and education', without mentioning women's conditions at all.[80]

However, one has to turn to her second book (*Democracy in England*, 1957) to get her views, which are somewhat patchy, on the question of women's suffrage or women's status in post-war Britain. She argues that democracy is the only possible form of government for any civilized state, although it is not the perfect one.[81] To make her point, she reconsiders the extension of the franchise in the nineteenth century which led to universal suffrage in 1928. Yet, she overlooked the impact of the suffragettes, as there is virtually no mention of their fight. Her analysis boils down to giving a few reasons why political parties in the nineteenth century did not push for female suffrage. For instance, according to her, 'opposition to women's suffrage was not based on any political theory, but either on mere unreasoning prejudice or, in the minds of Liberals, on a shrewd suspicion that women were more likely to vote Conservative than Liberal'.[82] Nothing proves that it would have been the case at the time. Her speculation might have resulted from her twentieth century biased perspective—that is the Conservative Party's strength to capture the women's vote in a disproportionate way in post-war Britain.

Moreover, she contends that the Utilitarians' ideas infiltrated the minds of the Tories: 'They were against giving the vote to women on the grounds that the interests of women and their husbands were the same, and therefore female suffrage was unnecessary'.[83] In other words, each man will be the best judge of his own happiness and therefore of his own interest alike to that of woman. The decision of the majority must produce the greatest happiness of the greatest number of men and women.[84] Diana Spearman's ideas are limited and, with hindsight, even flawed, as she did not offer a comprehensive analysis of the Conservative Party's attitude towards women's suffrage in the nineteenth century and this proved that she was much more interested in the issues of democracy and freedom after 1939. Lori Maguire, for instance, has argued that although 'traditionally, the Conservative Party has been represented as possessing a negative attitude on the question of women's suffrage, with a few exceptions, the reality is far more complicated, for the party's attitude on the question was decidedly ambivalent'.[85] Diana Spearman also views the 1918 extension of suffrage as a natural phenomenon of evolution than a revolutionary process. To her mind, 'women had done so much work of which they had previously been considered incapable, that it was felt absurd in all parties that they should continue to be shut out from political life'.[86]

Regarding post-war Britain women's issues, Diana Spearman reconsiders the idea of equality, which, in her eye, was a socialist tenet. Instead, she calls for equality of opportunity, so much in tune with Conservative principles. Looking at women's access to university in the 1950s, she only says:

> All that the most extensive political liberty can do is to remove legal barriers and prohibitions from as many activities as possible. (…) A policy which aims at giving everyone who can benefit by education a chance to go to a university is based on another and different idea, that of equality of opportunity.[87]

She contended that a woman should voice her opinion even beyond the typical post-war Britain women's issues identified by Pippa Norris as policies about the family, health-care provision, and food issues[88]: 'Tolerance, however is not natural; men and women, particularly men, have to be continually reminded of other people's right to disagree with them'.[89] That is exactly what she did. According to Geoffrey Foote, 'she gained a formidable intellectual reputation in Tory circles for her delight in argument and her erudition'.[90]

Diana Spearman's role in the Conservative Research Department and Hayekian influence on Enoch Powell and Richard Law (1949–1965)

This section will show that Spearman's trajectory after 1949 was all the more impressive since she did manage to make successful incursions into a series of male domains, such as the CRD and the Mont Pèlerin Society. The CRD, set up in 1930, was meant to be 'an Information-bureau providing data and briefs for leaders, and a long-term research body. (…) The CRD was seen as essential to the "postulation" of Conservative principles and their practical implementation through policy formulation'.[91] In fact, it was one essential apparatus to the Conservative Party's intellectual machinery, as were the Conservative Political Centre and the Advisory Committee on Policy and Political Education,[92] jointly in charge of 'reviving Conservatism'.[93] The CRD's goal was to become 'the indispensable engine of modernizing ideas',[94] and in order to achieve this, the revamped body needed talented young people who would provide memos and analyses to Conservative MPs and Lords so that the latter could fight against the Labour government's bills.[95] Rab Butler, freshly appointed at the head of the bodies of the Conservative Party's intellectual machinery, acknowledged:

> I was looking for people with great intelligence and constructive minds, essentially alert and preferably young. But they did not have to be from the same mould. Individual flair, imagination and even idiosyncrasy were to be encouraged, provided all concerned remained loyal to the party and did not go into rebellion on a major issue. (…) One of the abiding assets of the Conservative Party is its inflexibility—it can absorb a wide discrepancy of views among its members and still remain a coherent and unified entity.[96]

Although Butler had clearly indicated that he did not aim at providing the CRD with 'a hand-picked Brains Trust';[97] his famous 'backroom boys', forming 'a shadow civil service'[98] had to be talented to help the party prepare the next general election with ideas. Studies on the CRD[99] lay the emphasis essentially on the recruitment on young brilliant men (notably Enoch Powell, Ian Macleod or Reginald Maudling)—'destined for political fame in their own right'[100]—willing to enter Parliament and looking for seats. Indeed, in the eye of John Ramsden, '[working at the CRD] could give young men an intensive full-time preparation for their careers in politics, and in the meantime the Party would make use of them too'.[101] As for Alistair Cooke, he contended that working at the CRD was 'an excellent all-round training in politics in much the same manner as other able, ambitious people who were to pass through it over the years'.[102]

The CRD was almost an exclusively male political sphere, providing male recruits with an excellent springboard for prospective careers in the House of Commons. Diana Spearman was recruited again in the CRD in 1949, as 'a central figure in the economic policy section of the Research Department'[103],—with the intention to look for a seat again in the 1950s. She had typical so-called 'male' political characteristic as described by John Ramsden for example[104], such as ambition, brains (she was highly educated), a political network (her husband was an influential Conservative MP and she was a member of the MPS), money and experience (she contested two general elections). She thus fitted into a gendered paradigm, as she naturally became part of Rab Butler's 'backroom boys', having their qualities. Butler's memoirs show that he was seeking 'first rate staff in reliability and thoroughness' and 'ambitious people who were able to give their best in study'.[105] Diana Spearman was trained as a researcher and willing to fight against Keynesian ideas in order to revamp Conservative philosophy. This was precisely how Butler saw his team members.[106] It seemed unproblematic that she displayed masculine traits and it did not necessarily mean unsexing herself. Indeed, as Alistair Cooke and Stephen Parkinson put it, 'the famous Butler's boys and desk officers did not form an exclusive male preserve. A number of women forged successful careers in the Department. Diana Spearman was a prominent figure in the economics section for a number of years'. Two other women achieved a great deal at the CRD at the time; for instance, Elizabeth Briggs (now Buchanan) closely worked with Douglas Hurd's father, while Ursula Branston, who joined the CRD in 1946, eventually became head of its foreign affairs section in the 1950s.[107] All in all, that only amounted to a very limited number of successful women.

It is worth noticing that the decision to prepare a 'Women's Charter' under Rab Butler's initiative and the supervision of Evelyn Emmet, Lady Tweedsmuir and Marjorie Maxse, 'intended to modernize the Conservative position on women particularly with reference to social questions', was made in 1948 for the Annual Conference of the Party. Since Diana Spearman was recruited at the CRD a year later, it is impossible to assume whether or not she would have had any interest in the idea of introducing equal pay for men and women or fighting against discrimination against women, as she had never before defended a feminist agenda.[108]

In the late 1940s and early 1950s, Rab Butler did his utmost to revamp Conservative ideas in what was called 'New Conservatism' to quench criticisms that the Conservative Party had nothing to offer but 'pink Socialism', or 'me-too socialist ideas'.[109] At the same time, the Conservatives could not staunchly call for free-market and liberal ideas again as the 1930s—the devil's decade—had discredited the legitimacy of such policies. Hence Anthony Eden's statement at the 1947 annual Party Conference, which set a paternalist tone to mitigate nineteenth century unbridled capitalism:

> We are not a Party of unbridled, brutal capitalism, and never have been. Although we believe in personal responsibility and personal initiative in business, we are not the political children of the laissez-faire school. We opposed them decade after decade. (…) Conservatives were never averse to the use of legislation to deal with industrial and social problems.[110]

Therefore, 'the years between defeat in 1945 and the return to power in 1951 have acquired a legendary significance in the party's history'.[111] Many in the Conservative Party, as well as at the CRD, turned to Disraeli as 'a Sacred Flame'.[112] As Frank O'Gorman puts it, 'the historian of ideas notes the enduring power of Disraelian concepts and imagery for over a century after his death in 1881'.[113] However, Harriet Jones's research has shown that it would be misleading, in the very post-war period, to overlook the Conservatives' aim to stand up for the principle of 'liberty', while they chose to revive Disraeli's paternalist One Nation Conservatism: 'The task of the Conservative party is to wake up the British people to the fact that their liberty is being taken from them and that the Socialists have neither the wish nor the ability to give it back to them'.[114]

Diana Spearman was actually among the 'enthusiasts for the ultra-liberal economic philosophy of Frederich von Hayek',[115] and decided to promote his free market message in the battle of ideas in the context of Keynesianism and consensus policies. Not only did she draft a couple of reports on technical economic questions at the CRD to rule out the 'fallacy of Keynesian policies' and the drawbacks of a monetary system based on fixed exchange rates, but also to influence Conservative policies by spreading the free market and Hayekian ideas put forward within the MPS. Diana Spearman argued that Keynesian ideas justified state interference in the economy and 'economic planning' during the Second World War, but were not appropriate any longer in post-war Britain since Keynesian policies were 'unsuccessful in practice' as they could not account for and prevent unemployment and stagnation nor guarantee economic progress:[116]

> Keynesian economics has itself developed in two directions: On the one hand into an explanation of inflation and a theory of public finance as the mechanism for controlling not only the slump but also the boom; and on the other hand into an argument for Government control of investment and, in some writers, a complete system of economic planning.[117]

In her view, the fundamental issue of 'individual liberty in a free society' was jeopardized,[118] while inflation should not be apprehended through the Keynesian kaleidoscope, but through the 'quantitative theory of money linked to the amount of money circulating' or the 'over-investment theories' developed by Hayek and Robbins:[119] '[These theories] lead to recommendations as to policy exactly opposite to those which follow from the Keynesian diagnosis'[120]. Between 1948 and 1959, Diana Spearman also exchanged views on Labour's late 1940s unsuccessful economic and monetary policies with Lord Hailsham to gauge the harmful consequences on individuals.[121] Following the 1949 devaluation, she rued Labour's decisions 'not to introduce a more liberal payments system' and tackle 'the controversial question of the convertibility of sterling'.[122] She accounted for 'the Socialist Party's opposition to the case for convertibility', and claimed instead that 'convertibility [was] a condition of recovery' while the Labour Party had made 'inconvertibility a way of insulating our economic situation from that of the world'.[123] Her attendance of the Mont Pèlerin Society meetings led her to further address these issues. Not only did she publish a pamphlet on the ideas of 'liberty' and 'equality' to reject Socialism and state intervention in the economy, but she also tackled again the monetary questions of 'the floating exchange rates' in relation to a free market economy[124] and of inflation[125] for instance. She quickly became the advocate of the Hayekian principle of the 'spontaneous order of the market' free from state intervention.[126] In 1959, she had the honour to give a speech at the MPS meeting in Oxford. She explained again the failures of socialist policies in post-war Britain and promoted an alternative based on free-market ideas and the use of monetary policy:

> In 1951, the country was not intellectually convinced of the superiority of a free enterprise system. (…) No political leaders had put this forward as a consistent political alternative. (…) There is no doubt that we have at the moment a movement not only towards free enterprise but even in favour of property itself. This of course depends on the economic climate and on the continuance of explanations given by people like the distinguished members of this society,—one should particularly mention our President Professor Hayek—of how and why a free enterprise system does work.[127]

In the same vein as Hayek's *Road to Serfdom* and Adam Smith's *Wealth of Nations*, she also called for free market ideas: 'If every man were left to pursue his own interests, without the intervention of the State, he would achieve his own interest, but he would do so with the interests of others'[128]. Yet, she was aware that the State had a significant part to play in the protection of certain weak sections of society (children, the old and sick) and in the eradication of poverty as the Beveridge Report had highlighted this 'social giant'. To that extent, she challenged Samuel Smiles's unconditional principle of self-help but rejected the Socialists' idea of state interference in the economy:

> Most people now believe that free enterprise itself creates the monster that destroys it and that, therefore, the only way of achieving the maximum degree of economic welfare is to exchange the system of private enterprise for that of State ownership of all important industries, together with the detailed supervision by the State of all forms of economic activity.[129]

According to her, State interference in the economy would result in bureaucracy and a lack of efficiency, putting an end to profit incentives, while monopolies would distort the price system and free competition, leading to a maldistribution of resources. In the early Cold War context, she recalled the pernicious consequences of the 'Russian Revolution' that had brought about an absolute control of 'all aspects of economic life', which is 'alien to any conception of democracy that the Government should be able to decide what work a man shall do, involving, as it does in the end, also prescribing where he shall live, and what he shall earn'.[130] As she was close to philosopher Michael Oakeshott and to free-market economist Lionel Robbins from the London School of Economics, Andrew Gamble reckons that it allowed her 'to provide a bridge between intellectual Conservatism and the party politicians'.[131]

Likewise, Diana Spearman's husband, who was a diehard free-market Conservative, also dismissed any idea of consensus and Keynesian politics in the 1940s.[132] Richard Law said to Diana Spearman in the aftermath of the 1945 general election:

> I had lunch with Lionel [Robbins] before he went off to Washington. I told him that under your influence and Alec's, I had become a die hard, and he thought that that was a move in the proper, as well as the right, direction.[133]

More interestingly, he also added:

I wish that you and Alec could get us busy on the Tory reformers. (...) For my own part, I can't see that they have any distinctive principles except a vague impulse which we all share towards benevolence and votes. They give the impression the Party is much worse than it is.[134]

Since then, Diana Spearman had had tremendous influence on Richard Law[135] who published *Return from Utopia* in 1950. The book resulted from a lot of discussions he had with her and can be seen as a vindication of Hayek's *Road to Serfdom*.[136] Richard Law acknowledged his intellectual debt to Diana Spearman in his preface.

Diana Spearman's case is a good example of valuable contributions made by women, which afforded them 'a behind-the-scenes power'.[137] Diana Spearman also met Enoch Powell at the CRD and got him to read Hayek's *Road to Serfdom*.[138] While Powell's mind was trained in a Disraelian environment at the CRD, she was the trigger for Powell to start developing free market ideas in a Hayekian vein. She significantly influenced his thinking and convinced him that the Collectivist Age had to be fought against in the name of liberal ideas.[139] In her obituary, Enoch Powell praised her intellectual contribution to the battle of ideas: 'In this capacity of research at the Conservative Research Department, she became a powerful advocate of market economics, at least a decade before they acquired the label of Thatcherism'.[140]

The Longbow Group (1965)

After 'becoming active in the free market campaigns of the Institute of Economic Affairs (IEA)',[141] Diana Spearman thought in the aftermath of the Conservative Party's 1964 defeat:

> There is no future in simply trying to run the state economy more efficiently than Labour. Winning an election is not a matter of angling for this or that packet of votes, changing the fly as appropriate, but rather of putting forward a consistent and coherent political philosophy. There is only one line of approach which holds any promise of success. It is to establish again a free and competitive economic system which, in spite of its imperfections (or perhaps because of them), works for social and moral as well as for economic good.[142]

She had decided to leave the CRD in 1964 for 'she [found] herself increasingly out of sympathy with the Government's colonial policy'.[143] She had also been disappointed by Harold Macmillan's unwillingness to 'carry further liberal economic measures'.[144] According to Enoch Powell, 'the CRD, which she long adorned, must sometimes have been made uncomfortable by her searching demand for consistency with economic principle and compatibility with Tory ideals'.[145] Diana Spearman was critical of the role and the ideological position of the Bow Group; as a result, she launched the project of formulating a coherent Conservative philosophy of free market ideas by setting up what she called 'the Longbow Group', which included, for instance, John Wood of the IEA and T. E. Utley. There were nine male members while she was the only female one in charge of presiding over the Group.[146] They aimed to draft a Manifesto to offer fresh insight into free market ideas to revive the liberal branch of Conservatism. As 1965 was the year when the very first election for the party leadership had taken place, Diana Spearman pointed out that the 'manifesto would urge the need for a stronger emphasis on individual freedom and the competitive economy, at a time when the Conservative Party was supposed to be revising its policy and concentrating on measures rather than men'.[147] She could rely on Professor Jewkes (an MPS member) to provide the group members with a preliminary paper on the idea of 'individual freedom'. Furthermore, she did not want bad publicity, in her own words 'the Manifesto should be supported by the "right people" not individuals whom the media-crats could write off as the lunatic fringe'.[148] She surely expected Powell, who was becoming more influential within the Conservative party, to publicly promote such ideas of 'freedom' or 'a free economy', as that was the very moment when 'Powellism' appeared in the press (in *the Economist* in July 1965 for the very first time) as a distinctive doctrine calling for a free economy and a free society.[149]

The Longbow Group quickly drafted a manifesto called 'Manifesto for Freedom' supporting the primacy of a 'free economic system' in a Hayekian tone:

> There is indeed a strong argument for economic freedom, valid even for those who do not accept the primacy of individual over state interests. This is the superiority of the spontaneous order, created by the uncoordinated efforts of individuals, over the imposed order of authoritarian direction.[150]

It called for limited government in the economic sphere, no incomes policy, very few nationalized industries, low inflation and taxation. Instead, competition should be 'preserved' in a free market system. According to Richard Cockett, 'the document was very much a distillation of Hayek's political philosophy, and anticipated much of the Conservative Party policy in the 1980s, although it was far ahead of official Party thinking in 1965'.[151] Although little became of the short-lived Longbow Group or their putative manifesto, the attempt to redefine Conservatism from a free market perspective was crucial for different reasons. First, it represented a clear rejection of 'the Conservative version of consensus politics'.[152] This also meant a significant dismissal of the paternalist branch of Conservatism, which had been prevalent under Butler and Macmillan:

> The tendencies of a misconceived to make the individual's choices for him, not only cuts him off from many sources of happiness but also from the dignity of a responsible human being, and relegates him to the position of a child. (...) Freedom entails responsibility. It is the task of Conservatives to show that only Conservatism can provide conditions which make it possible.[153]

In addition, the Manifesto would help to 'move public and party opinion to the right',[154] as its ideas offered 'an intellectually based and firmly stated alternative'.[155] It was, in the view of Greenleaf, 'one factor crucial to the creation of that background of opinion from which the policies of the Thatcher government have emerged, policies which deliberately set out to challenge the dominant collectivist tendencies of the age'.[156]

Conclusion

Diana Spearman's case study has shown that she never managed to become an MP in the 1930s and 1940s as she was selected in Labour safe seats because she was a female candidate. Although she was not really interested in women's issues and only put forward very limited and unsophisticated ideas about them, it is fair to say that she was an important 'backroom woman' at the CRD and an influential thinker, making Enoch Powell and Richard Law discover the Hayekian philosophy of the primacy of the free market economy in the Collectivist Age. Even though her Longbow Group faded very quickly in 1965, their Manifesto was a crucial attempt to redefine Conservatism from a free market perspective, challenging the Middle Way and consensus politics and paving the way for Thatcherism. In the late 1960s, Spearman looked towards Enoch Powell as the 'eventual saviour'[157] to promote a free economy and a free society, and she strongly supported his stand against immigration, which, she was sure, had contributed towards the Conservatives' victory in the 1970 General Election.[158]

Richard Law, who then became Lord Coleraine, published a second book entitled *For Conservatives Only* in 1970. He rejected the myth of the middle ground and condemned the party for pursing it. It was reminiscent of Hayek's ideas and of those of the Longbow Group. Diana Spearman had thus trained minds of influential Conservative politicians who took part in the battle of ideas to revive the liberal branch of Conservatism from the 1960s onwards. Following Diana Spearman's path a decade later, Powell was eventually appointed member of the Mont-Pèlerin Society,[159] joining an international academy of liberal philosophers, economists and politicians where he would be committed to take part in the battle of ideas against Keynesianism and Socialism.[160] Even during the Thatcher years, Diana Spearman continued to praise Hayek's intellectual work and called for 'a crusade to abolish the constraints which interfere with freedom, to do away with subsidies to nationalized industries, the still excessive legal privileges of trade unions and the interventionist role of the Common Market'.[161] Throughout her life, Spearman was, in Powell's eye 'an outstanding and tireless philosopher of conservatism (...) [upholding] rigorously in books and articles the economic and social implications of Tory belief'.[162] Her role within the Conservative Party should therefore be acknowledged and she should be considered as a member of the pantheon of 'Iron Ladies'.

Notes

1. Sarah Childs & Paul Webb (2012) *Sex, Gender and the Conservative Party: from iron lady to kitten heels* (Basingstoke: Palgrave Macmillan), p. 3.
2. Ibid.
3. House of Commons Information Office (June 2010) 'Women in the House of Commons', Factsheet M4 Members Series Revised, p. 7, https://www.parliament.uk/documents/commons-information-office/m04.pdf [last retrieved 5 March 2017].
4. Ruth Hening & Simon Hening (2001) *Women and Political Power: Europe since 1945* (London & New York: Routledge), p. 1.
5. G. E. Macguire (1998) *Conservative Women: a history of women and the conservative party, 1874–1997* (Basingstoke: Macmillan Press), p. 149.
6. E. H. H. Green (2006) *Thatcher* (London: Hodder Arnold), p. 12.
7. Ibid., p. 13.
8. Ibid., p. 16.
9. Joni Lovenduski, Pippa Norris & Catriona Burness (1994) The Party and Women, in Anthony Seldon & Stuart Ball (Eds) *Conservative Century: the Conservative Party since 1900* (Oxford: OUP), pp. 611–635.
10. Joni Lovenduski & Pippa Norris (1996) *Women in Politics* (Oxford: OUP), p. 1.
11. Martin Pugh (1988) Popular Conservatism in Britain: continuity and change 1880–1997, *Journal of British Studies*, 27(3); (2015) *Women and the Women's Movement in Britain since 1914* (Basingstoke: Palgrave Macmillan).
12. Krista Cowman (2010) *Women in British Politics 1689–1979* (Basingstoke: Palgrave Macmillan), p. 3.
13. Sarah Childs & Paul Webb, *Sex, Gender and the Conservative Party*, p. 5.

14. Katie Haessly (December 2010) *British Conservative MPs and 'Women's Issues', 1950–1979* (Unpublished PhD, University of Nottingham).
15. Clarisse Berthezène (2016) Un Féminisme conservateur? Genre et politique en Grande-Bretagne 1928–1964, in Clarisse Berthezène & Jean-Christian Vinel (Eds) *Conservatismes en mouvement: Une Approche transnationale au XXe siècle* (Paris: éditions EHESS), pp. 409–434.
16. Ibid., p. 414.
17. Clarisse Berthezène & Julie Gottlieb (Eds) (2018) *Rethinking Right-wing Women: gender and the Conservative Party 1880s to the present* (Manchester: MUP), p. 2.
18. John Ramsden (1995) *The Age of Churchill and Eden 1940–1957* (London: Longman) and (1996) *The Winds of Change: Macmillan to Heath, 1957–1975* (London: Longman); Alan Clark (1998) *The Tories: conservatives and the nation state, 1922–1997* (London: Weidenfeld and Nicolson); Robin Harris (2011) *The Conservatives: a history* (London: Bantam); Tim Bale (2012) *The Conservatives since 1945: the drivers of party change* (Oxford: OUP); Timothy Heppell (2014) *The Tories: from Winston Churchill to David Cameron* (London: Bloomsbury Academic); Kevin Hickson (Ed) (2005) *The Political Thought of the Conservative Party since 1945* (Basingstoke: Palgrave Macmillan); Mark Garnett & Kevin Hickson (Eds) (2009) *Conservative Thinkers: the key contributors to the political thought of the modern Conservative Party* (Manchester: MUP); Richard Cockett (1995) *Thinking the unthinkable (think-tanks and the economic counter-revolution, 1931–1983)* (London: Fontana Press).
19. http://www.thepeerage.com/p58064.htm#i580633 [last retrieved 5 March 2017].
20. Anon, *Obituary: Diana Spearman* (1991). Archives, LSE Library, London, (Cockett Papers), COCKETT 1/5.
21. The Published LSE Register, 1895–1932.
22. LSE/Student File/Spearman Diana.
23. Constituency files on Poplar South for 1935, and Hull Central for 1945 did not survive in the Conservative Party Archives, Bodleian Library, Oxford—the majority of the constituency files survive from the late 1940s only [information from Jeremy McIlwaine, CPA archivist].
24. https://www.montpelerin.org/about-mps/ [last retrieved on 22 December 2017].
25. R. M. Hartwell (1995) *A History of the Mont-Pèlerin Society* (Indianapolis: Liberty Fund), pp. xiv–xvi.
26. Diana Spearman, *Letter to Hayek* (3 December 1948). Archives, Hoover Institution, Stanford University (Hayek Papers), Box 79, Folder 17.
27. They were all men.
28. Richard Cockett, *Thinking the Unthinkable*, p. 116; Geoffrey Foote (2006) *The Republican Transformation of Modern British Politics* (Basingstoke: Palgrave Macmillan), p. 138.
29. Oxford MPS meeting, 1959, https://digitalcollections.hoover.org/objects/52837/mont-pelerin-society-meeting-at-oxford?ctx=7009e8bd-9581-4a64-bb3a-8241ee9d319b&idx=0 [last retrieved on 22 December 2017].
30. Ibid.
31. Diana Spearman (1939) *Modern Dictatorship* (London: Jonathan Cape); (1957) *Democracy in England* (London: Rockliff); (September 1957) The Freedom of the Individual, *Swinton Journal*, 4(2), pp. 41–44.
32. *Correspondence with Diana Spearman*, 1965–1978. Archives, Hoover Institution, Stanford University (Register of the Institute of Economic Affairs Archives), Box 298, Folder 10.
33. Diana Spearman (Spring 1983) The Politics of Nature, *Salisbury Review*, pp. 7–9; (April 1987) Walter Scott as a Conservative Thinker, *The Salisbury Review*, pp. 29–32.
34. Anon. (1991) *Obituary of Diana Spearman, The Sunday Telegraph* (9 June), p. 20.
35. Simon Heffer (1999) *Like the Roman: the life of Enoch Powell* (London: Phoenix Giant), pp. 568 & 576.
36. Enoch Powell, *Diana Spearman* (1991). Archives, LSE Library, London (Cockett Papers), COCKETT 1/5.
37. Enoch Powell, *Memorial Address for Diana Spearman* (13 June 1991), pp. 1–2. Archives, Churchill College Archives Centre, Cambridge (Powell Papers), POLL 4/1/23.

38. Beatrix Campbell (1987) *The Iron Ladies: why women vote tory?* (London: Virago), pp. 1, 4 & 298.

39. Anon. *Obituary: Diana Spearman* (1991). Archives, LSE Library, London (Cockett Papers), COCKETT 1/5.

40. Sarah Childs & Paul Webb, *Sex, Gender and the Conservative Party*, p. 4.

41. Ibid.

42. William H. Greenleaf (1983) *The British Political Tradition (Vol. 2)* (London: Methuen), pp. 189–358.

43. Clarisse Berthezène, Un Féminisme conservateur?, p. 417.

44. ibid., pp. 417–418.

45. Diana Spearman (1986) The 'New Right' Radicals, *Economic Affairs Journal* (April-May), p. 35.

46. E. H. H. Green (2002) *Ideologies of Conservatism* (Oxford: OUP).

47. Alistair Cooke (Ed) (2009) *Tory Policy-Making: the conservative research department, 1929–2009* (Eastbourne: Manor Creative); John Ramsden (1980) *The Making of Conservative Party Policy* (London: Longman).

48. Anon. *Obituary: Diana Spearman.*

49. LSE/Student File/Spearman Diana.

50. https://www.revolvy.com/main/index.php?s=Oswestry%20(UK%20Parliament% 20constituency) [last retrieved on 22 December 2017].

51. Anon. *Obituary: Diana Spearman.*

52. Katie Haessly, *British Conservative MPs and 'Women's Issues', 1950–1979*, p. 45.

53. Diana Spearman, *Election Address* (1935). Archives, Bodleian Library, University of Oxford (CPA Archives), PUB 229/7/1 fo. 88.

54. Krista Cowman, *Women in British Politics, 1689–1979*, p. 121.

55. Anon. *Obituary: Diana Spearman.*

56. Joni Lovenduski, Pippa Norris & Catriona Burness, The Party and Women, p. 630.

57. G. E. Macguire, *Conservative Women*, p. 169.

58. Sarah Childs (2010) *Women and British Party Politics: descriptive, substantive and symbolic representation* (London: Routledge), p. xxiii; Krista Cowman, *Women in British Politics, 1689–1979*, p. 121.

59. Ibid., p. 121.

60. Ibid., p. 122.

61. Joni Lovenduski, Pippa Norris & Catriona Burness, The Party and Women, p. 629.

62. Katie Haessly, *British Conservative MPs and 'Women's Issues', 1950–1979*, pp. 45–46.

63. Anon. (1941) Scarborough Election Result, *The Times* (26 September).

64. E. Vallance (1979) *Women in the House: a study of women members of parliament* (London: Athlone Press), p. 27.

65. Mr. Hare, *Note of Interview* (6 May 1953). Archives, Bodleian Library, University of Oxford (CPA Archives), CCO 220/3/14/12. I would like to thank the Conservative Campaign Headquarters for permission to use and quote the file.

66. Diana Spearman, *Election Address* (1945). Archives, Bodleian Library, University of Oxford (CPA Archives), PUB 229/8/5 fo. 29.

67. Anon. *Obituary: Diana Spearman.*

68. G. E. Macguire, *Conservative Women*, pp. 166 & 170.

69. Mr. Thomas, *Note of Interview* (5 December 1946). Archives, Bodleian Library, University of Oxford (CPA Archives), CCO 220/3/14/12.

70. Mr. Hare, *Note of Interview* (28 July 1954). Archives, Bodleian Library, University of Oxford (CPA Archives), CCO 220/3/14/12.

71. Mr. Thomas, *Note of Interview* (5 December 1946).

72. Diana Spearman, *Candidate's File*. Archives, Bodleian Library, University of Oxford (CPA Archives), CCO 220/3/14/12.

73. Diana Spearman (1989) *A Time You Remember* (Braunton: Merlin), p. 9.

74. Joni Lovenduski, Pippa Norris & Catriona Burness, The Party and Women, p. 618.

75. Katie Haessly, *British Conservative MPs and 'Women's Issues', 1950–1979*, p. 16.
76. Sarah Childs & Paul Webb, *Sex, Gender and the Conservative Party*, p. 2.
77. Joni Lovenduski, Sex, Gender, and British Politics, *Parliamentary Affairs*, 1996, 49(1), p. 2.
78. Katie Haessly, *British Conservative MPs and 'Women's Issues', 1950–1979*, p. 17.
79. Diana Spearman (1948) The Competitive Order, *The Contemporary Review* (1 January) (173), p. 35.
80. Diana Spearman (1963) The Conformity of Non-Conformity, *The Spectator* (25 October), p. 525.
81. Diana Spearman, *Democracy in England*, pp. vii–viii.
82. Ibid., p. 135.
83. Ibid., p. 79.
84. Ibid., p. 78.
85. Lori Maguire (2007) The Conservative Party and Women's Suffrage, in Myriam Boussahba-Bravard (Ed) *Suffrage outside Suffragism: women's vote in Britain 1880–1914* (Basingstoke: Palgrave Macmillan), p. 52.
86. Diana Spearman, *Democracy in England*, p. 155.
87. Ibid., p. 195.
88. Joni Lovenduski, Pippa Norris & Catriona Burness, The Party and Women, p. 630.
89. Diana Spearman, *Democracy in England*, p. 197.
90. Geoffrey Foote, *The Republican Transformation of Modern British Politics*, p. 131.
91. Clarisse Berthezène (2004) Creating Conservative Fabians: the Conservative Party, Political Education, and the Founding of Ashbridge College, *Past and Present* (February) 182, p. 215.
92. Clarisse Berthezène (2011) *Les Conservateurs britanniques dans la batailles des idées* (Paris : Sciences Po Presses), pp. 374–382; John Ramsden, *The Making of Conservative Party Policy*, p. 105.
93. Mark Garnett (1999) *Alport: A Study in Loyalty* (Teddington: Acumen), p. 70.
94. S. Mitchell (2006) *The Brief and Turbulent Life of Modernising Conservatism* (Newcastle: Cambridge Scholars Press), p. 8.
95. Enoch Powell (28 May 1980), p. 3. Archives, LSE Library, London (BOAPAH Archives).
96. Rab Butler (1971) *The Art of the Possible: the memoirs of lord butler* (London: Purnell Book), p. 139.
97. Anon. *Rab 1945–51* [undated]. Archives, Bodleian Library, University of Oxford (CPA Archives), CRD 2/53/1.
98. John Ramsden, *The Making of Conservative Party Policy*, p. 104.
99. Alistair Cooke (Ed), *Tory Policy-Making*, p. 33; John Ramsden, *The Making of Conservative Party Policy*, p. 104.
100. Ibid.
101. Ibid., p. 105.
102. Alistair Cooke (Ed), *Tory Policy-Making*, p. 35.
103. Michael Kandiah & Harriet Jones (Eds) *The Myth of Consensus: new views on British history, 1945–64* (Basingstoke: Macmillan), p. 9.
104. John Ramsden, *The Making of Conservative Party Policy*, pp. 120–122.
105. Rab Butler, *The Art of the Possible*, pp. 138 & 140.
106. Michael Jago (2015) *Rab Butler: the best prime minister we never had?* (London: Biteback), p. 190.
107. Alistair Cooke (Ed), *Tory Policy-Making*, p. 37.
108. G. E. Maguire, *Conservative Women*, p. 147; Clarisse Berthezène, Un Féminisme conservateur, pp. 426–427.
109. Rab Butler, *The Art of the Possible*, p. 134.
110. Anthony Eden, *The New Conservatism* (1955), CPC, pp. 11–12. Archives, Bodleian Library, University of Oxford (CPA Archives), CCO 150/4/3/3.
111. J. Ramsden, *The Age of Churchill and Eden, 1940–1957*, p. 94.
112. D. Southgate (1977) From Disraeli to Law, in N. Gash *et al. The Conservatives: a history from their origins to 1965* (London: George Allen and Unwin), p. 125.

113. F. O'Gorman (1986) *British Conservatism: conservative thought from Burke to Thatcher* (London: Longman), p. 35.
114. Douglas Jerrold (1946) Editorial Comment, *The English Review*, (September) 13(3), in Harriet Jones (1992) *The Conservative Party and the Welfare State, 1942–1955* (Unpublished PhD, University of London), p. 117.
115. Simon Heffer, *Like the Roman: the life of Enoch Powell*, p. 212.
116. Diana Spearman, *Unemployment* (3 February 1954). Archives, Bodleian Library, University of Oxford (CPA Archives), CRD 2/53/13.
117. ibid., p. 24.
118. Diana Spearman, Letter to Hayek (2 May 1955). Archives, Hoover Institution, Stanford University (Hayek Papers), Box 51, Folder 9.
119. Diana Spearman, *Unemployment* (3 February 1954), pp. 9–11.
120. ibid., p. 11.
121. *Correspondence with Diana Spearman about inflation and economic data.* Archives, Churchill College Archives Centre, Cambridge (Lord Hailsham Papers), HLSM 2/42/4/16, HLSM 2/42/4/9 and HLSM 3/6/4.
122. Diana Spearman & John Wood, *Explanatory Notes on the European Payments Union* (17 July 1950), p. 4. Archives, Bodleian Library, University of Oxford (CPA Archives), CRD 2/34/5.
123. Diana Spearman, *A Note on Convertibility* (22 July 1952), pp. 1 & 6. Archives, Bodleian Library, University of Oxford (CPA Archives), CRD 2/53/13.
124. Diana Spearman (1953) *The Sterling Area* (London: CPC) 124, pp. 45–48.
125. Diana Spearman, *Note to Dance* (13 September 1957), p. 12. Archives, Bodleian Library, University of Oxford (CPA Archives), CRD 2/9/38.
126. R. Cockett, *Thinking the Unthinkable*, pp. 99; G. Foote, *The Republican Transformation of Modern British Politics*, p. 131.
127. Oxford MPS meeting, 1959.
128. Diana Spearman, Competitive Order, p. 31.
129. Ibid., pp. 31–32.
130. Ibid., p. 34.
131. A. Gamble (1974) *The Conservative Nation* (London: Routledge & Kegan Paul), p. 113.
132. Alec Spearman, *Draft* (4 January 1949). Archives, Bodleian Library, University of Oxford (CPA Archives), CRD 2/19/14.
133. Harriet Jones, *The Conservative Party and the Welfare State, 1942–1955*, p. 117.
134. ibid., p. 119.
135. R. Cockett, *Thinking the Unthinkable*, p. 99.
136. Stéphane Porion (2011) *Enoch Powell et le powellisme : entre tradition disraélienne et anticipation néo-libérale, 1946–1968* (Unpublished PhD, Sorbonne-Nouvelle University), pp. 148–151.
137. Joni Lovenduski, Pippa Norris & Catriona Burness (1994) The Party and Women, p. 618.
138. Simon Heffer, *Like the Roman, the Life of Enoch Powell*, p. 212.
139. R. Cockett, *Thinking the Unthinkable*, p. 99.
140. Enoch Powell, *Diana Spearman*.
141. Anon, *Obituary: Diana Spearman*.
142. Richard Cockett, *Thinking the Unthinkable*, p. 164.
143. Diana Spearman, *Letter to Sir Michael Fraser* (27 March 1962). Archives, Bodleian Library, University of Oxford (CPA Archives), CCO 220/3/14/12.
144. Diana Spearman, *Letter to Hayek* (13 January 1960). Archives, Hoover Institution, Stanford University (Hayek Papers), Box 79, Folder 17.
145. Enoch Powell, *Memorial Address for Diana Spearman*.
146. *Preliminary Meeting of Longbow Group* (23 February 1965). Archives, LSE Library, London (Cockett Papers), COCKETT 1/5.
147. Ibid.
148. Ibid.
149. Anon. The Importance of Being Enoch, *The Economist*, 17 July 1965, p. 217.

150. Longbow Group, *Manifesto for Freedom* (1965), p. 4. Archives, LSE Library, London (Cockett Papers), COCKETT 1/5.
151. Richard Cockett, *Thinking the Unthinkable*, p. 165.
152. W. H. Greenleaf, *The British Political Tradition (Vol. 2)*, p. 326.
153. Longbow Group, *Manifesto for Freedom*, p. 3.
154. W. H. Greenleaf, *The British Political Tradition (Vol. 2)*, p. 326.
155. T. Szamuely (1968) Intellectuals and Conservatism, *Swinton Journal*, 14(1) (Spring), p. 13. Archives, Bodleian Library, University of Oxford (CPA Archives), PUB 188/4.
156. W. H. Greenleaf, *The British Political Tradition (Vol. 2)*, p. 327.
157. Anon. (1991) *Obituary of Diana Spearman*.
158. Diana Spearman (1968) Enoch Powell's Postbag, *New Society* (9 May), pp. 667–668; Enoch Powell's Election Letters, in John Wood (Ed) *Powell and the 1970 Election* (Kingswood: Elliot Right Way Books), pp. 19–49.
159. *Mont-Pèlerin Society to Powell* (30 September 1965). Archives, Churchill College Archives Centre, Cambridge (Powell Papers), POLL 1/1/14.
160. *Powell to Mont-Pèlerin Society* (8 October 1965). Archives, Churchill College Archives Centre, Cambridge (Powell Papers), POLL 1/1/14.
161. Diana Spearman, The 'New Right' Radicals, p. 35.
162. Enoch Powell, Diana Spearman.

Acknowledgement

I would like to thank my two peer-reviewers for their useful recommendations, as well as Jeremy McIlwaine (Conservative Party Archives, Bodleian Library, Oxford), Katharine Thomson (Churchill College Archives Centre, Cambridge), Sue Donnelly (LSE Archivist) and Sarah Patton (Hoover Institution, Stanford University, California) for their valuable help.

Disclosure statement

No potential conflict of interest was reported by the author.

Housewives having a go: Margaret Thatcher, Mary Whitehouse and the appeal of the Right Wing Woman in late twentieth-century Britain

Jessica Prestidge

ABSTRACT

Margaret Thatcher and Mary Whitehouse have been described by Beatrix Campbell as 'populist heroines of the right', and an affinity between the two women was widely assumed throughout Thatcher's leadership. They were both suburban mothers with prominent handbags, calling for a return to the stabilising values of 'simpler times'. Their relationship, however, was far from straight-forward. By examining this relationship alongside its public presentation, this article will refine understandings of these important conservative women. Considering their shared cultural resonances will also enhance understanding of the late twentieth-century cultural and political contexts within which they operated.

Introduction

'Before Margaret Thatcher', wrote Anthony Andrew for the *Guardian* in 2012, there was 'another woman with firm convictions and an even firmer hairdo'.[1] Andrew was referring to Mary Whitehouse, the founder and elected president of pro-censorship campaign group, the National Viewers' and Listeners' Association. Describing Thatcher's relationship with Mary Whitehouse, Lynda Lee-Potter, writing for the *Daily Mail*, claimed that 'it was a case of Iron Lady meets Iron Lady … the two women are sisters under the skin'.[2] Jointly described by Beatrix Campbell as 'heroines of the right', similarities between Whitehouse and Thatcher are also emphasised in the academic literature. For Liza Filby they were 'remarkably similar' in both 'character and demeanour', their being middle-class suburban mothers 'armed with a handbag'.[3] Matthew Grimley begins his contribution to Jackson and Saunders' *Making Thatcher's Britain* with a comparison of these two 'middle-aged' women, and Lawrence Black has emphasised their common populist strategies.[4] Comparison, however, is generally made in passing, and the precise character of their shared cultural appeal warrants further consideration.

Thatcher's relationship with Whitehouse was complex, and changed over the course of her leadership. As Richard Vinen has argued, her moralist sympathies were strongest during the period between 1975 and 1979, with a lack of power enabling a freer articulation of support for typically populist causes.[5] Once Prime Minister, significant ideological differences prevented Thatcher from offering Whitehouse the support she had anticipated.

The enduring readiness of popular commentary to emphasise similarities speaks to the carefully constructed public images of both women, the cultural resonance of the values and ideals their public images mobilised and the strength of the gendered conservative stereotypes through which they were both understood. The discrepancy between the public image and private character of their relationship presents fruitful opportunities for analysis.

The premise of this article is that the prioritising of political office as the determining feature of comparison risks blunting analysis of Thatcher's public image, which was in many ways *incomparable* to the public images of male prime ministers. As a woman, Thatcher faced a different set of challenges to those of her male predecessors and successors. She was held to different standards, and also had a different set of 'tools' at her disposal. The visual and discursive resources she drew upon alternately emphasised and suppressed her gender, and the responses she generated were often equally gendered. Given the centrality of gender to her public identity, it is logical that this should be foregrounded in the structure of any comparative analysis. Comparison with Mary Whitehouse seeks to develop a more fruitful context for understanding the nuances of Thatcher's public image. By contextualising their shared cultural appeal and interrogating widely assumed similarities, this article will enrich understandings of how Margaret Thatcher's deeply moralistic public images operated. In doing so, it will also enhance understanding of 'Right Wing Women' stereotypes more broadly.[6]

I

The logic of a comparative analysis between Margaret Thatcher and the leader of a campaign group may not be immediately obvious. Within the expanded conception of 'politics' advanced by the New Political History, however, which emphasises the cultural history of 'the political' above a narrowly defined party establishment, Whitehouse should be recognised as a 'politician'. As Lawrence Black has argued, 'just as the Church was not the sum of religious history, nor was the party or government the sum of politics'.[7] Through her role as president of the National Viewers' and Listeners' Association, Whitehouse carved out a place for herself on the public stage, and her public career generated a wealth of historically rich documentary evidence. A skilled self-promoter, she published six memoirs, packed university debating chambers and found a willing platform for her organisation's views in the conservative leaning national press.[8] The NVALA archive clearly demonstrates the close attention the organisation paid to its media profile, with manuscripts, speeches and public statements filed alongside carefully compiled press clippings documenting their public incarnations. Whitehouse was the subject of at least one widely reviewed biography, by Max Caulfield, and one 'sociological enquiry'. The book *Whitehouse*, described by its authors Michael Tracey and David Morrison as an exploration of the 'gestation of moral protest', was conceived as an academic project with a limited press run. In response to widespread interest, however, it was launched by a high-profile press conference and promoted nationwide.[9] Tracey and Morrison spent three years studying Whitehouse and the NVALA through fieldwork, and their book provides a useful account not only of the Whitehouse's private motivations, but also of the social, cultural and political contexts that facilitated and shaped her public character.

This is not to suggest that coverage was universally—or even generally—positive. Whitehouse was a divisive figure who drew both mockery and contempt. Her background was in the Oxford Group, and later Moral Rearmament, making overt support all the less appealing for public figures on either side of the political spectrum. Following her successful prosecution of *Gay News* in 1977, for its publication of James Kirkup's poem depicting a sodomised Jesus Christ, banners in Trafalgar square read: 'Mary Whitehouse! Kill! Kill! Kill!'.[10] In 2008, *Telegraph* journalist Elizabeth Urdel described her as 'second only to Mrs Thatcher in the liberal hate stakes'.[11] In 1975 David Sullivan launched a pornographic magazine in her name, and *The Mary Whitehouse Experience*, a sketch show produced by the BBC in partnership with Spitting Image Productions, is an example of the irreverent and sexually explicit comedy the NVALA campaigned against. She was parodied as Mrs Smallgood in the short-lived television series *Swizzlewick*, and as the overzealous anti-sex campaigner Desiree Carthorse in *The Goodies*.

Whitehouse and her supporters regularly claimed to represent the 'silent majority', a loaded, amorphous phrase popularised by Richard Nixon in 1969.[12] The NVALA saw itself not as 'a noisy pressure group representing a tiny minority, but ... an awakening democracy conscious of its power and responsibility'.[13] Membership figures for the National Viewers' and Listeners' Association, which grew out of Clean Up TV in 1965, are hard to come by. Whitehouse claimed to represent 15,000 paying members in 1975, but argued that over a million people had demonstrated their support by signing the organisation's petitions.[14] But while Whitehouse's views may never have found the majority support she claimed, her appeal among certain groups was stronger than liberal critics were prepared to acknowledge. In 1967 the then editor of Woman's Hour, Monica Sims, argued against inviting Whitehouse to appear on the show for fear that 'a majority of our listeners might write to support her'.[15] For playwright Dennis Potter, she was 'standing up for all the people with ducks on their walls ... laughed at and treated like rubbish by the sophisticated metropolitan minority'.[16]

NVALA began life in 1964, when Whitehouse was working as an art mistress at Madeley School in Shropshire. Concerned by the effect that television appeared to be having on the sexual outlooks of the children she taught, she launched 'Clean Up TV' [CUTV] with her friend Nora Buckland, the wife of a vicar and an active member of the Church of England's Mother's Union. The specific motivation for the campaign was an episode of the BBC television show, *Meeting Point*, featuring the discussion between a headmistress, a clergyman and a bishop's wife on the subject of pre-marital sex. The programme led Whitehouse's students to conclude that pre-marital sex was acceptable. Outraged by the refusal of 'decent' Christian people to defend fundamental tenants of the Christian faith, she took action.[17] The brochure launching Clean Up TV accused the BBC of pandering to 'the lowest in human nature' by presenting promiscuity and drinking as inevitable, and called upon the broadcaster to 'encourage and sustain faith in God'. The petition collected 366,355 signatures.[18]

In the early stages of the campaign Whitehouse used her husband's initials, so that publicity material invited guests to speeches delivered by 'Mrs E R Whitehouse', the 'wife of a company director'.[19] Such reticence did not last long; once CUTV gathered momentum 'Mary Whitehouse' enthusiastically took centre stage. As the NVALA's dominant personality, Whitehouse proved herself to be a skilled campaigner, making effective use of the media platforms she so disparaged to publicise the Association's pro-censorship message. Described by Lawrence Black as 'Britain's most recognisable Christian', she quickly became a household name.[20]

The central and most consistent target of NVALA campaign activities was the BBC. Whitehouse believed that the licence fee entitled the public to influence over BBC content, and that denying this amounted to 'taxation without representation'.[21] Exploiting the languages of post-war consumerism and participatory politics, a draft recruitment poster urged viewers to join the NVALA in order to exert their rights as BBC 'shareholders'.[22] The broadcaster's rejection of its Reithian origins also threw the social and cultural shifts of the 1960s and 1970s into painfully sharp relief. Given its one-time status as a bastion of middle-class respectability, alienation from the BBC is likely to have been particularly difficult for Whitehouse and her supporters. The plaque located in the BBC headquarters at Broadcasting House provided a pointed reminder of the corporation's founding principles, and an English translation of its Latin transcription was regularly quoted in NVALA literature: 'This temple of the arts and muses is dedicated to Almighty God by the first Governors of Broadcasting'.[23] High profile private prosecutions of *Gay News* and Michael Bagdanov, the director of a National Theatre production of *Romans in Britain*, demonstrate that Whitehouse cast a wide net in her pursuit of moral turpitude.[24] Pop music, football hooliganism and pornography were further sites of anxiety. But while few cultural forms escaped the NVALA's attention entirely, television's intrusion into the domestic sphere was believed to make it a particularly potent threat to family life, and therefore to the life of the nation. While an individual might chose to read an 'offensive' book, or attend an 'offensive' play, the element of choice, Whitehouse argued, was diminished by television's immediate transmission of content into the sanctified, private realm of the home. By arguing that viewers should play a role in determining the television content projected into their homes, Whitehouse presented her pro-censorship campaign as a defence of truly free choice.[25] Indeed, she claimed that the promotion of liberal values effectively censored the views of 'ordinary' people.[26]

II

Upon Thatcher's general election success in 1979, Mary Whitehouse wrote to the new Prime Minister emphasising her hopefulness for the new parliamentary term: 'It was a wonderful thing to have a Prime Minister utter those marvellous words of St Francis before the whole world—already one senses a lifting of the spirit'.[27] Thatcher's religious commitments were consistently and deliberately publicised throughout her leadership, and her public Christianity, which has been discussed at length by authors such as Antonio Weiss and Liza Filby, was optimistically received by those hoping her premiership would usher in a period of re-moralisation.[28] The religious strictness of Thatcher's childhood, and the influence of her father's devout Methodism in particular, is duly emphasised in the rich biographical literature Thatcher's premiership has generated.[29] The Roberts children attended Church three times on a Sunday; their home life was 'austere, teetotal' and 'governed by strict rules'.[30] At Oxford University she joined the John Wesley Society, which regularly sent its members out to preach in surrounding villages. Thatcher readily joined in: she was 'a preacher before she was a politician'.[31] Although what might loosely be described as 'the moral lobby' was never motivated exclusively by religion, NVALA membership was overwhelmingly Christian, and the majority of letters in the NVALA archives are from non-conformists: Presbyterian, evangelical free churches and Baptist chapels.[32]

Whitehouse had grown frustrated with Callaghan, having 'received nothing but discouragement from the Labour government so long as it remained in power', while the 'cool corporatism' of Edward Heath had made him an equally reluctant supporter of a distinctly populist morality.[33] In the period preceding the 1979 general election Whitehouse urged NVALA members to petition their parliamentary candidates on moral issues, and circulated a questionnaire designed to assess their 'reliability' as advocates of 'the family'. Conservative candidates both returned the greatest number of surveys, and provided the most satisfactory replies.[34] In her capacity as Leader of the Opposition Thatcher had supported Whitehouse in her ABUSE petition, aimed at protecting children from pornography, and in reply to Whitehouse's letter of congratulation in 1979, Thatcher wrote that she hoped they would 'continue to communicate with one another over those issues about which we both feel so strongly'.[35]

Thatcher made Whitehouse a CBE in 1980, and in 1984 she presented an award for the BBC television programme *Yes, Minister* at the NVALA's television awards ceremony— her presence itself demonstrating public sympathy for the NVALA's aims. In her speech, she celebrated the organisation's founder: 'Let no-one ever again say "what can one person do?" Look at Mrs Whitehouse and see the answer'.[36] Keith Joseph's now infamous speech at Edgbaston in 1974 had similarly emphasised her individualistic achievements. Joseph urged his audience to 'take inspiration from that admirable woman, Mary Whitehouse', whom he described as a 'shining example of what one person can do single-handedly when inspired by faith and compassion'.[37] NVALA deputations received what Ben Thompson has described as 'exaggerated shows of respect' from Thatcher's ministers, and Mary Whitehouse played a key role in shaping Graham Bright MP's 'video nasties' bill, which successfully passed through parliament in 1984. The Video Recordings Act outlawed the selling or hiring of a cassette that had not been approved by a central censorship authority, made it an offence to sell 'adult' videos to children and banned certain titles outright.

Whitehouse believed that Thatcher's sex made her a natural ally. The National Viewers' and Listeners' Association was not only overwhelmingly Christian, but also overwhelmingly female. Morrison and Tracey estimated a 3:1 ratio in favour of female membership in 1979, whilst a journalist in attendance at the organisation's inaugural meeting at Birmingham Town Hall suggested that women outnumbered men by ten to one.[38] Members were likely to be either housewives or retired, and the majority were in their later middle age.[39] Reflecting a Victorian inheritance, Whitehouse believed that women were particularly well equipped to defend the nation's moral integrity. She had appealed to women specifically in the campaign's early days, and launched her Clean Up TV Manifesto under a slogan proclaiming 'we women of Britain believe in a Christian way of life'. Following the report of the Williams Committee in 1981, which argued against there being a causal link between pornography and violence, Whitehouse expressed confidence that Thatcher would reject its findings.[40] This was 'not only because she is prime minister but because she is a woman, and especially because she is a mother'.[41] Thatcher herself expressed a similarly 'Victorian' view of gender when she told her audience at the first Dame Margery Corbett-Ashby memorial lecture that 'Women know that society is founded on dignity, reticence and discipline'.[42] As will be developed below, her public image more broadly reflected an appreciation of women's special place within moralising discourses related to 'the family' and 'the home'.

However, early signs indicated that Thatcher's Conservative government would fail to fulfil NVALA's expectations. In 1979 Whitehouse complained in the *Viewer and Listener* of the vagueness surrounding the Prime Minister's pledge to 'insist' and 'ensure' that the BBC upheld its responsibilities, and in 1981 she described her 'disillusion and incredulity' at the Home Office's refusal to formally disown the Williams Report on obscenity.[43] Following the publication of the Hunt Report on Cable Expansion and Broadcasting Policy in 1982, she apprehensively urged NVALA supporters not to 'doubt the Prime Minister's concern for the family and for moral values' and apologetically suggested that 'her preoccupation with industrial and economic affairs' was understandable.[44] In 1985 Whitehouse wrote to Thatcher expressing her 'dismay' at the government's failure to legislate for the control of pornography, although she drew a distinction between 'a failure on the part of the Home Office' and Thatcher's 'great ... personal concern over these issues'.[45] The situation had escalated by 1986. Following a meeting with Douglas Hurd, the then Home Secretary, Whitehouse complained in a letter to Thatcher that she had 'never been more disappointed in any meeting with any Minister throughout the years of our campaigning'.[46]

Whilst Thatcher was never exactly a champion of the BBC, she was drawn more towards privatisation than a return to Reithian-style public service broadcasting, as was the ostensible ambition of Whitehouse. Thatcher's consistent emphasis on the moral superiority of personal freedom was incompatible with the statutory control for which Whitehouse campaigned. Indeed, her government licensed cable television in the name of consumer choice. As Matthew Grimley has emphasised, while moralist sections of the New Right gained strength as Thatcher's premiership progressed, the 'moral lobby' remained dissatisfied with the government's direction throughout Thatcher's premiership. Indices of divorce, abortion and illegitimacy continued to rise, and statutory intervention to redress these trends was generally withheld.[47] For Thatcher, the state was the cause of Britain's decline, both morally and otherwise, whereas for Whitehouse it proffered the means of redemption. Despite significant ideological differences, however, large sections of the media—both right and left—continued to imply an affinity between these 'populist heroines of the right'.

III

Heather Nunn's *Thatcher Politics and Fantasy* argues persuasively for the symbolic density of the female form, which is invoked in 'sublime nation-symbols' such as Britannia and Lady Liberty.[48] Nunn's work considers the construction of Thatcher as a symbolic figure, and to a lesser extent the symbolic construction of 'Thatcherism', drawing attention to the potent interaction between gender, nationalism and power that shaped Thatcher's public image. Although Nunn is primarily concerned with 'grand adversarial leadership' and the image of Thatcher at war, her emphasis on gendered fantasy as a key site of political discourse applies equally to the apparently mundane image of Thatcher-as-housewife, which exploited entrenched notions of Englishness, femininity, and feminine authority.[49] If Thatcher's reliance on the language and imagery of militarism constituted a strategy for warding off chaos and projecting a sense of control, as Nunn suggests, so too did her presentation of unsentimental domestic virtue, which called to mind authoritarian stock figures of 'Victoriana'—the nanny, the matron and the governess. Commenting on Thatcher's general election victory in 1983, for example, the author Julian Barnes antici-pated four more years of 'the cold showers, the compulsory cod liver oil, the finger nail inspection', whilst *Private Eye*'s comic sketch, Fifth Form at St Maggie's, depicted the Prime Minister as a disciplinarian head teacher.[50] Thatcher-as-housewife recalled an easily recognisable, and apparently endangered, female 'type', exploiting the novel public image opportunities associated with her gender whilst simultaneously assuring voters that her unprecedented female power would not threaten the established, gendered order.

Whitehouse and Thatcher presented domestic identities to advance their political agendas. Whilst cultural politics has traditionally been considered the preserve of the New Left, Whitehouse and Thatcher made the personal political long before second-wave feminists, using the domestic sphere to demonstrate their commitment to certain values and a particular way of life. 'The housewife' is a richly symbolic figure. While fem-inist scholarship of the 1970s and 1980s emphasised that *being* a housewife was a job, 'the housewife'—taken abstractly—was a symbol, whether of female subjugation or of whole-some 'family values'. The housewife figure was ubiquitous in advertising, film, on televi-sion and in literature throughout the post-war period. Frequently depicted as a 'natural' feature of the social landscape, 'the housewife' was routinely used as short-hand for the 'ordinary' woman.[51] This belies a complex history. As Catherine Hall has emphasised, the 'meaning' of 'the housewife' fluctuates across time and between social and cultural locations, underlining the need to analyse domestic ideals within carefully delineated contexts.[52]

The 'housewife' image dominated Thatcher' public image from 1974 to 1982, and the presentation of domestic virtue continued to define her communication with female audi-ences thereafter. This emphasised the importance of Thatcher's relational, familial identity despite her professional achievements. Images of the prospective Prime Minister wielding her shopping basket—its contents depleted by purportedly Labour induced inflation—became a hallmark of the 1979 general election campaign, and she was regularly photo-graphed doing 'everyday' domestic tasks, such as washing up.[53] During a pre-election visit to a factory in Bristol in 1979 Thatcher was presented with a new broom; obligingly adopting the 'aggressive' sweeping pose requested of her by a press photographer , she promised to 'sweep [the opposition] out of Whitehall'.[54] In interviews Thatcher minimised the domestic disruption caused by her political career, routinely emphasising, for example, the seriousness of her commitment to the wifely preparation of Denis Thatcher's break-fast.[55] Domestic rhetoric made sound political practice analogous with domestic respon-sibility: inflation became 'prices' and the budget became what every housewife knew. The 'appalling' state of 'national housekeeping' had to be addressed, and who better than a housewife to do this? Thatcher was not the first party leader to speak of 'household econ-omics', but as a woman she did so with novel authority.[56]

Within the discourses of the Women's Liberation Movement, which emerged in Britain in the late 1960s, the housewife figure was widely understood as a symbol of women's oppression. Betty Friedan's *The Feminine Mystique* presented a particularly vivid picture of domestic discontent.[57] As such, Thatcher's celebration of domesticity is fre-quently interpreted as a strategy for sustaining the patriarchal systems that confined women to the home. While, however, there was undoubtedly a prescriptive element to Thatcher's housewife image, it was primarily a publicity tool, and overemphasis on prescriptivism risks undermining the extent to which it reflected popular and political values, assumptions and prejudices. Thatcher-as-housewife was a calculated attempt to *widen* her appeal beyond traditionally Conservative circles; to demonstrate her uniquely feminine competency as well as the 'ordinariness' commonly projected by politicians . It was a distinctly classed image designed to counteract the 'Tory lady in a hat' caricature with which Thatcher had become associated.[58] Through marriage to millionaire-businessman Denis, Thatcher had acquired what Wendy Webster has described as the 'emblems of upper middle class womanhood', including domestic 'help'.[59] Whilst this made her candidacy more 'respectable' internally, as a prospective party leader she had to convince the party of her ability to appeal to a wider cross section of voters. Described by one journalist as sounding like she was 'always wearing a hat' and 'opening a village fete', her acquired class identity came to be perceived as an electoral liability.[60] The 'housewife' ideal celebrated a particular type of femininity believed to resonate across the political spectrum, and with certain target groups, such as the working-class woman, in particular.

In the lead up to the 1979 General Election the Conservative Party's strategy rested on attracting working-class votes. The C2 voter, a longstanding target of the Conservatives, gained particular prominence in internal campaign documents. The wives of traditional Labour voters—especially those in council houses—were also defined as a social group likely to be amenable to the Conservative message.[61] This proved to be an effective campaign strategy; polls conducted on behalf of the Labour party between 7 and 30 April 1979 revealed that Labour had lost support among 'young housewives in the C2 group'.[62] As Gordon Reece, the adviser most closely associated with Thatcher's 'housewife' transformation, wrote in November 1979, 'research has clearly shown we won the last election by a change in the voting behaviour of the working classes, and especially women in working-class homes'.[63] The presentation of Thatcher's class identity shifted significantly in 1974, and her domestic image presented plentiful opportunities to imply affinity with 'ordinary' voters. Importantly, though, she did not *become* a housewife upon announcing her candidacy for the Conservative leadership. Her Dartford adoption speech, which took place before she was married, encouraged the government to do 'what any good housewife would do' and take care of its accounts.[64] She was routinely photographed with her children throughout the 1960s, and upon her appointment as Parliamentary Secretary to the Minister for Pensions in 1961, a newspaper headline celebrated 'The housewife who became a Minister'.[65] Rather, her presentation shifted from a wealthy middle-class housewife towards a lower middle-class housewife affected by inflation to the extent that, as she told the *Daily Mail* in 1977, she had been left unable to buy a new winter coat, or a new pair of curtains.[66] Dubbed 'Maggie' in the tabloid press, Thatcher's humble, Grantham background assumed new public prominence as a means of authenticating her public persona as a 'typical' wife and mother.[67] In 1970 she had spoken of the importance of hiring a good 'English nanny'.[68] By April 1979 she was presenting herself as a hardworking 'mum' forced to 'cope' with the demands of raising a family once 'Dad has gone to work'.[69]

As Joanna Bourke has written of the period from 1890 to 1960, 'of all the dreams dreamt by working class women, marriage followed by full time domesticity was the most widely shared'.[70] There is a considerable literature supporting and explaining this statement. Hannah Gavron's the *Captive Wife*, published in 1966, emphasises young working-class women's romanticised investment in their anticipated identities as wives and mothers, and Ann Oakley's *The Sociology of Housework* describes the enduring cultural importance of female domesticity to working class life.[71] More recently, Stephen Brooke's examination of mid-century literature has demonstrated the importance of the figure of the working-class mother—or 'mam'—as a means of stabilising and reinforcing working-class identity in the context of anxiety about the corrupting effects of affluence.[72] The practical realities of working-class life also encouraged an enduring attachment to domestic identities. Working-class women were likely to have children at a younger age than their middle-class contemporaries, and less likely to pursue higher-level careers— although it should be emphasised that women of all classes remained underrepresented in the professions, and overrepresented in low paying fields such as retail, clerical and care work.[73] Given that employment opportunities were incredibly limited, domesticity was regarded by many working-class women as a viable and rewarding strategy for demonstrating their familial indispensability: by making the most of scarce resources they were able to demonstrate their economic value to the family unit. In invoking domestic authority Thatcher and Whitehouse therefore drew on an established source of female power, particularly resonant among older women from lower-middle and working-class backgrounds.

The historic success of the Conservative party among female voters has generated a distinguished literature. The work of David Jarvis, David Thackeray and Ina Zweiniger-Bargielowska helpfully chronicles the Conservative party's effective mobilisation of 'the housewife vote' from female enfranchisement through to the 1950s. A 'well developed typology of Conservative woman' emerged in the interwar period, represented in the pages of the Conservative party magazine *Home and Politics* by middle-aged Char lady Mrs Maggs. Described by Jarvis as 'a bastion of common sense and homely wisdom', Mrs Maggs, though not a housewife herself, represented the virtues integral to political constructions of the housewife throughout the twentieth century.[74] As Thackeray has shown, 'the housewife' functioned within conservative discourses of the period as a strategy for contesting the stereotypical image of Conservative women as well-do-to 'Lady Bountifuls' with scant understanding of life beyond their social class.[75] The success of the Conservative party of the 1950s is widely attributed to its appeal to the consumer interests of women against a back-drop of post-war austerity. To counter the Labour party slogan 'Ask your Dad', which encouraged voters to consider the unemployment of the interwar years, the Conservative party urged, 'Ask their Mums'.[76] The idea that the Labour party had forgotten about (middle-class) women, who had enjoyed plentiful food and consumer goods in the 1920s and 1930s, exploited Labour's image as a party dominated by masculine interests.[77] While a substantial body of historical literature seeks to explain the female move away from the Conservative Party in the 1980s, the narrowing of a gender gap was the result of younger women's increased preference for Labour. Middle-aged and older women continued to demonstrate a strong preference for the Conservative party, and for Thatcher specifically.[78]

The most pertinent context in the formation of what would become known as 'Thatcherism', is the top-down 'permissive' revolution of the 1960s and early 1970s, which saw homosexuality and abortion legalised, divorce laws relaxed and capital punishment outlawed. As Stuart Hall has argued, these changes helped to generate the sense of crisis that lay at the heart of Thatcherism's mobilisation of consent for its authoritarian programme.[79] A rapid series of legal reforms threatened cultural norms and destabilised established identities premised on a traditional interpretation of the Christian faith. As Callum Brown has shown, secularisation was not a 'long, inevitable' process as conventionally described, but 'remarkably sudden and culturally violent', with the greatest gradient of religious decline occurring after 1958 and religiosity in free fall from 1963.[80] The Nationwide Festival of Light [NFOL], which saw 35,000 Christians gather in Trafalgar Square to protest the erosion of moral values in 1971, is one demonstration of the anxiety this generated.[81] The centrality of piety to nineteenth and early twentieth century constructions of femininity meant that feminine identity was a particularly acute register of secularisation. Feminist femininities of the Women's Liberation Movement represented a direct challenge to the 'respectable' domestic woman of the mid-century. With reference to the magazines *Jackie* (launched in 1964) and *Cosmopolitan* (launched in 1972), Brown has argued that 'feminine identity was now conveyed by everything other than family, domestic routine, virtue, religion or "respectability"'.[82] Within this context, the housewife—an established emblem of 'family values'—emerged as a powerful means of articulating Conservative discontent with the developing moral consensus. The image of the religiously motivated woman—exploited by Thatcher and Whitehouse—became a particularly pertinent symbol of what Britain had lost.

Crucially, cultural change was presented as having been imposed upon 'ordinary' citizens by an elite, metropolitan minority. The quintessentially suburban housewife assumed discursive significance as an embattled representative of the 'ordinary' individual defending traditional values (or 'family values') against the encroaching powers of a permissive state. Thatcher and Whitehouse reflected a tradition of 'militant' domesticity associated with the mid-century housewives association, the British Housewives League. They were not 'angels in the house' but housewives 'having a go'.[83] As Lawrence Black has emphasised, their ideological stridency put them beyond the pale of establishment Conservatism, and squarely among the grass-roots middle class, taxpayer revolts of 1970s' 'respectable rebels'.[84] Ferdinand Mount's *The Subversive Family*, which was first published in 1982, articulates the disruptive power of domesticity. Mount, who was then head of Thatcher's Policy Unit, argued for the family as the one true source of individual freedom against the competing demands of Church, state and trades unions. Far from being socially enforced and restrictive, the family was the unit towards which the majority of people naturally aspired, while its internal loyalties made it threatening to establishment powers.[85] The spread of liberalism from the late 1960s onwards made it possible for conservatives to present social traditionalism as a form of defiance, or even rebellion.

Both Whitehouse and Thatcher used 'housewife' images to emphasise their opposition to 'elite' institutions such as universities, the BBC and—crucially—the Church of England, whose leadership espoused a political ideology at odds with its core constituency. Criticism of Thatcher's Government from within the Church left Conservative-voting congregations feeling personally affronted.[86] Such disaffection with Church leaders enhanced popular enthusiasm for the unapologetically conservative Christianity of Whitehouse and Thatcher, who spoke publically of their own disappointment with the Church establishment. In her speech to the General Assembly of the Church of Scotland in 1988, Thatcher urged that 'Christianity is about spiritual redemption, not social reform', and a decade earlier she had emphasised, in a speech at St Lawrence Jewry, that the 'Bible as well as the tradition of the Church tell us very little directly about political systems or social

programmes'.[87] Whitehouse and her supporters blamed the Church's response to secularisation, as much as secularisation itself, for the nation's moral decline.[88]

The image of a housewife compelled to public action was used either as part of a David-
and-Goliath narrative to amplify Whitehouse's reputation for courage, or read as symbolic
testament to the provincial, backward-looking views widely associated with the NVALA.
The former certainly applies to Keith Joseph's celebration of Whitehouse as an:

> unknown middle-aged woman, a schoolteacher in the Midlands [who] set out to protect ado-
> lescents against the permissiveness of our time. Look at the scale of the opposing forces. On
> the one side, the whole of the new establishment, with their sharp words and sneers poised.
> Against them stood this one middle-aged woman.[89]

Whitehouse, like Thatcher, revelled in her oppositional status. The NVALA was deliberately unsophisticated in both its language and campaigning strategies, speaking regularly
of the need for 'common sense' and relying on housewife-friendly, 'DIY' methods such as
letter writing.[90] In the *Oxford Dictionary of National Biography* entry on Mary Whitehouse, Mary Warnock argues that her unrelenting confidence in her own 'common
sense' world view 'seriously obstructed her success'.[91] While, as a caricature of overzealous,
provincial moralism, Whitehouse was the consistent 'object of sneers and widespread
calumny', the ridicule she incurred mobilised particular sections of society disenchanted
by a patronising and increasingly alien establishment stance on issues that were central
to their social identities.[92] As Kenneth Thompson has argued, the loosening hold of 'Victorian morality' had 'a particularly strong impact on the precariously balanced lower
middle class from which Mrs Whitehouse and many of her supporters came'.[93] BBC director General Hugh Greene was 'amused by Mrs Whitehouse', whom he regarded as 'an
absurd and reactionary embodiment of the lower middle classes at their primmest and
most narrow minded'.[94] The *Humanist Times* noted that she was 'not rich ... not educated ... single minded and energetic'.[95] Similar charges were levied at Thatcher, who
drew enthusiastic support from the skilled-working and lower-middle classes whilst
being sneered at as 'philistine in chief' by leading cultural figures.[96] In the context of
such anti-institutionalism, it is important to recognise that the derision that Whitehouse
and Thatcher incurred authenticated their claims to represent and speak for 'ordinary'
people.

Thatcher, plainly, was not a housewife. And having sat her final exams for the Bar a
mere three months after giving birth to twins, she never really had been. Her husband's
money paid for domestic 'help', and the brief period she was without this left her
feeling 'nothing more than a drudge'.[97] Whitehouse's extensive and high profile campaign
work meant that her 'housewife' identity was similarly fictitious. A *Daily Mail* article from
1972, chronicling Whitehouse's '17 hour day' does not mention a single domestic task, and
before dedicating herself to the NVALA full time she had worked as a teacher.[98] Unlike
Thatcher, however, she had taken a prolonged absence after the birth of her first son,
and her autobiography suggests self-consciousness about the decision to return to work
at all. Having been left weak from illness, Whitehouse claimed that paid employment—
a less demanding occupation than full-time housewifery—was a necessary means of
financing domestic help.[99] To mark Queen Elizabeth II's accession to the throne in
1952, Margaret Thatcher rejected the idea of female employment being detrimental to
family life, and urged women to 'fight harder' to play a 'leading part in the creation of

a glorious Elizabethan era'.[100] Conversely, in 1953 Mary Whitehouse appeared on Woman's Hour to advise her audience that 'dedication' to the Queen could be conveyed by 'the caring details [she] put into the tiny details of [her] everyday life, even the washing up'.[101]

The point remains, however, that both Thatcher and Whitehouse persuasively presented themselves as housewives despite demanding public careers. 'Housewife', then, was an identity that referred to feminine characteristics not reducible to, or even dependent upon, full-time domestic labour. A 1951 edition of *The Citizen Housewives' Guide* makes this point explicit by addressing the 'countless married women who have a whole or part time job' as well as the 'single woman working nine-to-five'. 'The word 'housewife'', argued the guide, 'no longer only describes a married woman with a family'.[102] In this respect the category of 'housewife' operates similarly to Rupa Huq's conceptualisation of 'suburbia'. Both are to some degree 'metaphorical', referring to 'mindset [s]' rather than precise criteria.[103] Roger Silverstone has likewise emphasised that 'suburbia is a state of mind ... constructed in imagination and in desire.'[104] Mary Whitehouse and Margaret Thatcher were 'housewives' not because they performed domestic labour, but because they represented apparently threatened 'domestic' values.

IV

Affinities between Margaret Thatcher and Mary Whitehouse were rooted in notions of 'Victorian Values', which came to define the moral character of Thatcher's leadership.[105] The phrase 'Victorian Values' was coined by the Labour MP turned journalist Brian Walden in a television interview with Thatcher, aired in January 1983, and was critically intended. Despite this, it became one of the defining moral concepts of Thatcher's premiership. In response to Thatcher's complaint of increased state dependency, Walden contended that the values she advocated did not 'have a future resonance'. Rather, they resonated with 'Victorian times, when there was great poverty, great wealth, etc ... you've really outlined an approval of what I would call Victorian values'.[106] Thatcher went on to praise the philanthropy of Victorian people, who she claimed 'gave great voluntary things to the State' as they prospered. This particular celebration of Victorian values as a testament to philanthropic spirit, however, soon gave way to her expression of a broader admiration for 'honesty and thrift and reliability and hard work and a sense of responsibility for your fellow men'.[107] By May, Thatcher would write to the Labour MP John Evans explaining that the term referred to 'respect for the individual, thrift, initiative, a sense of personal responsibility, respect for others and their property' as well as, importantly, 'all the other values that characterised the best of the Victorian era'.[108] The main target of a revival of Victorian values, then, was clearly the individual's relation to the state. Indeed, when accused by a member of the public of promoting, amongst other things, a 'frigid morality', Thatcher merely responded that the viewer had it 'mixed up', before going on to explain the economic vitality and self-reliance she saw as characteristic of the period.[109]

The flexibility of the term, however, suggested by Thatcher's letter to Evans, is significant. While there is little evidence of Thatcher using Victorian values explicitly to condemn 'permissiveness', the connection between Victorian values and moral authoritarianism was widely assumed. Indeed, in a radio interview for IRN, Peter Murphy suggested that the pragmatism of Thatcher's response to AIDs ran contrary to her professed commitment to 'Victorian values and family values'.[110] The economic focus of Thatcherite morality—which included, but was by no means limited to an elevation of nineteenth century individualism—has been used to argue for the instrumentality of Thatcher's moralising rhetoric. Presenting Thatcher's moralistic rhetoric as 'window dressing' in the sale of unpalatable economic policies, however, rather ignores its significance in terms of the reception of Thatcherism. Indeed, Thatcher's forceful emphasis on good and evil, right and wrong, was fundamental to the presentation of ideological consistency implied by the word 'Thatcherism' itself. A limited legislative record on 'moral' or 'family' issues should not be used to undermine the moralistic tone of Thatcherism, which consistently articulated a vision of politics bound up in a fundamentally moral battle. As Thatcher famously put it to the *Sunday Times* in 1981, 'Economics are the method; the object is to change the heart and soul.'[111]

The speed and enthusiasm with which 'Victorian values' was taken up as a catch-all statement of Thatcherite morality is indicative of the extent to which the phrase resonated with popular conceptions of what Thatcherism offered, whether this was regarded positively or not. With its roots in the 'law and order' Conservatism of the party's women's groups, the authoritarian populism that characterised both Whitehouse and Thatcher reflected the Conservative party's gendered past. That the fears of the 1980s were primarily framed as women's fears—either for themselves or their children—helped to mobilise entrenched notions of female conservatism, tied to what Beatrix Campbell has described as the 'hang 'em and flog 'em brigade' of the 1950s and 1960s.[112] The Law and Order lobby was galvanised by the media landscape of the 1980s, which following the 'Murdoch revolution' emphasised the apparently increasing threat to women and children in ever more sensationalistic terms. In response to the roadside murder of the heavily pregnant Marie Wilks in 1988, the *Daily Mail* ran an article under the title 'Is nowhere safe for a woman?', while *The Times* claimed that 'the fear of crime on the roads is creeping into our daily lives just as the possibility of being raped or mugged now restricts a woman's choice about whether to go out in the evening'.[113] As Philip Jenkins argues, popular identification of social problems is a cumulative process, and as the 1980s progressed a rich fund of 'socially available knowledge' appeared to present a society bedevilled by an insidious and unavoidable evil.[114] 'Victorian values', which spoke of discipline and moral fortitude, certainly chimed with the traditional, social concerns of the party's women's groups. More than this, however, Thatcher's Victorian values created 'a metaphorical space for the expression of moral anxiety' that resonated beyond the 'moral lobby'.[115]

However, it is important to recognise that in the 1970s and 1980s 'Victorian' was commonly used as a pejorative description. In 'A Public Disservice', an undated campaign booklet produced by the NVALA, Whitehouse addressed and refuted the popular image of her organisation as being 'anxious to re-impose a caricature of Victorian values', and as recently as 1981 Harold Macmillan had denounced the Victorian period as 'simply an interruption in Britain's history'.[116] Thatcher had in 1979 dismissed socialism as a 'Victorian ideology'. As Raphael Samuel argued in 1992, 'in Mrs Thatcher's lexicon 'Victorian' seems to have been an interchangeable term for the traditional and the old fashioned', thus reflecting a broader tension between the radical and traditional elements of Thatcherite discourse.[117] In aligning herself with a contestable value system Thatcher demonstrated her willingness, even desire, to be regarded as a champion of the unfashionable: 'what mattered was less the words themselves than the character she projected of one who was not afraid of sounding reactionary'.[118] Thatcher's reappraisal of the Victorians should therefore be understood as a concerted demonstration of her populist credentials.

The simplistic, reductionist quality of the phrase 'Victorian values' itself was bound to rile academic arbiters of the Victorian past, and attracted considerable academic condemnation. Eric Sigsworth's edited volume of essays, *In Search of Victorian Values*, published in 1988, is largely an academic rebuttal of Thatcher's unduly celebratory vision of the Victorians. 'Given the way in which [Victorian values] is being bandied about', Sigsworth argued that the phrase needed to be 'examined critically'.[119] Demonstrating, for example, the invalidity of Thatcher's 'Victorian' admiration of 'cleanliness' as being 'next to Godliness', however, seems to miss the rather obvious point that the cultural resonance of political rhetoric is rarely attributable to historical accuracy. The Raphael Samuel article from which I have quoted was also published as part of an edited volume exploring 'Victorian Values' and 'the great contemporary interest' they generated, although only Samuel's article engaged explicitly with their political resonances under Thatcher. This was the product of a collaborative symposium organised by the British Academy and the Royal Society of Edinburgh in 1990, demonstrating considerable academic attention. Given Thatcher's anti-intellectualism, academic opposition to her appropriation and redefinition of 'Victorian Values' served only to cement her oppositional status. 'Elitist' criticism of Victorian Values was condemned as 'patronising' by a report published by the Centre for Policy Studies in 1987.[120]

While the virtues of the nineteenth century may have been academically disputed, the late twentieth-century fascination with the Victorian period is widely recognised by social and cultural historians, who emphasise the proliferation of television adaptations of Victorian literature, the vogue for Victorian collectables and the upmarket refurbishment of Victorian terrace houses for affluent buyers.[121] This popular appetite for Victoriana preceded Thatcher's premiership. Whereas in the 1960s 'Victoriana' referred narrowly to the collectable remnants of material, Victorian culture, by the late 1970s 'its reference had widened to embrace a complimentary miscellany of evocations and recycling of the nineteenth century'.[122] Reaction to Labour's refusal to 'save' Mentmore Towers, a high Victorian country house faced with private sale, is a pertinent example of the growing value attached to 'heritage'.[123] The backward-looking emphasis of Thatcherite rhetoric made use of, and augmented, but certainly did not create popular desire for the explanatory certainties of a particular version of British history.

Thatcher's public Christianity and the appeal of her moralising public image more broadly, must be understood within this context. Unlike Whitehouse, Thatcher understood that British Christianity was diffuse and cultural; part of the national heritage but not an active part of the majority of people's daily lives. She spoke regularly of the country's 'Judeo-Christian' inheritance and referred to a 'way of life' derived from 'a specifically Christian civilisation', but made no claims about the active religious commitments of ordinary British people.[124] In 1979, for example, Thatcher told the Central Conservative Council that the 'quiet majority have continued to live their lives by the largely unwritten rules that have governed decent behaviour for generations'. These 'unwritten rules' were only implicitly Christian. Her appeal, As Matthew Grimley has argued, was to a 'silent majority' who no longer attended Church but 'had some folk memory of religious stories and symbols'.[125] In his analysis of working-class autobiographies, Callum Brown has described religion as the 'central symbol of lost worlds', evocatively suggesting the nostalgic resonance of Christianity in a rapidly secularising society.[126] Perusing the visitor book at the Church of St Lawrence in Dorset, a *Spectator* journalist noted in 1980 'how unfamiliar visitors were with religion': descriptions were affectionate but evoked the sense of a museum.[127] Christianity's waning social hold arguably sharpened its cultural significance. Through Christianity, and Christian femininity in particular, Thatcher presented herself as the defender of Britain's apparently besieged cultural heritage.

Conclusions

The public images of Margaret Thatcher and Mary Whitehouse drew on a complex repertoire of cultural and political significations. Feminine domesticity spoke not only of practical competence learned through the daily trials of household management, but also of moral goodness. It represented commitment to traditional values and suggested an authoritarian moral stance associated with Conservative women's groups. An acutely gendered image, it exploited discourses of feminine identity rooted in Britain's Christian past, suggesting a bygone age of political, economic and cultural stability. At the same time, however, it poised 'common sense' female authority against the wisdom of an overwhelmingly male Establishment, threatening disruption and promising change. Ben Thompson has described Mary Whitehouse's 'unique blend of alarm and reassurance' as 'her unique selling point as a public figure'. This article has argued that Thatcher's public image negotiated a similar combination.[128]

Mary Whitehouse was not a comfortable figure to accommodate, and the apparently sympathetic relationship between Whitehouse and Thatcher encouraged the amplification of some of Thatcher's more divisive qualities. Whitehouse was largely understood through caricature, and detractors considered her a backward-looking reactionary determined to impose an out-dated and discriminatory moral framework on modernising institutions. However, as Thatcher's elevation of 'Victorian values' demonstrates, a willingness to be seen to be reactionary could be considered a strength, and both Whitehouse and Thatcher emphasised their readiness to speak 'unfashionable' truths.[129] Had Thatcher turned her back on Whitehouse, she would have been widely perceived as rejecting the very position upon which she had campaigned in 1979. Both the public profile that Whitehouse was able to develop and popular interest in Thatcher's 'Victorian values' testify to pronounced contemporary concern for moral issues. The ideological differences between Whitehouse and Thatcher had little impact on the public image of their relationship, which emphasised shared 'suburban' qualities, whether positively or negatively conceived.

Thatcher's handling of Whitehouse emphasises the discrepancy between her moralising rhetoric and her willingness to legislate on moral issues. However, far from suggesting the superficiality of Thatcher's moralistic stance, this emphasises the importance of tone and style to the character of Thatcher's leadership. As Raphael Samuel argued, 'as a political leader, [she] was happiest in the role of an evangelist confronting the country with uncomfortable truths'.[130] Whitehouse and Thatcher preached the value of respectability in decidedly undeferential tones, and argued for the fundamental importance of family life while pursuing demanding full time careers. Thatcher's moral authoritarianism may have been a matter of 'style', more than 'substance', but the political significance of 'style' should not be underestimated.

Notes

1. Anthony Andrew, 'Letters from the Mary Whitehouse Archive', *Guardian*, November 11, 2012, https://www.theguardian.com/books/2012/nov/11/mary-whitehouse-ban-this-filth-review
2. Lynda Lee Potter, 'The Woman Who Never Gave Up', *Daily Mail*, April 14, 2001.
3. Liza Filby, *God and Mrs Thatcher: the Battle for Britain's Soul* (London: Biteback, 2015), 03.
4. Matthew Grimley, 'Thatcher Morality and Religion', in *Making Thatcher's Britain*, eds. Ben Jackson and Robert Saunders (Cambridge: Cambridge University Press, 2010) and Lawrence Black, 'There was Something about Mary: The National Viewers' and Listeners' Association and Social Movement Campaigning', in *NGOs in Contemporary Britain: Non-State Actors in Society and Politics Since 1945*, eds. Nick Crowson, Matthew Hinton and James McKay (Basingstoke: Palgrave Macmillan, 2009).
5. Richard Vinen, *Thatcher's Britain* (London: Pocket Books, 2010) 279.
6. For discussion of 'right wing woman' stereotypes see Sara Childs, *Women and British Party Politics* (London: Routlegde, 2010); Beatrix Campbell, *Iron Ladies: Why Women Vote Tory* (London: Virago, 1987).
7. Lawrence Black, *Redefining British Politics: Culture Consumerism and Participation* (Basingstoke: Palgrave Macmillan, 2010), 1.
8. See Mary Whitehouse, *Cleaning Up TV* (London, 1967); *Who Does she Think she is?* (London, 1971); *Whatever Happened to Sex?* (Hove, 1977); *A Most Dangerous Woman?* (Tring, 1982); *Mightier than the Sword* (Eastbourne, 1985); *Quite Contrary: An Autobiography* (London, 1993).
9. *Middlesbrough Evening Gazette*, October 4, 1979, NVALA archive, Essex University, box 76.
10. Michael Tracey and David Morrison, *Whitehouse* (London: Macmillan, 1979), 17.
11. Elizabeth Udall, 'Mary Whitehouse: Sometimes I Denied she was my Mother', *Telegraph*, May 28, 2008, http://www.telegraph.co.uk/news/features/3636761/Mary-WhitehouseSometimes-I-denied-she-was-my-mother.html
12. See, for example, 'The Importance of Being Mary', *Daily Mail*, June 14, 1980.
13. *Viewer and Listener* (Summer 1970), NVALA archive, box 1.
14. Lawrence Black, 'Mary Whitehouse, The National Viewers' and Listeners' Association', *Campaigning for Change: Lessons from History*, 2016, 137.
15. Sims memo, 16 January 1976, quoted in Black, 'There was Something about Mary', 186.
16. Ben Thompson, ed., *Ban this Filth! Letter from the Mary Whitehouse Archive* (London: Faber and Faber, 2012), 173.
17. Black, *Mary Whitehouse*, 129.
18. Ibid., 134.
19. Thompson, *Ban this Filth*, 14.
20. Black, *Redefining*, 124.
21. CUTV 'Draft Constitution', NVALA archive, box 1.
22. CUTV draft poster, Thompson, *Ban This Filth*, p. 60.
23. Thompson, *Ban This Filth*, p. 38.
24. Whitehouse brought legal proceedings under the Sexual Offences Act, in the grounds that the simulated rape constituted gross indecency. She withdrew the case before it went to trial, arguably to avoid the indignity of an expected loss, but had by this point succeeded in puncturing the legal invulnerability of theatre.
25. Black, 'There was Something about Mary', 184.
26. Whitehouse, *Cleaning Up TV*, 152.
27. Whitehouse to Thatcher, 9 May 1979 in Thompson, *Ban this Filth*, 365.
28. Antonio Weiss, 'The Religious Mind of Mrs Thatcher' (unpublished masters thesis, University of Cambridge, 2011) and Lisa Filby, *God and Mrs Thatcher*.

29. See, for example, Hugo Young, *One of Us* (London: Macmillan, 1989); John Campbell, *The Iron Lady* (London: Vintage Books, 2012); Charles Moore, *Margaret Thatcher: The Authorised Biography, Volume I* (London: Allen Lane, 2013).

30. Campbell, *The Iron Lady*, 4.

31. Ibid., 12.

32. Black, 'There was Something about Mary', 189.

33. Mary Whitehouse, *Quite Contrary* (London: Sidgwick & Jackson, 1993), 23; and Campbell, *Iron Ladies*, 99.

34. 62% of the 280 responses were returned by Conservative candidates, 32% by Labour candidates, 2% by Liberal candidates and 4% 'other'. Of the 105 Conservative replies, 18 refused to define their moral position. Of the 90 Labour replies, 34 refused. *The Viewer and Listener*, October 1978, NVALA archive, box 15.

35. Thatcher to Whitehouse, 24 May 1979, NVALA archive, box 59.

36. Thatcher, Speech for BBC1 *Yes, Prime Minister*, 20 January 1984, MTFW: 105519.

37. Speech at Edgbaston, 19 October 1974, MTFW: 101830.

38. *Evening Mail*, 6 May 1964, NVALA archive, box 1.

39. Michael Tracey and David Morrison, 'Opposition to the Age', NVALA archive, box 76, p.27.

40. The committee, chaired by the atheist philosopher Bernard Williams, had been tasked by Callaghan's Labour administration with reviewing the laws relating to obscenity, indecency and violence. Reflecting on the necessary balance between freedom of expression and the obligation of Government to protect against offence, the report came down firmly on the side of the former. In relation to pornography specifically, the report argued that it should be regarded an epiphenomenon of social change, more effect than a cause of the changes Whitehouse and her allies railed against: 'to regard pornography as having a crucial or even a significant effect on essential social values' is to get the problem 'out of proportion'. See *Report of the Committee on Obscenity and Film Censorship* (London, 1981), 96.

41. Whitehouse quoted in Durham, *Sex and Politics: The Family and Morality in the Thatcher Years* (Basingstoke: Macmillan, 1991), 79.

42. Thatcher, Women in a Changing World, 26 July 1982, MTFW: 105007.

43. Thompson, *Ban this Filth*, 371.

44. Ibid., 374.

45. Whitehouse to Thatcher, 21 October 1985, NVALA archive, box 59.

46. Thompson, *Ban this Filth*, 373.

47. Grimley, 'Thatcherism, Morality and Religion', 79.

48. Health Nunn, *Thatcher, Politics and Fantasy: the Political Culture of Gender and Nation* (London: Lawrence and Wishart, 2002), 10.

49. Ibid., 13.

50. 'Matron Plays the Virgin Queen', *Observer*, June 12, 1983.

51. For example, the short stories included in women's magazines of the 1950s and 1960s frequently depicted women who sought adventure only to find true contentment in a happy marriage. See Niamh Baker, *Happily Ever After?: Women's Fiction in Britain 1945–1960* (Baskingstoke: Macmillan, 1989), 3.

52. Catherine Hall, 'The History of the Housewife', in *The Politics of Housework*, ed. Ellen Malos (London: Allison and Busby, 1980), 44.

53. Radio Interview for BBC Radio 2 *Jimmy Young Programme*, 19 February 1975, MTFW: 102500. Young asks Thatcher whether 'the ballyhoo and the publicity that went with [the leadership election]' was 'really necessary': 'I mean the William Whitelaw kiss and he was doing the washing up and you were doing the washing up and so on'.

54. Remarks visiting Bristol, 17 April 1979, MTFW: 104014.

55. 'With the Breakfast to Cook', *Manchester Evening News*, May 1, 1975, MTFW: 102682.

56. As early as 1923, Stanley Baldwin described himself as the 'housewife of the nation'. See David Thackeray, *Conservatism for the Democratic Age: Conservative Cultures and the Challenge of Mass Politics in Early Twentieth Century English* (Manchester: Manchester University Press, 2013), 171.

57. Betty Friedan, *The Feminine Mystique* (London: Victor Gollancz, 1963).
58. Wendy Webster, *Not a Man to Match Her* (London, 1990), 28–48.
59. Ibid., 43.
60. Ibid., 29.
61. The embarrassing 'unreliability' of the wives of Trade Union members had been recognised by Transport House as early as 1959. See A. Black and S. Brooke, 'The Labour Party, Women and the Problem of Gender', *Journal of British Studies* 36 (1997): 434.
62. D. Butler and D. Kavanagh, *The British General Election of 1979* (London, 1980), 343.
63. Transition to power: Gordon Reece minute to Thatcher, 27 November 1979, MTFW: 112176.
64. 'Conservatives to Fight at Election', *Erith Observer*, March 4, 1949, MTFW: 100821.
65. 'Interview on becoming a Minister', unidentified cutting, 10 October 1961, MTFW: 101112.
66. 'Feeling Rich? No I'm Saving for a Pair of Curtains', *Daily Mail*, February 8, 1977.
67. For example, in 1985 she told Dr Miriam Stoppard in an interview for Yorkshire Television, 'Home was really very small and we had no mod cons and I remember having a dream that the one thing I really wanted was to live in a nice house'. 2 October 1975, MTFW:105830.
68. BBC Panorama Profile, 1970
69. Quoted in Campbell, *Iron Ladies*, 101.
70. Joanna Bourke, *Working Class Cultures in Britain 1890–1960* (London: Routledge, 1994), 62.
71. Hannah Gavron, *The Captive Wife: Conflicts of Housebound Mothers* (Middlesex: Penguin, 1975); and Anne Oakley, *The Sociology of Housework* (London: Robertson, 1974).
72. Stephen Brooke, 'Gender and Working Class Identity in Britain During the 1950s', *Journal of Social History*, 34 (2001): 788.
73. Gerry Holloway, *Women in Work in Britain Since 1840* (London: Routledge), 209. See also Michael Argyle, *The Psychology of Social Class* (London: Routledge, 1994), 80–84.
74. David Jarvis, 'Mrs Maggs and Betty: The Conservative Appeal to Women Voters in the 1920s', *Twentieth Century British History* 5 (1994): 133–34.
75. David Thackeray, 'Home and Politics: Women and Conservative Activism in Early Twentieth-Century Britain', *Journal of British Studies* 49 (2010): 834.
76. Ina Zweiniger-Bargielowska, 'Rationing, Austerity and the Conservative Party Recovery after 1945', *Historical Journal* 37 (1994): 182.
77. See Martin Francis, 'Labour and Gender', in *Labour's First Century*, eds. Duncan Tanner, Pat Thane and Nick Tiratsoo (Cambridge: Cambridge University Press, 2000); and Amy Black and Stephen Brooke, 'The Labour Party, Women and the Problem of Gender', *Journal of British Studies* 36 (1997).
78. Laura Beers, 'Thatcher and the Women's Vote', in *Making Thatcher's Britain*, eds. Ben Jackson and Robert Saunders, 120–23.
79. Stuart Hall, 'The Great Moving Right Show', *Marxism Today*, 1979, 19.
80. Callum Brown, *The Death of Christian Britain* (London: Routledge, 2001), 188.
81. Amy Whipple, 'Speaking for Whom? The 1971 Festival of Lights and the Search for the 'Silent Majority', *Contemporary British History* 24 (2010): 319.
82. Brown, *The Death*, 177.
83. Beatrix Cambpell aligned Margaret Thatcher and Mary Whitehouse with Victoria Gillick, Tina Turner and Brookside's Sheila Grant as women having a go'. Campbell, *Iron Ladies*, 190.
84. Black, Mary Whitehouse, 137.
85. Ferdinand Mount, *The Subversive Family: An Alternative History of Love and Marriage* (London: Unwin Paperbacks, 1993).
86. Filby, *God and Mrs Thatcher*, 101.
87. Thatcher, Speech to General Assembly of the Church of Scotland, 21 May 1988, MTFW: 107246 and Thatcher, Speech at St Lawrence Jewry, 30 March 1978, MTFW: 103522.
88. Black, 'There was Something about Mary', 191.
89. Speech at Edgbaston, 19 October 1974, MTFW: 101830.
90. Black, 'There was Something about Mary', 187.
91. Mary Warnock, 'Whitehouse', ODNB.
92. Max Caulfield, *Mary Whitehouse* (London, 1975), 134.

93. Keith Thompson, *Moral Panics* (London, 1998), 125.

94. Jeremy Lewis, *Shades of Greene: One Generation of an English Family* (London, 2011), 444.

95. Quoted in Black, There was Something about Mary, 188.

96. Ian Gilmour is reported by his Amersham constituents to have warned that Thatcher's leadership threatened a 'retreat behind the privet hedge'. See Wendy Webster, *Not a Man* (London: Women's Press, 1990), 29. Charles Moore, *Margaret Thatcher, the Authorised Biography: Volume II* (London: Allen Lane, 2015), 635–38.

97. Thatcher, Finding Time, *Onward*, 1 April 1954, MTFW:100939

98. 'The Woman Who Never Switches Off', *Daily Mail*, June 23, 1972.

99. Whitehouse, *Quite Contrary*, 7.

100. Thatcher, 'Wake Up Women', *Sunday Graphic*, February 17, 1952, MTFW:100936.

101. Mary Whitehouse, 'Thoughts of a housewife on the coronation' transcript, NVALA archive, box 72.

102. *The Citizen Housewives' Guide* (Glasgow, 1951), 5.

103. Rupa Huq, *Making Sense of Suburbia Through Popular Culture* (London: Bloomsbury, 2013), 6.

104. Roger Silverstone, ed., *Vision of Suburbia* (London: Routledge, 1997), 13.

105. Black, 'There was Something about Mary', 183.

106. TV interview for London Weekend Television, 16 January 1983, MTFW: 105087

107. Thatcher, Speech to Glasgow Chamber of Commerce, 28 January 1983, MTFW: 105244

108. Thatcher to John Evans, 5 May 1983, MTFW: 132330.

109. TV interview for BBC One Nationwide, 24 May 1983, MTFW: 105147.

110. Murphy, Radio interview for IRN, 23 January 1987, MTFW: 106731.

111. Thatcher, Interview for *Sunday Times*, 3 May 1981, MTFW:104475.

112. Campbell, *Iron Ladies*, 99.

113. Unattributed, *Daily Mail*, June 22, 1988, and H. Kirby, 'Lessons that Could be a Lifesaver', *Times*, June 27, 1988.

114. Philip Jenkins, *Intimate Enemies: Moral Panics in Contemporary Great Britain* (New York: Aldine de Gruyter, 1992), 13.

115. Raphael Samuel, *Island Stories, Theatres of Memory Volume II* (London: Verso, 1998), 335.

116. Harold Macmillan quoted in A. Briggs 'Victorian Values' in *In Search of Victorian Values* (Manchester: Manchester University Press, 1988), 11.

117. Raphael Samuel, 'Mrs Thatcher's Return to Victorian Values', *Proceedings of the British Academy* 78 (1992): 9.

118. Ibid., 17.

119. Sigsworth, *In Search*, 1.

120. Gertrude Himmelfarb, *Victorian Values and Twentieth-Century Condescension* (London: CPS, 1987).

121. Kate Mitchell, *History and Cultural Memory in Neo Victorian Fiction* (Basingstoke: Palgrave Macmillan, 2010).

122. Cora Kaplan, *Victoriana: Histories, Fictions, Criticism* (Edinburgh: Edinburgh University Press, 2007), 3.

123. Patrick Wright, *On Living in an Old Country: The National Past in Contemporary Britain* (London: Verso, 1985), 29.

124. Speech to Greater London Young Conservatives, 4 July 1977, MTFW:103411. See also Whipple, 'Speaking for Whom?', 335.

125. Grimley, 'Thatcherism', 93. See also Grace Davie, *Religion in Britain Since 1945: Believing Without Belonging* (Oxford: Blackwell, 1994).

126. Brown, *The Death*, 185.

127. Faith and Charity, *Spectator*, September 20, 1980, reprinted in Philip Marsden-Smedley, ed.1991, *Britain in the Eighties* (London: Paladen, 1991), 267.

128. Thompson, *Ban this Filth*, 377.

129. Samuel, 'Mrs Thatcher's Return', 17.

130. Samuel, *Island Stories*, 339.

Disclosure statement

No potential conflict of interest was reported by the author.

Free markets and feminism: the neo-liberal defence of the male breadwinner model in Britain, c. 1980–1997

Ben Jackson

ABSTRACT

Although neo-liberalism is often seen as a set of ideas that prioritises the individual, in fact, neo-liberals have always seen the traditional family as the critical social institution that is to be protected from the state and to be granted new freedoms by greater access to market opportunities. A male bread-winner model of economic life was therefore as central to the worldview of neo-liberalism as it was to post-war social democracy. How did the advocates of market liberalism on the British right conceptualise the shifts in gender norms that took place during the 1980s and 1990s? How far did they try to adapt their free market objectives to this new social reality and how far did they try to resist it? How did they react to the growing salience of feminist arguments and policies on the left of British politics, and in particular Labour's growing enthusiasm for a social democratic politics that integrated some feminist insights? This article investigates these questions through an examination of the political thought of Britain's market liberals. The picture that emerges is two-fold: in the first instance, a concerted, although unsuccessful, effort by the free market right to resist some of this social change, but secondly greater ideological success for neo-liberals with respect to the role that could legitimately be played by the state rather than the market in addressing the social challenges posed by shifting gender roles.

The most far-reaching social changes of the late twentieth century in Britain (and many other advanced industrialised nations) were the rise of market liberalism in economic policy and a marked cultural shift towards less unequal gender norms. The rise of what became dubbed 'neo-liberalism' and the rise of second-wave feminism therefore coincided with one another and were the most influential ideologies in British public life after the 1970s. But could we strengthen this statement and identify some connection between the success of neo-liberal and feminist ideas? One argument that might be posed along these lines is that the rise of feminism—or at least the changing role of women in British society—unintentionally weakened the economic model of traditional social democracy by unsettling the male breadwinner model of family life.[1] On this account, the traditional social democratic vision of political economy was based on a gendered division of household labour, full male (but not female) employment in paid work, and a welfare state structured to allocate benefits and services to families with a male earner and female carer. The 1970s and 1980s were characterised by rising divorce rates; an increase in single parent families and in the number of children born to cohabiting rather than married couples; an increase in the employment of women, including married women and women with children (a trend that had already been underway since 1945); and a rise in male unemployment (especially in those manufacturing industries that were the targets of the economic restructuring pursued by the Thatcher government). All of these changes, it might be argued, opened up new social risks that had not been contemplated by social democracy's founding fathers and complicated the valourisation of male working class labour that was at the heart of the left's identity and guiding purpose.

While this argument is correct as far as it goes, it is also important to recognise that the changing role of women in society, and the rise of feminist ideas, posed an equally serious challenge to neo-liberalism and to the new market economy that neo-liberals envisaged as the ultimate product of a period of strenuous economic reform.[2] Although neo-liberalism is often seen as a set of ideas that prioritises the interests of the individual, in fact neo-liberals have always seen the traditional family as the critical social institution that is to be protected from the depredations of the state and to be granted new freedoms by greater access to market opportunities. As Florence Sutcliffe-Braithwaite and Melinda Cooper have pointed out, the leading exponents of neo-liberalism ultimately sought to substitute family responsibility for state responsibility in social policy and saw the incentive of providing for one's children as a more moral guide to economic conduct than contributing to the impersonal welfare bureaucracies created by socialists and progressive liberals after the Second World War.[3] Neo-liberals sought social arrangements that would enable families to run their own affairs and to look after themselves, independent of public support. But they were also usually clear that the most efficient organisation of the family would involve a gendered division of labour and that such an arrangement was also likely to be the overwhelming choice of most men and women. A male bread-winner model of economic life was therefore as central to the worldview of neo-liberalism as it was to traditional social democracy.

During the 1980s and 1990s, the British left, including the Labour Party, slowly and inconsistently adapted to changing gender roles and relations and increasingly accepted certain feminist arguments about the need to alter economic and social policy accordingly.[4] But how did the advocates of market liberalism on the British right conceptualise and respond to these shifts in gender norms? How far did they adapt their free market objectives to these new social trends and how far did they resist them? How did they react to the growing salience of feminist arguments and policies on the left of British politics, and in particular Labour's growing enthusiasm for a social democratic politics that integrated some feminist insights? This article investigates these questions through an examination of the ideas of Britain's neo-liberals—the network of British experts, commentators, and political leaders committed to the market liberal ideas disseminated internationally by the Mont Pèlerin Society (MPS) and the string of think-tanks and advocacy groups that it inspired.[5] These were the ideological outriders and technocratic experts who shaped the policy priorities and language of Thatcherism and in the course of the 1980s came to dominate the discourse of Conservative policy-making. This article demonstrates that their response to shifts in gender roles was two-fold: in the first instance, a concerted, although unsuccessful, effort to resist some of this social change, but secondly, greater success in delimiting the role that could legitimately be played by the state rather than the market in addressing the social challenges posed by shifting gender norms.

Traditionalist conservative opposition to the liberalisation of gender identities and sexuality—although not absent—was more muted in Britain than the United States during the high watermark of the New Right in the 1970s and 1980s.[6] But while the regulation of sexuality and reproductive rights remained largely orthogonal to the core policy objectives of Thatcherism, the implications of changes in gender roles for social and economic policy raised issues that were central to Margaret Thatcher's desire to foster a new Britain based around self-sufficient families. Although it took some time for this issue to surface in right-wing policy circles, it became a topic that attracted significant attention during the 1990s as the profound implications of changing patterns of family life became clearer and some of the heat was lost from the economic policy battles waged during the 1980s. However, this timing also meant that much of the subsequent unease expressed by right-wing commentators about these changes came too late, since new forms of social behaviour had already become established and would be hard to reverse.

Like other strands of British neo-liberal thought, the ensuing debate about the proper response of the right to the family drew extensively on authors, concepts and evidence from the United States, deriving intellectual authority from American expertise and political energy from the more full-throated critique of the growth of women's rights and feminism to be found on the American New Right.[7] Social trends in the United States and Britain were in fact sometimes bundled together by British neo-liberals in an unhelpful and misleading way. A more distinctive feature of the British neo-liberal engagement with the family and gender roles, however, was that these discussions brought to the fore a number of important female writers, an exception in the hitherto male-dominated intellectual culture of free market think-tanks and policy debate. The field of family policy was therefore one in which there was greater space for women to stake a claim for expertise. The discourse that was generated by a wide range of neo-liberal thinkers, and sponsored by key think-tanks such as the Institute of Economic Affairs (IEA), the Social Affairs Unit, the Centre for Policy Studies (CPS) and the Adam Smith Institute (ASI), was not homogenous, but it broadly sought to challenge the key claims and political achievements of post-1960s feminism while recognising that a different form of more market-friendly feminism might nonetheless represent a viable route forward for the right. This was a difficult line to tread and it is doubtful that all of the contributors to this literature managed to do so. At times a more unvarnished anti-feminist rhetoric became the dominant note instead. The defence of what was thought to be an earlier model of family life and marriage seemed on the surface to be the chief concern of many of these authors, but by the time the Conservatives lost office in 1997 it was clear that the practical policy upshot of much of this analysis had resolved into a focus on market rather than state solutions to the provision of childcare (and perhaps the rebalancing of fiscal policy to recognise the importance of marriage), but not, as some of these thinkers had hoped, a tightening of divorce law, a repeal of equal opportunities legislation, or even a return to the norm of a family wage for male breadwinners.

Home economics

An important—although ambiguous—intellectual resource for neo-liberals writing about the family was the new economic analysis of the household that emerged during the 1970s and was given an authoritative intellectual statement by the Chicago economist and MPS member Gary Becker in his 1981 book, *A Treatise on the Family*.[8] While an economic approach of considerable sophistication—which could even be said to meet feminism half-way insofar as it sought to recognise the household as a site of labour and economic production—the analysis it generated was nonetheless susceptible to a reading that was congenial to the traditional family policy preferences of the neo-liberal right. One influential implication of this economic analysis of the family, which Becker himself offered support for, was that the 'traditional' division of domestic labour in a marriage, in which men undertook paid work and women domestic work, reflected rational economic decision-making, in that each sex had (in part for biological reasons) their own area of specialisation and this complementarity in married life generated efficiency gains that would not be available under alternative social arrangements.[9] This basic idea was widely used in a more popularised form in the pamphlets and articles issued by the neo-liberal right to maintain that a traditional family structure and division of labour was in fact justified to maximise the economic well-being of family members. In its policy recommendations, this argument arrived at similar conclusions to the functionalist sociology of Talcott Parsons, which was widely invoked in the 1960s to justify the rationality of a gendered role specialisation in the family, but Becker used a rational actor theory based on the pursuit of individual economic advantage rather than Parson's concern for social stability and continuity. This economic argument was therefore one that fitted more easily within a neo-liberal framework, since Parsons's functionalism posited social structures and values that at the most abstract level leading neo-liberals considered to be dangerously collectivist.[10]

One of the first attempts by a British neo-liberal think-tank to analyse family life from this perspective was the IEA's 1980 pamphlet, *For Love or Money?*, written by Ivy Papps. The aim of the pamphlet was to present for the first time to a British policy audience some of the key insights that could be gleaned from the economic analysis of the family pioneered in the United States. Papps was a lecturer in economics at Durham University who later became an economic consultant, and who had completed her PhD at Chicago under the supervision of Gary Becker and George Stigler. Papps's pamphlet was published before Becker's *Treatise* emerged into print, but it drew on articles that Becker had already published on the subject and a familiarity with Becker's work from her time at Chicago in the early 1970s (Becker himself acted as a referee on an earlier draft of the pamphlet), as well as related work undertaken by economists such as Cynthia Lloyd and Theodore Schultz.[11] Papps offered a variety of examples of the kind of analysis that could be generated by approaching the family as a unit of production, but perhaps the most striking claim was that from this perspective women had a comparative advantage in household work and men in market work, even if a man and a woman with the same amount of education were equally productive in the market when they left school and were equally productive at domestic labour—because women will nonetheless have a comparative advantage in 'the bearing and nursing of children.'[12] Indeed, Papps continued, it could well be that the clustering of women in jobs that bear some relation to domestic labour 'such as catering, nursing, teaching of small children' is from this perspective 'economically rational', since the skills gained from engaging in such paid work would also make women more efficient at their household tasks.[13] All of this went to show, Papps argued, that marriage and family life should be understood as an arrangement entered into for mutual gain and based on the greater efficiency yielded by complementarity in

the domestic division of labour. Citing the work of Germaine Greer, Ann Oakley and
Sheila Rowbotham, Papps rejected the feminist argument that marriage should be seen
as a relationship that exploits women on the grounds that individuals choose to get
married and thus would not voluntarily enter into a relationship in which they would
be worse off than when they were single. In terms of whether the distribution of the
'additional output' that resulted from marriage could be seen as unequal, Papps suggested
that from a market perspective this would vary according to supply and demand—men
would be able to acquire relatively more from marriages at a time in which there were
fewer eligible men, women at times when there were fewer women.

However, in a disarming footnote Papps observed that it was quite likely empirically
that men would have the advantage in most circumstances, since factors such as wars,
the greater likelihood of female children surviving into adulthood and so on would 'restrict
the number of men relative to the number of women. It seems that the arguments of the
"Women's Movement" have some *a priori* support from economic theory.'[14] This was a
characteristic move, in that Papps sought several times in the pamphlet to debunk arguments made by feminists but subsequently endorsed reformulated versions of those same
arguments.[15] In what initially seemed a startling and radical analysis, Papps appeared to
mount an economic critique of equal opportunities legislation on the classic market liberal
grounds that it interfered with employers' capacity to make efficient allocations of positions according to their own best judgements about employee productivity. This was a
familiar line of argument in neo-liberal circles, ultimately going back to Gary Becker's
1957 book, *The Economics of Discrimination*.[16] But Papps qualified this assessment by
noting that such laws might nonetheless be valuable as transitional measures insofar as
they would accelerate women's investment in their market work skills relative to household skills when new economic opportunities for women become available outside the
household, something that might otherwise take a long time to come about.[17] She also
mounted a defence of the objectives of the women's movement as not, in fact, about
effacing the efficiency benefits of specialisation in marriage but rather about seeking to dissociate the division between household and market work with gender differences. From an
economic perspective, she argued, little could be said either way on the merits of this question, although she did note that in this scenario 'the costs of searching for a suitable
partner would, however, be increased.'[18]

Papps was more critical of the 1970s feminist case for wages for housework. Although
she applauded this measure for recognising the economic point that work in the home was
productive, she argued that it ignored the other insight of the economic theory of the
family, namely

> that the benefits of such productive work are received by members of the family. There seems
> to be little reason for the family to receive an extra benefit in the form of a payment from the
> state simply because the family contains a woman.[19]

Furthermore, unless the wages were paid to all women, the policy would distort market
behaviour in the sense that it would either (if paid to all married women) be a subsidy
from single people to married couples or (if given to married women not in paid work)
would create an incentive for women to undertake household rather than market
work.[20] Papps was likewise unconvinced of the fairness and efficiency of policies geared
towards the provision of free or subsidised nursery provision, since in her view this

would transfer resources from childless people to those with children and would increase the incentive for women to undertake market work but without reflecting any change in their market productivity, creating 'an inefficient allocation of time.'[21] The other side of this unflinching application of economic criteria was that Papps was sceptical of attempts to use the tax system to create incentives for marriage. As she later argued, she thought the state should be neutral on value judgements relating to whether or not to get married or whether or not women should work outside the household, since these were ultimately matters that in a free society should be the province of individual choice.[22] She was critical of the creation of the Family Policy Group by the Thatcher government in 1982 on the grounds that it did not recognise that at the core of Conservative philosophy was individual choice and the construction of policies that did not distort those choices by artificially altering incentives to behave in a certain way. Papps was unusual among neo-liberals in regarding the individual, and not the family, as 'the basic unit for the criteria of social policy', since 'only individuals can create families' in the light of their own preferences and choices about how they want to live.[23]

Although Papps's work was pioneering in its application of economic theories to family policy, it was ultimately notable as a harbinger of future neo-liberal analysis rather than a work that was itself widely discussed by policy-makers. The immediate reception of her pamphlet by the press was a mixture of bafflement and amusement.[24] In part, this was because in 1980 the application of economic principles to non-economic domains was still a novel and rather heterodox development in British political discourse. But Papps's work also had less resonance than later neo-liberal interventions in this field because she offered a more libertarian view of the state's role in relation to the family than most commentators and intellectuals on the right were willing to entertain, particularly during the later 1980s and 1990s, as the Conservative government became firmly embedded in Whitehall and the social behaviour of men and women continued to depart from what were thought to be the well-established norms of the past.

The family way

By the late 1980s, as the period of high Thatcherism began to give way to the more uncertain times of Thatcher's final years in office and John Major's tenure as Prime Minister, the Conservatives and allied neo-liberal think-tanks began to pay more attention to the family and its implications for social policy.[25] As significant changes in family life became more apparent to policy-makers, and as the facts about rising poverty and disadvantage under the Conservatives became harder to gainsay, the relationship between the family and the market graduated to a more important place in the discourse of the neo-liberal right. The line of argument that was subsequently developed was strongly opposed to what was perceived to be the legacy of post-1960s feminism and its apparent success in shifting public policy against traditional family structures. Faced with the challenge of explaining why the liberalisation of the British economy had coincided with higher rates of poverty and unemployment, the exponents of Thatcherism attributed this growing social polarisation to the decay of the conventional model of family life, synthesising traditional conservative ideas with concepts taken from neo-liberalism. Two key sponsors of this analysis were the Social Affairs Unit, founded as a spin-off from the IEA in 1980 by a former sociology lecturer, Digby Anderson, to examine sociological and social policy questions, and the IEA's own Health and Welfare Unit, founded in 1986 with an initial remit to analyse the NHS but which quickly widened its ambit to include the whole range of social policies. The Health and Welfare Unit was run during this period by David Green, a former Labour councillor and academic who had moved to work at the IEA in 1984.[26] Similar ideas were also articulated around the same time in the publications of the Centre for Policy Studies, which was closer to the leadership of the Conservative Party, as well as in more popular form by leading newspaper commentators.

The most trenchant and prolific contributor to British Conservative debates on the family in this period was Patricia Morgan, an academic sociologist who had been based at the LSE from 1979 to 1982. Morgan subsequently established a career writing and commentating on family policy and criminology, chiefly for right-wing think-tanks and publications, as well as later holding a Visiting Fellowship at the University of Buckingham.[27] In spite of her ubiquity in the publications of neo-liberal think-tanks in this period, Morgan in some respects departed from a more orthodox market liberalism to offer instead a hybrid communitarian-neo-liberal position on family policy. Morgan's intellectual trajectory was a complex one. Her first book, *Child Care: Sense and Fable* (1975), was a robust critique of the maternal attachment theory of John Bowlby, marshalling a considerable body of research to demonstrate that Bowlby's emphasis on the unique importance of the bond between mothers and their children, and its psychanalytic foundations, were without merit. Morgan concluded from this that a less maternalist approach to childrearing was necessary, one that recognised the importance of other family members and the wider community in caring for and developing young children. The 'isolated, independent, child-centred' family needed to be augmented by a wider creation of intermediate social institutions between the family and the state, while men and women should both be able to pursue careers and 'creches and nursery schools' should 'be created as an integral part of housing units.' There should be 'an opening up of the nuclear family, a sharing of parental functions by people who become involved with children not biologically theirs.'[28] There were intimations here of some of Morgan's later positions, since this argument was also embedded within a wider concern about a child-centred psychology that paid no attention to the need to communicate to children a clear set of moral and social rules.[29] Morgan subsequently became more worried by changes in family structure and social morality, which she initially expressed through a sceptical analysis of the treatment of juvenile delinquency by parents, teachers, liberal intellectuals and social workers. She argued that progressive opinion wrongly treated delinquency as a product of social deprivation rather than a failure to transmit and enforce moral and legal rules.[30]

When Morgan then emerged in the 1980s as a leading commentator on social change in the publications of think-tanks such as the IEA and the CPS, she focused on what she saw as a feminist-influenced attempt to downplay the role of fathers in raising children; on her assessment of the disadvantages of the emergence of dual-earner households for family life; and on what she regarded as the damaging social consequences of the rise of single parent families. Her first major contribution to these debates to some extent built on her earlier work, in the sense that she argued strongly on the basis of a large body of empirical evidence for the importance of fathers as well as mothers in parenting children, a point she contrasted with a feminist tendency 'to disestablish men's ties to families, where support for "carers" (men appear to be disqualified from occupying his position by their sex membership), will be provided by the state.'[31] But it was also framed as an objection to the maternal attachment literature she had earlier criticised, which she argued had served to marginalise the importance of fathers in child-rearing.[32] Morgan defended the importance of men's breadwinning as a contribution to family life that should itself be recognised as a crucial form of care and recommended that 'values, rules and institutions' were needed to root men in family life, including (she implied) some recognition of the value of marriage within the tax system.[33] Morgan's later work became more explicit about this point and about her view that the state should be much clearer about which forms of family life were better than others. Some of this research involved a detailed critique of non-parental childcare. Morgan argued that the available evidence showed that extensive use of nurseries rather than parental care would lead to bad outcomes for young children, including poor socialisation, greater aggression and emotional insecurity. She also reviewed the experience of other countries, particularly Sweden, to show that the widespread use of child-care had been unsuccessful elsewhere. Finally, Morgan argued that the provision of sufficiently high quality nurseries would in any case be unaffordable, either in the public or private sector.[34] Indeed, Morgan later strengthened this analysis to argue that the dual earner couple was 'probably the most effective contraception ever devised', since the need for two incomes to maintain living standards changed the calculus of advantage in having children.[35] She drew on a loosely household economics framework to explain this point, citing Becker, and arguing that women's increased employment made child rearing a more expensive use of women's time and undermined the efficiency of a gendered division of labour between domestic and market work.[36] This was compounded by changes in state policy that had taken away the material incentives for couples to have children or run a household as a single (male) earner family. Instead, she argued, state policy now overwhelming presented an incentive for the formation of single parent households, which were of course predominantly headed by women.[37]

But Morgan departed from the standard neo-liberal script in that she saw decision-making about families as also shaped by the availability of secure, well-paid employment for men. She was clear that the collapse of male manufacturing employment during the 1970s and 1980s (and a more general deregulation of the labour market) had played a causal role in forging communities in which it was harder to have a family. 'The growth, not merely of unemployment, but of jobs which neither pay much nor survive very long' had, Morgan said, 'produced a momentous change in the marital as well as the economic opportunities of populations.'[38] With the decline of secure male employment, she argued, men were less likely to get married or more likely to defer it.[39] In her view, it was therefore 'the ideology of both feminism and the free market' that was undermining family life, since 'the fashion for translating all life, including the family, into one big market' was undermining the 'moral economy' of family 'relationships, obligations and responsibilities' that ultimately 'sustained and subsidised' both the state and the economy.[40] Morgan's recommendation was therefore two-fold: first, that the tax and benefit system should be altered to recognise and incentivise marriage, including an expansion of personal and occupational family allowance schemes, and second, that secure, high skill manufacturing jobs for men should be created, which would enable a return to the male bread-winner role and ideally to the old idea of a 'family wage' for men. This might even entail, she hinted, a move away from the use of unemployment as 'a tool of anti-inflationary policy.'[41] Rather than offer state support for childcare, whether in the form of vouchers, tax relief or subsidies, Morgan argued that 'what is needed is help for parents, male and female, that allows them to choose whether they spend family allowances on their own care or that of substitutes.'[42] For her part, Morgan was certain that, if given such a choice, most women would elect to remain at home caring for their children when young rather than undertake paid work outside the home, and she located this position as in continuity with an earlier, maternalist strand of feminism that advocated 'measures to foster the special contribution of mothers' and had been displaced by the new women's movement after the 1960s.[43]

Another, equally radical contribution to the family policy debate on the right was made by Hermione Parker, a researcher at the House of Commons for a number of Conservative MPs, and an important social policy writer, particularly on the idea of a basic income (she was one of the founders of the Basic Income Research Group in 1984 and one of the MPs she worked for was Sir Brandon Rhys Williams, a key advocate for a basic income).[44] Parker presented a basic income scheme as a solution to the negative impact that the British tax and benefit system had on work and saving incentives and on family life. The basic income, she argued, would have the effect of removing the disadvantages of the current system for 'the traditional two-parent, single-earner family.' With a basic income for every individual, 'non-earners (particularly non-earning mothers)' need no-longer feel the pressure to enter the labour market, which, Parker said, 'has nothing to do with women's emancipation, which is about freedom of choice, but has more to do with an outdated socialism, which sees everybody's salvation in the labour market.'[45]

The redistributive policy implications of the arguments of Morgan and Parker were ignored or downplayed by their Conservative readers. A similar fate met the interventions of the eminent sociologists A. H. Halsey and Norman Dennis, whose writings on the importance of two parent families, and in particular fathers, to children's life chances were published by the IEA but were embedded within a wider argument for an ethical socialism that was neither laissez-faire in economics nor social behaviour.[46] It was the attention Morgan, Parker, Dennis and Halsey paid to the interaction between the welfare state and family structures, and to the disadvantages of both the single parent and dual-earner models of family life, that found a ready audience on the right and were echoed in numerous other publications. The most prominent argument along these lines was the widely discussed intervention by the American conservative Charles Murray in British social policy debate. Murray brought his concept of an 'underclass' to bear on data from Britain and wrote high profile articles for the *Sunday Times* in 1989 and 1994 (subsequently reprinted by the IEA), which sought to make the case that, like the United States, Britain faced a growing social problem with an excluded section of the poor set apart from the rest of society by their anti-social behaviour.[47] Murray's argument was a wide-ranging one, but a central theme was the dangerous social consequences attendant on a social welfare system that made it 'more expensive to raise children within marriage, less expensive to raise children outside it.'[48] Murray denied that a return to full employment would change the central problem of 'illegitimacy' and doubted that the British state could afford to pay subsidies to married couples. He therefore prescribed a radical cut back in social welfare entitlements, including 'eliminating benefits for unmarried women altogether.'[49] Patricia Morgan noted that Murray was inconsistent in regarding some economic incentives as important, namely those associated with the welfare state, but dismissing others, namely those that flowed from stable and secure employment. She therefore dissented from what she saw as his simplistic solution of cutting back social welfare entitlements, favouring instead the combination of welfare reforms and active labour market policy discussed above.[50] But insofar as Morgan's work had a political impact, it was the former and not the latter suggestions that were taken up in public debate.[51]

Conservative responses

There was in fact substantial disagreement among Conservative policy-makers about how best to respond to this debate over changing family structures. The most consequential tension here was over how far the state should subsidise childcare for working parents. The traditional, reflexive view of many Conservatives was that if both parents (or a single parent) wished to take on paid work, then they were of course entitled to do so, but they could not expect any financial support for childcare from the state, since that would unfairly disadvantage parents who chose to stay at home with their children. But as the Thatcher government drew to a close in 1990, it became clear that there was an emergent current of opinion in the Party, associated particularly with female government ministers such as Gillian Shepherd and Angela Rumbold, and eventually with John Major, which on the contrary supported greater state spending on childcare.[52]

The traditional view was well expressed by Keith Joseph in a 1990 pamphlet for the CPS that acknowledged Morgan's influence, and which sought to advance her proposal to modify the tax system to ensure that single-earner, two-parent households were granted the same tax advantages as single parent or dual earner households.[53] The aim was to give women a genuine choice between working or not 'without the financial factor predominating'.[54] While Joseph noted the decision about whether or not the mother of a family would undertake paid work was for the families themselves to decide, he added that children's need for 'secure and deep attachment to someone who is responsible for his or her care' would mean that 'many mothers will want to be in the company of their children in their early years as much as possible.' But he also conceded that participation in paid work could have benefits beyond the financial: 'it is true that often part-time work may help a young mother to be more cheerful and lively than if she had no paid work.'[55] However, Joseph also adopted Morgan's critique of childcare outside of the home on the grounds that 'crèches and nurseries are not ideal; they tend to be impersonal with changing staff. Would it not be better if playgroups run by the mothers themselves—either paid or on a rota or both—were encouraged by government?'[56] Government, Joseph firmly concluded, should 'not provide taxpayers' money to subsidise crèches.'[57] This was also the view expressed by Margaret Thatcher after leaving office in her autobiography. Reflecting on her efforts towards the end of her time in government to support family life, Thatcher noted: 'There was great pressure, which I had to fight hard to resist, to provide tax reliefs or subsidies for childcare. This would, of course, have swung the emphasis further towards discouraging mothers from staying at home.'[58] Perhaps recognising that this view was somewhat in tension with her own life experience, she added:

> I believed that it was possible – as I had – to bring up a family while working, as long as one was willing to make a great effort to organise one's time properly and with some extra help. But I did not believe that it was fair to those mothers who chose to stay at home and bring up their families on the one income to give tax reliefs to those who went out to work and had two incomes.[59]

A similar line of argument was expressed by David Willetts in a 1991 CPS pamphlet. Willetts at that time worked for the CPS and was a Conservative parliamentary candidate, having previously served in the No. 10 Policy Unit. Representing a younger generation of Conservatives than Thatcher and Joseph, his conclusions nonetheless followed the lines that they set out. Indeed, Willetts had earlier disagreed publicly with Gillian Shepherd on this issue at a CPS conference in 1990, with the pair clashing over whether greater state support for dual earner households constituted an 'intrusion into family life' or encouraged 'personal responsibility and choice.'[60] In his pamphlet, Willetts reviewed some empirical evidence about the changing patterns of family life in Britain, concluding that women were indeed increasingly undertaking paid work—partly, he thought, because the liberalisation of the British economy in the 1980s had opened up new opportunities for part-time and more flexible work patterns, and partly because house price inflation necessitated higher family incomes. But Willetts also argued that the evidence showed that only a small proportion of women worked outside the home when their children were very young, with full-time work only becoming common once the children were about 10. This, he said, reflected 'the general, intuitive belief that when a child is very young it is likely the mother will be around for much of the time.'[61] Like Joseph, Willetts broadly seemed to agree that this was the right pattern for most families. He argued that the evidence showed that 'very young children (under three years old) may not thrive if they spend long periods in anonymous institutional settings' because they lack 'a close attachment to their mothers, or some other special individual.'[62] While the private sector would be free to offer childcare, he concluded that 'it would be wrong to use the tax and benefit systems to encourage mothers with young children back into the workforce.' The core principle of family policy-making, argued Willetts, was that the state 'should be neutral between mothers who choose to go out to work and those who wish to spend more time with their children.'[63]

Willetts agreed with Joseph that there should be a child tax allowance to direct more financial support to families with children, coupled with an enhanced child benefit for children under five. Willetts regarded the latter as a more effective and more Conservative measure than the introduction of childcare vouchers, since it would allow mothers 'the greatest possible choice in what they do with the money', including but not limited to spending it on childcare.[64] Perhaps the most significant point about the targeting of increased child benefit at children under five was that Willetts also saw it as a response to the pattern of family life he had sketched earlier in the pamphlet—it was primarily intended to compensate families for the loss of income they would suffer when mothers exited the labour market for a few years while their children were of pre-school age.[65] Fundamentally, though, Willetts's worry about the childcare conundrums faced by modern families was that they threatened to unleash new demands for large-scale public expenditure by the state:

> Families are perfectly entitled to buy childcare, but do we want a big new public expenditure programme as well? The real solution will come from the steady improvement in women's education and employment opportunities, enabling both families and employers to buy more childcare.[66]

The market for childcare

The line taken by Willetts—an uneasy halfway house between a male breadwinner and a dual-earner model of social policy—proved unsustainable. The political ground on the question of childcare shifted rapidly in the 1990s, as it moved to the centre of the Labour Party's policy-making and became increasingly salient to the Conservatives, developments which in turn reflected the rising electoral demand for policies to support dual-earner families.[67] The ascendant view among Conservative ministers became that the government could indeed play a legitimate role in enabling parents to access childcare and nursery education, a development that was officially sanctioned by John Major's pledge to the 1994 Conservative Party conference to offer nursery places to all four year olds whose parents wanted them.[68] Nonetheless, even within this new Conservative thinking there was some ambiguity about the government's objective. Major's pledge was to expand nursery education rather than day care, although he sought to do so by enabling nurseries and playgroups to act as education providers alongside schools. Ultimately, this Conservative thinking did not distinguish very clearly between nursery education and day care, or explore the extent to which the former would help with the latter.

As the debate within the Conservatives progressed, the state neutrality that Willetts had prized between working and non-working mothers, although not absent in later neo-liberal discourse, became displaced as the right's core political objective by a novel—and ultimately more achievable—aim: preventing public expenditure on childcare translating into a new universal state service. The alternative, distinctively neo-liberal model that now took shape was that the state would offer explicit financial support for childcare, but in the form of vouchers that parents could spend on private childcare services. The IEA and allied think-tanks continued to publish highly critical analyses of feminist politics during the 1990s, including robust libertarian critiques of sex discrimination legislation, positive discrimination, equal pay for equal work, no-fault divorce and other aspects of family law, and indeed state subsidies for childcare.[69] But while this generated an anti-feminist rhetoric that held a certain appeal on the right of British politics, in policy terms there was little political momentum behind any of these as practical reform agendas beyond a small circle of commentators and politicians. One idea which did retain a tenacious longevity in the Conservative Party all the way to 2013 was the introduction of tax incentives for marriage, a measure finally introduced in an attenuated form under David Cameron. Apart from this, it was the debate about childcare, and its subsidy by the state, that placed the neo-liberal response to feminism at the heart of public policy discussions.

Sheila Lawlor, Deputy Director of the CPS and a former academic historian and advisor in the Conservative Research Department, offered a clear exposition of the revised neo-liberal approach to this question in a 1994 pamphlet, *Nursery Choices*. Like her neo-liberal predecessors on this subject, Lawlor was sceptical of many of the claims made for nursery education as a tool to narrow social disadvantage and boost educational standards, and she even echoed some of their points about its unfairness as a use of public money to boost women's ability to undertake paid work:

> Why should the one-earner family which makes the decision not to send its young children out to a nursery place, because the mother and father hold that it is better for them to stay at home, in effect have to subsidise, through the taxes they pay, the two-earner family which decides, equally conscientiously, to take up whatever nursery provision is available?[70]

In spite of this rather sceptical starting point, Lawlor nonetheless argued that there was a case for the state to subsidise childcare in order to enable all parents to be able to choose for themselves whether or not to use it. Since wealthy parents already enjoyed that choice, Lawlor argued that it should be the Conservative mission to extend that choice to all sections of society. Lawlor's chief concern was rather that the childcare system should not force parents to send their children into a state system 'over which they have little or no control', by which she meant one that was run by Local Education Authorities (LEAs).[71] The solution to this dilemma, she concluded, was to use vouchers for childcare. Lawlor proposed a universal scheme, in which all parents of three and four year old children would receive a voucher worth the equivalent of a full-time place at a playgroup or a half-time place at a nursery.[72]

The significance of this proposal was that it brought into the debate a voucher system for childcare. A similar idea was proposed shortly afterwards for the ASI by David Soskin, who, significantly, was the founder of a chain of private day nurseries and prep schools that sought to replicate the success of American childcare chains in Britain.[73] The ASI worked closely with Soskin and American childcare companies looking to expand into the British market to persuade the Conservative government that, as ASI President Madsen Pirie argued, it would be possible to combine state funding with 'supply led by the private sector so that it will have the variety and quality that parents as customers will demand.'[74] Soskin himself was subsequently appointed to the No. 10 Policy Unit under John Major in April 1995.[75] Soskin's ASI pamphlet, published before his appointment in January 1995, accepted without further quibbling that some form of universal pre-school provision would now be a legitimate goal of government policy but argued that leaving this as a local authority service was inefficient and inhibited parental choice. Instead, he proposed a scheme where childcare vouchers would be issued for all three and four year olds, but their value would vary according to parental income, with the full costs of a nursery place covered for the poorest families, 60% of the costs paid to basic rate tax payers and 20% to higher rate tax payers. As Soskin summarised his proposals: 'For all who wanted them—pre-school places would become available. The market will provide the solution'.[76]

The use of vouchers was a concept that had long gripped the imagination of neo-liberal economists and policy entrepreneurs, stretching back to Milton Friedman's original advocacy of it as a mechanism by which individual choice in the field of education might be realised while retaining the equity of access to education achieved in the existing state-dominated system.[77] Rather than the state directly providing education, neo-liberals argued, it should restrict itself to providing the necessary purchasing power for families to select for themselves the school they wanted from a market of state, voluntary and private providers. Neo-liberal think-tanks in Britain had pushed this argument on the Conservative government after 1979, to no avail, and leading figures such as Arthur Seldon remained bitterly disappointed by the failure of even sympathetic ministers such as Keith Joseph to make any moves in this direction.[78] Pre-school education and childcare therefore appeared to be a promising new front for these arguments, since it represented a relatively fresh policy area in which there were as yet few of the path dependencies that had led Conservative ministers to reject vouchers as impractical, while the existing structure of childcare provision that had emerged by the 1980s was one that was favourable to a private sector, market-based solution.[79]

After a protracted internal debate, the Major government did indeed initiate a limited voucher scheme for nursery school places for four year-olds, the first time vouchers had been used in the British education system.[80] This was reported as a victory for the No. 10 Policy Unit—and its argument that vouchers 'expand parental freedom of choice'— over the resistance of both the Department for Education and Treasury, although John Major's firm endorsement of the scheme should also be seen in the context of the Conservative leadership election of 4 July 1995, in the run-up to which Major had affirmed his support for nursery vouchers as an indicator of his Thatcherite ideological commitments.[81] Major's scheme was ultimately truncated by Labour's arrival in power in 1997 with a different agenda for childcare, but it indicated how the neo-liberal stance on family life had been forced to shift ground, from one which regarded parental working patterns as a matter for families themselves to decide upon (but with a hefty steer in the direction of women leaving the labour market while their children were young) to one which sanctioned state subsidies to families to facilitate dual-earner households. However, the crucial ideological dimension of this commitment was to preserving a market for childcare services through subsidising demand rather than instituting a new universal public service. The launch of the Labour Party's National Childcare Strategy in 1998 did mark a significant break with the Conservative approach insofar as it ended the Conservative voucher scheme and more generally deployed significant government resources in developing and co-ordinating childcare provision. But while Labour invested in some new service provision by the state, it also used supply side subsidies to childcare providers and retained the Conservative emphasis on demand side transfers, channelling significant new funds to parents to spend on state, private or voluntary sector childcare provision. This ultimately meant that British childcare policy retained significant continuities with the path first charted by the neo-liberal right in the 1990s.[82]

Conclusion

How important was neo-liberalism to the construction of Conservative policy on the family in this period? In the first place, neo-liberal ideas played a blocking role by furnishing Conservatives with new intellectual resources that could be used to downplay or contest a feminist analysis of modern gender relations.[83] The immobility of the Conservatives in government on childcare policy was legitimised for a number of years in the late 1980s and early 1990s by the belief that the state must remain neutral over mothers entering the labour market and by a ferocious critique of what was purported to be the alternative model of family life offered by feminists. To some extent, however, these neo-liberal ideas simply gave a modernist garb to existing and deeply entrenched Conservative values and assumptions. In the long run, the greatest impact of neo-liberal ideas occurred when Conservative policy-makers eventually accepted that the state would have to play a role in supporting dual-earner households. At that point, neo-liberal think-tanks effectively promoted market-based policies for funding the demand side for childcare rather than the supply, interventions that were important in shaping nascent Conservative thinking on this question but more broadly in channelling subsequent childcare policies of all parties away from the creation of a new state childcare service. Although some of the most incisive treatments of British childcare policy have regarded the failure of the state to intervene more decisively on the supply side—particularly after 1997—as the product of a liberalism with deep historical roots in British political culture, this underestimates the distinctiveness and potency of the neo-liberal policy analysis of the 1990s. The dominance of this worldview among policy-makers prevented other approaches to the issue gaining a purchase in political debate and framed decision-making in terms designed to avert a new universal public service.

From this perspective, neo-liberal family policy was relatively successful. But there were also significant limits to it as a broader framework for right-wing thinking about gender roles in society. One of the striking aspects of this debate was the extent to which neo-liberals found it difficult to engage with the hardest questions posed to public policy by feminism, in spite of the fact that those questions could themselves be formulated in ways that had common ground with key neo-liberal principles. One such question was how to promote freedom and choice for both men and women, a point that could be made in terms acceptable to neo-liberals, or at least made the subject of a productive exchange about precisely what a freely chosen life might look like. Yet many contributors to free-market publications insisted on representing feminist ideas in terms that ignored the ideal of liberty at their core. The rhetorical strategy of arguing specifically against second-wave feminism disguised the extent to which neo-liberalism, like feminism, was a child of the 1960s and the rise of popular demands for greater individual autonomy and self-expression.[84] It also placed a movement that benefited politically from running with the grain of significant social and economic changes in the 1970s and 1980s in tension with arguably the most significant sociological transformation in Britain in the late twentieth century, namely changing gender norms.

A related question posed by feminism was how to create conditions in which individuals would be able to access both a family life and paid work. Neo-liberal commentators found it difficult to appreciate that family life and relationships were central feminist concerns. But here too a more constructive dialogue could be imagined. As Jane Lewis has pointed out, the gradual evolution of an 'adult worker model' for social policy, which treats men and women as individual contributors, has brought with it dangers for women, insofar as it ignores the more complex social reality in which women are still more likely to work part-time outside the household and perform more unpaid care work.[85] But the difficulty for neo-liberals was that the solution proposed by feminists to this problem was not—as the right imagined— efforts to somehow compel all women into full-time paid work, but rather reforms to the nature of working life for both men and women that would enable a more equal sharing of care work and more generally the ability to combine paid work and family life more easily. Among other things, this would inevitably involve the state introducing new regulations about working practices that the neo-liberal right was ideologically ill-equipped to entertain. As a result, the 'free-market feminism' that neo-liberals had developed by the turn of the century was one that did not in fact succeed in seriously grappling with the pressures on contemporary family life that they had diagnosed.

Notes

1. In this article I follow the definition and analysis of the male breadwinner model in Jane Lewis, 'The Decline of the Male Breadwinner Model: Implications for Work and Care', *Social Politics* 8 (2001): 152–69; see also Jane Lewis, 'Gender and the Development of Welfare Regimes', *Journal of European Social Policy* 3 (1992): 159–73.

2. Nancy Fraser, *Fortunes of Feminism: From State-managed Capitalism to Neo-liberal Crisis* (London: Verso, 2013), 209–26.

3. Florence Sutcliffe-Braithwaite, 'Neo-liberalism and Morality in the Making of Thatcherite Social Policy', *Historical Journal* 55 (2012): 497–520; Melinda Cooper, *Family Values: Between Neo-liberalism and the New Social Conservatism* (New York: Zone, 2017), esp. 58–63.

4. Sarah Perrigo, 'Women and Change in the Labour Party, 1979–1995', *Parliamentary Affairs* 49 (1996): 116–29; Meg Russell, *Building New Labour* (Basingstoke: Palgrave, 2005), 96–128; Claire Annesley, Francesca Gains, and Kirstein Rummery, eds., *Women and New Labour: Engendering Politics and Policy?* (Bristol: Policy Press, 2007); Stephen Brooke, *Sexual Politics: Sexuality, Family Planning and the British Left from the 1880s to the Present Day* (Oxford: Oxford University Press, 2011), 185–268.

5. Richard Cockett, *Thinking the Unthinkable* (London: HarperCollins, 1995); Philip Mirowski and Dieter Plehwe, eds., *The Road from Mont Pèlerin* (Cambridge, MA: Harvard University Press, 2009); Ben Jackson, 'At the Origins of Neo-liberalism: The Free Economy and the Strong State, 1930–47', *Historical Journal* 53 (2010): 129–51; Angus Burgin, *The Great Persuasion* (Cambridge, MA: Harvard University Press, 2012); Daniel Stedman Jones, *Masters of the Universe: Hayek, Friedman and the Birth of Neo-liberal Politics* (Princeton, NJ: Princeton University Press, 2012); Ben Jackson, 'The Think-Tank Archipelago: Thatcherism and Neo-liberalism', in *Making Thatcher's Britain*, eds. Ben Jackson and Robert Saunders (Cambridge: Cambridge University Press, 2012), 43–61; Ben Jackson, 'Currents of Neo-liberalism: British Political Ideologies and the New Right, c. 1955–79', *English Historical Review* 131 (2016): 823–50.

6. Martin Durham, *Sex and Politics: The Family and Morality in the Thatcher Years* (Basingstoke: Macmillan, 1991); Jennifer Somerville, 'The New Right and Family Politics', *Economy and Society* 21 (1992): 93–128; Jennifer Somerville, *Feminism and the Family* (Basingstoke: Macmillan, 2000), 125–66; Anna Marie Smith, *New Right Discourse on Race and Sexuality: Britain 1968–1990* (Cambridge: Cambridge University Press, 1994); Matthew Grimley, 'Thatcherism, Morality and Religion', in *Making Thatcher's Britain*, eds. Ben Jackson and Robert Saunders (Cambridge: Cambridge University Press, 2012), 78–94.

7. Jackson, 'Think-Tank Archipelago', 49–50, 60.

8. Gary Becker, *A Treatise on the Family* (Cambridge, MA: Harvard University Press, 1991 [1981]).

9. Becker, *Treatise*, 30–53; for criticism of Becker's approach to gender, see Marianne Ferber, 'A Feminist Critique of the Neoclassical Theory of the Family', in *Women, Family and Work*, ed. Karine Moe (Oxford: Blackwell, 2003), 9–23.

10. Talcott Parsons and Robert F. Bales, *Family, Socialisation and Interaction Process* (Glencoe, IL: The Free Press, 1956); Betty Friedan, *The Feminine Mystique* (London: Penguin, 2010 [1963]), 99–118; Carol Ehrlich, 'The Male Sociologists' Burden: The Place of Women in Marriage and Family Texts', *Journal of Marriage and Family* 33 (1971): 421–30.

11. 'Ivy Papps', TECIS Ltd Economic & Social Consultants, http://www.tecisltd.co.uk/who-we-are/ivy-papps/ (accessed July 19, 2017); Shoshana Grossbard, 'The New Home Economics at Columbia and Chicago', in *Jacob Mincer: A Pioneer of Labor Economics*, ed. Shoshana Grossbard (New York: Springer, 2006), 41–3; I. Papps, *For Love or Money? A Preliminary Analysis of the Economics of Marriage and the Family* (London: IEA, 1980), 8–9; Cynthia Lloyd, ed., *Sex, Discrimination and the Division of Labor* (New York: Columbia University Press, 1975); Theodore Schultz, ed., *Economics of the Family* (Chicago: University of Chicago Press, 1974).

12. Papps, *Love or Money?*, 28–9.

13. Papps, *Love or Money?*, 29.

14. Papps, *Love or Money?*, 30–2.

15. This is a feature of the pamphlet that Beatrix Campbell overlooked in her brief critique of it in her, *Iron Ladies: Why Do Women Vote Tory?* (London: Virago, 1987), 227–8.

16. Gary Becker, *The Economics of Discrimination* (Chicago: University of Chicago Press, 1957).

17. Papps, *Love or Money?*, 51–3.
18. Papps, *Love or Money?*, 53–4.
19. Papps, *Love or Money?*, 55.
20. Papps, *Love or Money?*, 55.
21. Papps, *Love or Money?*, 55–6.
22. Papps, *Love or Money?*, 56–8; I. Papps, 'Husbands and Wives – Taxes and Choices', *Economic Affairs* 1 (1981): 238–9; I. Papps, 'Do We Need a Policy for the Family?', *Economic Affairs* 3 (1983): 252–5.
23. Papps, 'Do We Need a Policy for the Family?', 255.
24. Frances Cairncross, 'Ideal Homes Exhibition', *Guardian*, May 20, 1980.
25. David Willetts, 'Put the Family in the Foreground', *The Times*, May 21, 1990; Ruth Lister, 'Back to the Family: Family Policies and Politics Under the Major Government', in *The Politics of the Family*, eds. Helen Jones and Jane Millar (Aldershot: Avebury, 1996), 11–31; Martin Durham, 'The Conservative Party, New Labour and the Politics of the Family', *Parliamentary Affairs* 54 (2001): 459–74; Jane Lewis, 'Is Marriage the Answer to the Problems of Family Change?', *Political Quarterly* 72 (2001): 437–45.
26. Cockett, *Thinking the Unthinkable*, 279–80; Christopher Muller, 'The Institute of Economic Affairs: Undermining the Economic Consensus', *Contemporary British History* 10 (1996): 102, 104–5; 'Advert for Health and Welfare Unit', *Economic Affairs* 12 (1992): 16.
27. Lee Rodwell, 'Suffer and be Happy; Women Who Believe that Unhappy Marriages Do Not Make Unhappy Children but that Working Mothers Can', *The Times*, August 19, 1988; Patricia Morgan, *The War Between the State and the Family* (London: IEA, 2007), 8.
28. Patricia Morgan, *Child Care: Sense and Fable* (London: Temple Smith, 1975), 11–20, 27–8, 175–81, 317–8, quotes at 338, 331. On the influence of Bowlby and 'Bowlbyism' on the post-war welfare state, see Mathew Thomson, *Lost Freedom: The Landscape of the Child and the British Post-war Settlement* (Oxford: Oxford University Press, 2013), 79–105.
29. Morgan, *Child Care*, 12–13, 20, 318–38.
30. Patricia Morgan, *Delinquent Fantasies* (London: Temple Smith, 1978); Patricia Morgan, 'The Children's Act: Sacrificing Justice to Social Worker's Needs?', in *Criminal Welfare on Trial*, ed. Digby Anderson (London: Social Affairs Unit, 1981).
31. Patricia Morgan, 'Feminist Attempts to Sack Father: A Case of Unfair Dismissal?', in *Family Portraits*, eds. Digby Anderson and Graham Dawson (London: Social Affairs Unit, 1986), 39.
32. Morgan, 'Feminist Attempts', 53–4.
33. Morgan, 'Feminist Attempts', 55, 59–60.
34. Patricia Morgan, *Families in Dreamland: Challenging the New Consensus for State Childcare* (London: Social Affairs Unit, 1992); Patricia Morgan, *The Hidden Costs of Childcare* (London: Family Education Trust, 1992); Patricia Morgan, *Who Needs Parents? The Effects of Childcare and Early Education on Children in Britain and the USA* (London: IEA, 1996).
35. Patricia Morgan, *Farewell to the Family? Public Policy and Family Breakdown in Britain and the USA* (London: IEA, 1995), 80.
36. Patricia Morgan, 'Double Income, No Kids: The Case for a Family Wage', in *Liberating Women ... From Modern Feminism*, ed. Caroline Quest (London: IEA, 1994), 11–12, 17–19, 23; Morgan, *Farewell*, 52–3, 76, 78–81
37. Morgan, 'Double Income', 14–16; Morgan, *Farewell*, 3–26.
38. Morgan, *Farewell*, 61.
39. Morgan, 'Double Income', 12–13; Morgan, *Farewell*, 54–65, 76.
40. Patricia Morgan, 'To the Banks, A Child', *The Times*, September 16, 1989; Patricia Morgan, 'Not Just Taxing But Shooting the Family Fox', *Guardian*, August 28, 1995; Patricia Morgan, 'A Time for Women', *Guardian*, April 29, 1996.
41. Morgan, 'Double Income', 24–5; Morgan, *Farewell*, 93–112, 150–1, 154–5, 63, quote at 63.
42. Morgan, 'Double Income', 25.
43. Morgan, 'Double Income', 21–2, quote at 21; Morgan, *Farewell*, 67–8. Morgan was in effect endorsing the standard view of women's 'dual roles' among policy-makers and social scientists before the challenge to this view posed by second-wave feminism in the 1970s: Helen

McCarthy, 'Social Science and Married Women's Employment in Post-war Britain', *Past and Present* 233 (2016): 269–305.

44. Susan Raven, 'Obituary: Hermione Parker', *Citizen's Income Newsletter* no. 3 (2007): 4.
45. Hermione Parker, *Taxes, Benefits and Family Life: The Seven Deadly Traps* (London: IEA, 1995), 101, 88–9.
46. Norman Dennis and George Erdos, *Families Without Fatherhood* (London: IEA, 1992), with a foreword by A.H. Halsey; Norman Dennis, *Rising Crime and the Dismembered Male* (London: IEA, 1993).
47. John Welshman, *Underclass: A History of the Excluded since 1880* (London: Bloomsbury, 2013), 163–84.
48. Charles Murray, 'Underclass: The Crisis Deepens', in *Charles Murray and the Underclass: The Developing Debate*, ed. Ruth Lister (London: IEA, 1996 [1994]), 112. Murray drew on data he had been given by Patricia Morgan to make this case: see 120.
49. Murray, 'Underclass: The Crisis Deepens', 124–8, quote at 126.
50. Morgan, *Farewell*, 93–5.
51. See for example the discussion of Patricia Morgan's work by Janet Daley, *The Times*, January 5, 1995 and Melanie Phillips, *The Observer*, November 10, 1996.
52. Nicholas Wood, 'Minister in Family Policy Clash', *The Times*, June 29, 1990; Teresa Hunter, 'Women's Votes Mean Childcare is Vital in the Mother of all Election Battles', *Guardian*, January 18, 1992.
53. Keith Joseph, *Rewards of Parenthood? Towards More Equitable Tax Treatment* (London: CPS, 1990), 2.
54. Joseph, *Rewards*, 12.
55. Joseph, *Rewards*, 12.
56. Joseph, *Rewards*, 13.
57. Joseph, *Rewards*, 13.
58. Margaret Thatcher, *The Downing Street Years* (London: HarperCollins, 1993), 630–1.
59. Thatcher, *Downing Street Years*, 631. Some glimpses of the childcare arrangements in the Thatcher household, including the employment of a full-time nanny, can be gleaned in John Campbell, *Margaret Thatcher Volume 1: The Grocer's Daughter* (London: Pimlico, 2001), 98–106; Charles Moore, *Margaret Thatcher: The Authorised Biography Volume 1: Not for Turning* (London: Penguin, 2013), 118–22.
60. Wood, 'Minister in Family Policy Clash.'
61. David Willetts, *Happy Families? Four Points to a Conservative Family Policy* (London: CPS, 1991), 18–19, quote at 18.
62. Willetts, *Happy Families?*, 20.
63. Willetts, *Happy Families?*, 21.
64. Willetts, *Happy Families?*, 30–2, quote at 32.
65. Willetts, *Happy Families?*, 24–5.
66. Willetts, *Happy Families?*, 10.
67. Vicky Randall, *The Politics of Child Daycare in Britain* (Oxford: Oxford University Press, 2000), 76–107; Jane Lewis, 'Continuity and Change in English Childcare Policy 1960–2000', *Social Politics* 20 (2013): 368–77.
68. John Major, 'Leader's Speech to Conservative Party Conference', Bournemouth, October 13, 1994, http://www.britishpoliticalspeech.org/speech-archive.htm?speech=140 (accessed July 19, 2017).
69. See for example Caroline Quest, ed., *Equal Opportunities: A Feminist Fallacy* (London: IEA, 1992); Jon Davies, ed., *The Family: Is It Just Another Lifestyle Choice?* (London: IEA, 1993); Caroline Quest, ed., *Liberating Women … From Modern Feminism* (London: IEA, 1994); Robert Whelan, ed., *Just a Piece of Paper? Divorce Reform and the Undermining of Marriage* (London: IEA, 1995); David Conway, *Free-market Feminism* (London: IEA, 1998).
70. Sheila Lawlor, *Nursery Choices: The Right Way to Pre-school Education* (London: CPS, 1994), 16–21, quote at 21.

71. Lawlor, *Nursery Choices*, 5, also 21–2. Lawlor was a long-standing critic of the role of LEAs in running schools: Lucy Hodges, 'The Right-hand Woman of Education's Right-wingers', *Independent*, May 15, 1996.

72. Lawlor, *Nursery Choices*, 34–5.

73. Derek Harris, 'Nursery Schools Spell Success', *The Times*, October 18, 1993.

74. Fran Abrams, 'American Nurseries Want Your Vouchers', *Independent*, March 26, 1995.

75. Barry Hugill, 'Nursery Boss Joins Tory Think-tank', *The Observer*, April 2, 1995.

76. David Soskin, *Pre-schools for All: A Market Solution* (London: Adam Smith Institute, 1995), 15–18, 25–8, quote at 28. The ASI's earlier, less far-reaching proposals in this area had advocated tax exemption for parents who used workplace childcare: Madsen Pirie, *Mind the Children* (London: Adam Smith Institute, 1989).

77. Milton Friedman, 'The Role of Government in Education', in *Economics and the Public Interest*, ed. R. Solo (New Brunswick, NJ: Rutgers University Press, 1955), 123–45; Milton Friedman, *Capitalism and Freedom* (Chicago: University of Chicago Press, 1962), 85–107. The British version of the education voucher scheme was first outlined by Alan Peacock and Jack Wiseman, *Education for Democrats* (London: IEA, 1964) and E.G. West, *Education and the State* (London: IEA, 1965).

78. Arthur Seldon, *The Riddle of the Voucher* (London: IEA, 1986); Andrew Denham and Mark Garnett, *Keith Joseph* (Chesham: Acumen, 2001), 369–73.

79. Jane Lewis, 'The Failure to Expand Childcare Provision and to Develop a Comprehensive Childcare Policy in Britain during the 1960s and 1970s', *Twentieth Century British History* 24 (2013): 249–74.

80. Randall, *Politics of Child Daycare in Britain*, 95–102.

81. Paul Gosling, 'Why Vouchers are for Grown-ups Too', *Independent*, July 5, 1995; Judith Judd and Fran Abrams, 'A Child of Four Could See the Problems: At Long Last the Right Has Got a Voucher Scheme Off the Ground. But Will it Work?', *Independent*, July 7, 1995.

82. Jane Lewis, 'Developing Early Years Childcare in England, 1997–2002: The Choices for (Working) Mothers', *Social Policy and Administration* 37 (2003): 219–38; Mary Daly, 'Shifts in Family Policy in the UK under New Labour', *Journal of European Social Policy* 20 (2008): 433–43; Eva Lloyd, 'The Interface Between Childcare, Family Support and Child Poverty Strategies Under New Labour: Tensions and Contradictions', *Social Policy and Society* 7 (2008): 479–94.

83. The supply of alternative sources of expertise to cast doubt on an emerging policy consensus has been a core function of neo-liberal think-tanks in many different contexts: Thomas Medvetz, *Think Tanks in America* (Chicago: University of Chicago Press, 2012), 176–212; Philip Mirowski, *Never Let a Serious Crisis Go to Waste* (London: Verso, 2013), 223–323.

84. Fraser, *Fortunes*, 224–6; Emily Robinson, Camilla Schofield, Florence Sutcliffe-Braithwaite, and Natalie Thomlinson, 'Telling Stories About Post-war Britain: Popular Individualism and the "Crisis" of the 1970s', *Twentieth Century British History* 28 (2017): 268–304.

85. Lewis, 'Decline of the Male Breadwinner Model', 161–6.

Acknowledgement

I am grateful to Helen McCarthy, Jeremy Shearmur and Zofia Stemplowska for their comments on an earlier version of this article.

Disclosure statement

No potential conflict of interest was reported by the author.

From 'I'm not a feminist, but … ' to 'Call me an old-fashioned feminist … ': conservative women in parliament and feminism, 1979–2017

David Swift

ABSTRACT

Feminism is generally not associated with Conservative politicians. Yet in 2018, politicians as diverse as Theresa May, Amber Rudd and Nadine Dorries claim to be feminists, and argue that their beliefs— such as limited taxation and a reduced state—do not impede their feminism. This article analyses the relationship between female Conservative Parliamentarians and feminism, from the time of Thatcher to May, and argues that Conservative women have projected an abstract version of feminism which helped them construct their own identity; both through distancing themselves from it during Thatcher's era, and co-opting it during the present day.

Introduction

Feminism is not a concept closely associated with the British Conservative Party. Despite being the only major party to have had a permanent female leader–and providing both of the United Kingdom's two female Prime Ministers–some would argue that being a feminist and a Conservative are mutually exclusive.[1] Although Angela McRobbie has claimed that 'conservative feminism' is 'part of the everyday vocabulary', featuring in 'newspaper articles, blogs and TV appearances', the concept has not penetrated much beyond those familiar with contemporary political culture.[2] Furthermore, many women (and men) in British politics would deny that the two terms are compatible. Speaking in the House of Commons debate occasioned by the death of Margaret Thatcher, the Labour MP Glenda Jackson, while conceding that Thatcher was 'the first Prime Minister denoted by female gender' continued: 'but a woman? Not on my terms'. Jackson thereby implied that Thatcher's brand of Conservatism precluded her not merely from being a feminist, but from being female.

Certainly, Thatcher and other leading female Tories of her era disavowed feminism and explicitly denied that they were feminists. Thatcher herself even left the women's section of the Party as, according G.E. Maguire, she did not find it 'to her taste'.[3] In 1974 *the Observer* quoted her as saying she 'owe[d] nothing to women's lib', and in an interview with the *Hornsey Journal* four years later she declared that she was 'not a feminist'. After being pressed on where she felt feminism had 'gone wrong'. Thatcher replied:

> I think they've become too strident. I think they have done great damage to the cause of women by making us out to be something we are not ... You don't say: 'I must get on because I'm a woman, or that I must get on because I'm a man' . You should say that you should get on because you have the combination of talents which are right for the job.[4]

During her premiership, in a speech at the Institute for Electrical Engineers on 'Women in a Changing World', she claimed that

> the battle for women's rights has been largely won. The days when they were demanded and discussed in strident tones should be gone for ever. And I hope they are. I hated those strident tones that you still hear from some Women's Libbers.[5]

Her former aide Paul Johnson claimed that in the same year she told him she did not blame feminists for hating her: 'For I hate feminism. It is poison'.[6] This approach worked with some female voters, as Patrick Cosgrave has argued, particularly in the case of:

> Young youngish married working women whose husbands were Labour voters with old-fashioned views on the place of women. These ladies ... had been touched by the Women's Movement to the extent of feeling some discontent with their lives, but they were not radical feminists.[7]

In contrast, by the time Theresa May became Prime Minister in 2016 she had stated her feminism on many occasions, including through wearing the Fawcett Association t-shirt proclaiming 'This is What a Feminist looks Like', and urging other Tory women to do the same. May is not alone: current and former Cabinet ministers such as Amber Rudd, Andrea Leadsom, Anna Soubry and Nicky Morgan have all claimed to be feminists. This transformation of the relationship between Tory women and feminism in a period of around thirty years poses the question whether it is the Tory Party that has changed, or the nature of 'feminism'.

The word feminism and the designation feminist have always been contested. As Valerie Bryson and Timothy Heppell have noted, there has never been a 'cohesive ideology or a unified political movement' around feminism, and its history 'has been one of discontinuity and fragmentation rather than a clear narrative of progress'. Nonetheless, it should be possible to sketch a broad definition of exactly what these terms mean. Bryson and Heppell claimed that 'an idea or policy [can] be feminist, or at least compatible with feminism, if it recognises the collective, structural and socially produced nature of men's domination and women's disadvantage'.[8] According to these criteria, a broad range of beliefs could be said to be feminist: socialist or economically radical feminism, which sees gender and material inequality as fundamentally interlinked; liberal feminism, which seeks to remove barriers to women's advancement; and conservative feminism, which argues that aspects of modernity undermine the position of women.

There is a broad corpus of work concerning conservative or neoliberal interpretations of feminism, and there is a growing literature into the co-option of feminist labels by the political Right.[9] In 1987, Beatrix Campbell claimed that Conservatives could be feminists, but 'their feminism is rooted in liberalism and ... tends to end where contemporary feminism starts: with investigating and organising against the social system of sexual oppression, and mapping the connections between class and sex'.[10] More recently, Angela McRobbie has described the co-option of feminism by some Tory women as part of the 'emergence of a new moment in the unfolding of contemporary neoliberal hegemony which sees the political potential in creating strong connections with liberal feminism'.[11] Over a number of essays, Sarah Childs, Rosie Campbell, Karen Celis and Paul Webb have analysed the 'feminization' of the Party initiated by David Cameron's election as leader in 2005. Campbell and Childs concluded that despite the increased number of female Tory MPs, 'women's substantive representation does not equal feminist substantive representation', and 'Conservative actors may ... conceive of women's interests in ways that feminists will contest'.[12]

In terms of grassroots feminism, Childs and Paul Webb have investigated whether the increase in feminist language and arguably feminist policies at the elite of the Conservative Party have been taken up by ordinary members, and concluded that—for female members at least—some of the feminism of prominent Tory women appears to be present at the base.[13] Bryson and Heppell examined whether the feminisation of the Conservative Party had produced policies compatible with different interpretations of 'feminism', and argued that 'there are a number of long-standing, significant and sometimes unexpected overlaps and resonances between some ideological tendencies within the Conservative Party and some elements of feminist thought'.[14]

This article is concerned less with the actions of Conservative women towards advancing gender equality than with the explicit identification or otherwise of female Tories as 'feminists', and their use of the word 'feminism'. For this reason, the source base is dominated by Hansard records of speeches in the Houses of Parliament, augmented by interviews, newspaper coverage, election manifestos, and the 2008 pamphlet *Women in the World Today*. The systematic use of Parliamentary speeches allows for an analysis of every single instance where Tory Parliamentarians have used the terms 'feminist' and 'feminism'. There is no mention of the words 'feminist' or 'feminism' in Conservative Party manifestos during this period—indeed the 2001 and 2005 manifestos do not contain the words 'women' or 'woman'—and the discussions of feminism by female Tory councillors and activists are more difficult to trace. Therefore, this article is concerned only with the women at the apex of the Conservative Party—in the Houses of Commons and the Lords—and not with lower-level elected representatives, party activists and workers, or committed Tory voters. Thus the transformation in the relationship between feminism and Tory Parliamentarians is not necessarily representative of the rest of the Party; as Childs and Webb have noted, when it comes to feminism, there is an attitudinal difference between the 'Theresa Mays' at the top and the 'Anne Widdecombes' at the bottom of the Party.[15]

During the 1980s, Tory women disavowed the word 'feminist', despite some of their legislative proposals and career trajectories arguably providing examples of a type of feminism. In the 2010s, by contrast, senior Tory women go to great lengths to explicitly declare that they are indeed 'feminists', while implementing policies that disproportionately harm women.[16] The purpose of this article therefore is to analyse the shift in the relationship of female Conservatives with 'feminism' and the word 'feminist', and question what this shift can tell us about feminism in the early Twenty First century.

The first section considers the relationship of Tory women with feminism in the 1980s, a period in which a female leader presided over a party with a number of vocal and prominent female MPs, who nonetheless stridently disavowed feminism. An analysis of the language used by these women reveals they drew a distinction between policies that might benefit women on the one hand, and the ideology of 'feminism' and a caricatured 'feminist' subject on the other, with the latter two held as inherently radical and representative of lazy tabloid clichés. The article will then analyse the claims to feminism of modern Tory Parliamentarians, postulate the reasons behind this change in language, and examine the new kind of feminism and feminist subject constructed by contemporary Conservative women. The final section evaluates the nature of this modern Conservative feminism, and examines what the adoption of feminism by right-wing women reveals about the contested nature of 'feminism' today.

Ultimately, this article claims that the words 'feminist' and 'feminism' are used by Tories of different stripes to mean different things and justify different positions: in the 1980s they were used by Tory women to signify everything that they were not; now they are an important part of their public image. Many aspects of modern British Conservatism are indeed compatible with traditional feminist objectives, in terms of career opportunities for women, domestic violence and female genital mutilation, and the claims to feminism by some Tory women are doubtlessly sincerely held. This change was facilitated by the significant socio-economic change of the period, specifically the rise of dual-income households and single-parent households, the latter usually headed by a woman. This can be seen as an unexpected consequence of Thatcher-era policies, in terms of deindustrialisation, the increase in service-sector employment and the rise of a more 'casual' labour market, and welfare reforms. Furthermore, the notably increase in female MPs after 1997 both made the Labour Party look more modern and in touch with social change, and legitimised similar moves in the Conservative Party; and the increased number of women in the House of Commons provided a less hostile environment, and reduced the concern of the few female Tory MPs to be pigeon-holed as being concerned with 'women's issues'.

This does not mean, however, that the adoption of feminism by leading female Tories owes nothing to political pragmatism; the socio-economic change of the period has actively encouraged overt expression of feminism by elite Tory women. The co-option of feminism by prominent Conservatives is politically painless, does not require extra spending or taxation, and may win votes—it is thus a relatively straightforward choice for career-minded Parliamentarians. Furthermore, these claims to feminism are not reflected in policy in areas such as taxation and welfare provision.[17] Therefore, while the transformation in the relationship of senior Tory women to feminism can be seen as both principled and expedient, in suggests that nature of 'feminism' itself has changed, from something associated with collectivism and political radicalism, to an individualistic, aspirational doctrine.

'I'm not a feminist, but … ': Tory women and 'feminism', 1979–2005

There were Tory women advancing 'feminist' positions from the first days of female representation in Parliament. Nancy Astor supported birth control, equal pay, employment of married women, and nursery schools, although since she was also a firm believer in gender essentialism and separate spheres, it would be difficult to describe her as a feminist in the modern sense of the word.[18] In the inter-war years, prominent Tory the Duchess of Atholl allied with veteran feminist Eleanor Rathbone against female genital mutilation, and the noted feminist Irene Ward was elected as a Conservative MP in 1931.[19] Although the vast majority of female Tories in the first half of the Twentieth century were strongly committed to traditional morality and family values, they nonetheless had a clear idea of Tory female identity, and were offended when women of the Left attempted to monopolise feminine politics. For example, a 1940s meeting of leading female Conservatives reacted with fury to an article by the journalist Dorothy Thompson concerning prominent British women. They noted that the women listed were mostly of the Left—including the 'Communist' Vera Brittain—and were infuriated by the 'impertinence' of Thompson—a Leftist, and an American Leftist at that—to presume to identify leading British women.[20]

Three decades later, while still disavowing 'feminism', Tory women were quick to take umbrage at inaccurate or outdated caricatures of female Conservatives. The Vice Chairman's Papers at the Conservative Party Archive contain the drafts of an angry letter to *The Sunday Times*, written in response to a 1974 piece by Jilly Cooper, 'Look, I am a Tory Lady!' which they felt traded on inaccurate stereotypes.[21] As Beatrix Campbell has written of this episode:

> They were very upset when the *Sunday Times* report carried pictures of the only two women wearing hats—real Tory ladies no longer wear hats—but even these weren't the hair-hiding felt hats, they were the cheeky pillboxes of the woman who dresses for a party conference as if it weren't a congregation but a cocktail party.[22]

Despite their concern for the public perception of 'Tory Ladies', prominent Tory women of this time almost uniformly denied that they were 'feminists'. Furthermore, the language used by female Conservative Parliamentarians of Thatcher's era with regards to 'feminism' reveals the construction of an abstract, mythologised ideology which was never precisely delineated, but allowed to stand for all the things right-thinking Tory women should be against. Beatrix Campbell has argued that Thatcher's own ascendency to the apex of the Conservative Party and to 10 Downing Street was driven partially by the unease of rank-and-file Tory women with the evolution of gender roles from the 1940s and 1970s.[23] In the minds of many Conservatives—and voters—'feminism' was associated with the identitarian politics of the 'New Left', and it was believed political gains could be had through portraying Labour as the party of race relations, homosexual rights, and feminism.[24] Therefore, it made political sense to advocate policies that reflected the increasing number of women in the workplace, while at the same time using the spectre of 'feminism' as a stick to beat the Left. Laura Beers notes that a 1987 MORI survey found Harriet Harman, Jo Richardson and Joan Ruddock made women less likely to vote Labour, thus suggesting that 'feminism was not a winning proposition with most voters, male or female'.[25]

Campbell has highlighted the 1983 Gillick case as an example of Tory 'feminism' in this period: Victoria Gillick had campaigned against allowing doctors to prescribe contraception to girls under sixteen without parental consent. Campbell argued that what animated the support of many Tory women for Gillick was 'to do with their feelings about women and men and the sense that a strong *feminine* identity could be defeated by sex and men'.[26] That is to say, some Conservative women held a view women's increased access to contraception could itself challenge femininity. Nonetheless, it was not until the Twenty First century that Conservative women would explicitly use the term 'feminism' as a means to challenge reproductive rights.

For most of the period 1979–2005, female Conservatives might advocate policies consistent with feminism, but this would be accompanied with strident denials that they were feminists. Campbell noted in 1987 that right-wing women often prefixed their advocacy of women's rights with the phrase 'I'm not Women's Lib but … ' and the same was true with feminism.[27] Female Tories were quick to deny that they—or the women whom the quoted approvingly—were feminists. For example, Baroness Denton, before quoting Jacqueline Onassis in a House of Lords debate, noted that 'by no stretch of the imagination could she [be] called a feminist':

> What is sad for women of my generation is that they weren't supposed to work if they had families. What were they to do when the children were grown—watch the raindrops coming down the window pane? Women are beginning to realise that it is not possible to get too much education.[28]

Thus, the arguments of Onassis and Denton in favour of women's education and careers were given greater weight by the fact that they were *not* feminists. Similarly, Baroness Elles, speaking in a 1996 reading on the Family Law Bill, put forward her concerns about how the Bill might affect women, particularly those with young children, but prefaced her point by saying that she was 'sorry to inject a note of feminism into this debate'.[29] Earlier in that year, Baroness Strange was unequivocal: 'Without being a feminist, I believe in fair and equal treatment for men and women'.[30] Similarly, Baroness Oppenheim-Barnes claimed that she had

> spent my political life promoting the role of women, but I have never been dedicated or even attracted to numbers, percentages and the feminist cause. However, I wholeheartedly believe that any society which is underrepresented by women loses out on a huge resource.[31]

In a debate on a sex discrimination bill, Anna McCurley MP argued that she had 'no wish to arrest the effort that is being made to remedy some of the appalling discriminations against my sex'. Yet she felt unable to support the legislation, as despite 'many nuggets of good sense in the Bill but they are buried in an overwhelming mass of dross, mostly of an ill-conceived and illogical nature, which is heavy with feminist overtones'. She went on to chide feminists that

> historically we cossetted men because from conception the female is stronger than the male. It is still a biological fact that more females than males are born and that there are fewer baby boys than baby girls. Only modern medicine helps them to survive.[32]

This statement had notable similarities with the language used by (male) Tory MPs opposing the equalisation of the Parliamentary franchise in 1928: that women did not reach 'maturity' until a later age, but this was a compliment, for in the animal kingdom the most advanced beasts had the longest adolescence.[33] Discussing the ineligibility to retired persons caring for a disabled relative to claim Invalid Care Allowance (ICA, now known as Carer's Allowance), Edwina Currie MP noted that the situation was worse for married women, who could not claim ICA even if they were not married to the person they were caring for. Nonetheless, she felt compelled to confirm that 'I am not a feminist and the House will not hear me advancing feminist arguments', before arguing that 'the result is iniquitous'.[34]

In a 1986 debate on the avoidance of politicisation in education, Baroness Faithful warned that the training of social workers was subjection to 'infiltration' by Marxists and feminists.[35] In a similar vein, debates around sex education in schools saw Tory women associate feminism with the premature sexualisation of children. Sally Oppenheim MP described a 'disturbing case in my constituency where a girl [was] given a book called "Sexual Politics" about feminism, sexuality and such matters ... That girl had a nervous breakdown and was withdrawn from school'.[36] In a debate on religious education, Lady Olga Maitland warned 'The Department for Education must ensure that religious education is about genuine religious study and not political debates about western imperialism, feminism, gay rights and the allegation that Christ's teaching is little more than Eurocentric education'.[37]

Virginia Bottomley MP claimed it was 'exactly right' that the 'rabid ideas of feminism are not the best approach to bringing up children and that children need mothers as well as fathers'.[38]

Similarly, Baroness Olga Maitland assured the House of Lords that she had 'no feminist angst about the use of "he" or "she". I do not believe in butchering the English language, and think that it is appropriate at times to use the generic term. "He" will suffice very nicely here'.[39] As late as 2000, during a debate on child welfare, Baroness Carnegy argued that the lack of a cap on Child Benefit 'was crude social engineering ... an inadvertent giving-in to feminism'.[40]

Nonetheless, Conservative female Parliamentarians occasionally took up positions designed to further women's rights. Webb and Childs have described a conservative feminism that 'rejects those feminist arguments that adopt a "male" model of careerism and public achievement as female goals, thereby denying women's needs for intimacy, family and children'.[41] They also found anecdotal evidence that the prospects of aspiring female politicians could be stymied by 'older women activists in constituency associations' who were presumably 'uncomfortable with the implications for the traditional model of family life of a woman having a demanding and public job such as being a member of Parliament'.[42] Yet many Tory women in Parliament during the 1979–2005 period felt career advancement and equal opportunities in the workplace were one area where they could advocate nominally 'feminist' positions, even if they were careful not to be mistaken for feminists. In the House of Lords in 1985, Baroness Lane-Fox claimed that 'being myself no feminist, I believe that there are subtle, and not so subtle, differences between men and women which generally should not be altered'. Nonetheless, the 'question of equal work is quite another story. There can be no justifiable excuse why women who do the same job as men, and sometimes do it better, should receive less pay than the men'.[43]

Baroness Perry, after registering her concerns about the growth of pregnancy through artificial insemination, and fearing the redundancy of fathers, she claimed that 'the changing position and aspirations of women have created great strains within the family'. Nevertheless, she did not believe that:

> We need to return to the pattern of the family where its stability and strength rested on the self-immolation of the mother who gave up her own aspirations and interests in the world outside in order to hold the family together. Modern feminism and modern women are no longer concerned with an irrational pursuit of some kind of self-sufficiency at the expense of others, nor is there any great satisfaction any longer among modern women in competitive and aggressive competition with men out in the market place. I believe that women today are seeking a partnership with men both in their homes, in the sharing of tasks in the home, and in working life.[44]

Marion Roe MP, while expressing pleasure in the increase in women working outside of the home between 1930 and 1987, said she suspected it was 'despite the direction of Government [and] zealous feminists that women are managing to combine work with having a family'.[45] In a similar vein, Baroness O'Cathain postulated that:

> Some might maintain that the increase in the numbers of women in the labour force is the result of a natural evolutionary process begun by the breaking down of barriers at the beginning of this century when women first began attending universities in significant numbers, when women became active in politics and when feminism developed to encourage women to have faith in their own abilities and to work for equality of opportunity. There is almost certainly some credence in that, but I feel that the developments over the past decade have been so marked that there must be other factors at work.

Specifically, she felt that the premiership of Thatcher, the Equal Opportunities Commission (which led to a 'genuine dawning of the realisation that women were a greatly underused asset'), improvement in infrastructure, and childcare facilities made a larger contribution than feminism.[46]

Edwina Currie would occasionally link 'feminism' with the advancement of career opportunities for women, although usually suggesting that the latter had led to the former. During a healthcare debate in 1987, she claimed that

> the fall in child mortality [has led] us in the West to have smaller families because we know with confidence that our children will grow up and that makes it easier for women to have careers. The development of feminism, in my opinion, owes a great deal to disease prevention earlier in the century.[47]

Currie was suggesting that disease prevention, and the subsequent reduction in child mortality, had led to smaller families and thus enabled women to combine paid work outside the home with motherhood.

Perhaps unsurprisingly, female Tory MPs occasionally put forward fairly radical proposals in terms of increasing female representation in Parliament, even if they combined these with reassuring conservative bromides. Teresa Gorman MP, for example, proposed that General Election ballots should have both a male and female candidate:

> I disagree with positive discrimination. I disagree also with the idea that there should be a Minister for women's affairs. Neither of those matters would be political issues, however, if it were natural for every voter in Britain to have the opportunity on his ballot paper to vote for both a man and a woman. By adopting that approach we would take the issues of women's politics and feminism outside the deliberations of the House.

In this (ultimately unsuccessful) initiative she was supported by the Labour MP Clare Short, and the Tories Edwina Currie and David Amess.[48]

Yet even ostensibly 'feminist' policies supported by female Tories could still reinforce patriarchal values, as with the introduction of independent taxation for married women in 1990. Bryson and Heppell have argued that this appeared like a 'liberal assertion of the right to privacy and independence' for married women, but because it was combined 'with a tax allowance for married couples that … automatically went to the husband', it reaffirmed the '"normality" of traditional gender roles as well as the value of marriage'.[49]

A common theme in the speeches of leading Tory women vis-à-vis feminism was a dichotomy between woolly, ideological 'feminism' on the one hand, and practical, common sense measures to improve the position of women on the other. As late as 2013, in a speech in the House of Lord's debate on International Women's Day, Baroness Heyhoe Flint noted that when she argued in favour of female equality she was 'talking not from a feminist standpoint but about a practical, common-sense approach'.[50] Twenty-five years earlier, in a debate on women's health, Edwina Currie posed the question:

> Why women's health? Why not health in general? Is it not somewhat artificial to separate out "women's health", along with "women's issues", "women's rights" and other, as Private Eye would put it, "loony feminist nonsense"? I am no feminist. When I was asked to take on responsibility for women's health in 1986 I wondered whether, apart from maternity, there were indeed any separate issues. There are two answers: we should look at women's health because it is completely different from men's health at almost every stage in our lives, and because many aspects of women's health and women's role in the health of their families have perhaps received far less attention in the past then they merited, not just from men but also from the women.[51]

In another debate, after noting that she and Virginia Bottomley were two of the few MPs to claim child benefit ('I have my book in my handbag and am grateful for the £54.80 which we receive every month') Currie claimed it was fair to 'criticise benefit payments to families which do not need them'. She then claimed that

> we should not perpetuate the idea that children need only their mother and that only the mother is capable of taking that responsibility. That is nonsense. That sort of philosophy, borne of feminism, has created far too many single-parent families and deprived far too many men of their children.[52]

Similarly, Baroness Olga Maitland claimed that:

> The ideals of Emmeline Pankhurst, who campaigned vigorously for the vote, have not been upheld by what I call the angry feminist brigade. The difficulty is that the women of that brigade have clouded the real issues. Emmeline Pankhurst would turn in her grave if she could see the way in which they have brought the issue of sexism into the whole subject and their personal style of sexuality into the workplace, which has become offensive … We want straightforward, down to earth common sense and we want to get on with it … The best barometer of progress is in my constituency. Angry feminism has never entered their heads, but women play a key role in our society. Not one has ever mentioned to me that she has been a victim of sex discrimination. They all reflect the progress that has been greatly helped by the Government's down-to-earth, practical approaches.[53]

Angela Rumbold MP, speaking in an immigration debate in 1982, related how her first experience as a constituency Member:

> Involved a young girl who, after attending school and working here, went back to her native home with her parents. She married, subsequently returned here, and has borne her husband's child. She is still trying to get her husband into the country. That caused me considerable concern, because it aroused in my breast an unusual feminist streak that told me that had she been wearing trousers rather than a skirt she would not have encountered the same difficulty.[54]

In the same year, Baroness Hornby-Smith averred that she could not 'claim to be anything like a militant feminist', for the curious reason that 'throughout my life I have always been attended by male doctors. I have never been attended by a woman doctor in my life'.

Nonetheless, 'however much we may deplore it, the complete dominance of many Arab and Asian males, and some Africans, in dealing with the womenfolk in their families is very real indeed'.[55]

This use of 'feminism' to attack black and minority ethnic Britons was a constant throughout the period covered in this essay. For example, the 2008 Conservative Women's Policy Group document *Women in the World Today*, which delineated Tory policy towards women under David Cameron's leadership, claimed that Labour's' attachment to multiculturalism has led them to ignore women's rights in Black and Minority Ethnic communities'.[56] Similarly, the 2017 election manifesto argued that 'extremism, especially Islamist extremism, strips some British people, especially women, of the freedoms they should enjoy', and set out an 'integration strategy, which will seek to help people in more isolated communities to engage with the wider world, help women in particular into the workplace, and teach more people to speak English'.[57]

In addition to advocating women's rights at the same time as condemning supposedly 'foreign' practices, Tory women also used feminism as a means to attack the class-based politics of the Left. Speaking in a debate on wage councils, Angela Rumbold argued that the councils often suppressed women's entrepreneurship and ingenuity in setting up their own small businesses. This drew criticism from some (male) Labour MPs, who claimed that Rumbold had no experience of working-class women, the many obstacles that limited their entrepreneurship, and the many ways in which wage councils protected them. Rumbold criticised the Liverpool MP Eddie Loyden as:

> Not willing to show the decency of allowing that women of any origin have the ability to move forward for themselves. We do not need to be supported indefinitely by the opinions or views of the male sex. This is the first time in my life that I have ever been moved to make such a feminist and pro-feminist speech. But I find that increasingly in this place the number of times men wish to tell women what they are capable of doing and what they should do with their bodies and their lives is becoming quite intolerable.[58]

The weaponisation of 'feminism' by Conservatives to attack labour rights was not necessarily as disingenuous as it might seem. The welfare state itself was based upon patriarchal values-in particular the assumption of a single salary of the male 'breadwinner' and a woman at home to raise the children-while trade unions had an inglorious history sexism in and outside of the workplace.[59] The reforms of the 1997–2010 Labour governments-such as the increase in Child Benefit, the opening of Sure Start centres, and the expansion of childcare provision-resulted in a welfare state more attuned to women's needs, particularly single mothers. Thus by 2010s the use of feminism by female Tories to attack the Left was more dubious, as many of the welfare reforms of the Conservatives in power disproportionately hurt women.

Conservative Parliamentarians' support for ostensibly feminist positions while resolutely disavowing 'feminism' was consistent with the language and policies of official Tory documents during this period. The 1992 manifesto spoke of their proud record of introducing 'independent taxation of husbands and wives [and] giving married women full eligibility for tax allowances'. It claimed the party was 'determined to ensure that women in the work-force realise their full potential' and that it was 'vital that the education system should attract back women who have taken a career break to raise a family'. In a designation section on 'Women and Opportunity', they pledged to encourage the development of part-time work within a framework which safeguards employees from exploitation, break down 'artificial barriers to women's advancement based on prejudice or lack of imagination' and to 'stimulate the provision of childcare'. Noting that 'after-school childcare is an area of particular importance to many working mothers', the manifesto pledged to 'introduce a new initiative to encourage the provision of after-school facilities by schools, employers and voluntary groups across the country'.[60]

Nonetheless, while the appeal to the electorate in 1992 had many policies specifically designed to help women spread across the manifesto, in the 1997 manifesto this was limited to one brief paragraph on 'opportunities for women', and another section on 'families'. It could be that 1992 was a recognition of the changing socio-economic environment, whereas 1997 was a result of the 'back to basics' campaign to reassert 'traditional' values, coupled with a reaction to the so-called sleaze scandals that had beset the party during the 1990s.

Even during Thatcher's era, there were occasions when Tory women would speak positively of feminism, although they were exceedingly rare. While speaking in favour of a bill to prohibit female genital mutilation, Baroness Gardner of Parkes lamented:

> I have heard a lot about feminism, and I often feel that as the United Kingdom representative [on the United Nations Status of Women Commission] I have had feminism thrust upon me; but there is a good deal of good to be said for a lot of it, too.[61]

In a similar vein, Emma Nicholson MP, speaking in favour of the ordination of women priest argued:

> My hon. Friend the Member for Kemptown—in a way that I found unsatisfactory, unattractive and denigratory of many hon. Members and millions of people outside the House— added feminism to his list of the religions whose members should not participate in the debate. I found that profoundly shocking, not just for the obvious reason that feminism is clearly not a religion—neither a faith nor a belief in God—but because my hon. Friend, perhaps without realising it, sought to debar from the debate on this important subject, and presumably also on other matters, men and women who would argue today that women can be doctors, lawyers, sailors, bus drivers, Members of Parliament, peers, Prime Ministers, queen, Cabinet Ministers, stockbrokers and teachers.

She also noted that until recently women of

> quality ... would have been debarred from debating in this Chamber ... would not have been allowed to put her name down to speak this morning. Indeed, she would presumably have been classified as a feminist and therefore not allowed to speak on those grounds alone.

She concluded that the debate was:

> Related to gender, but not, in my view, to feminism, which is something different. I agree that feminism is a secular matter. It is about equal rights and opportunity for all people—men, women, children, young, old, black, white or any other colour. Feminism is a strand of the human rights debate, but not a strand of the theological debate ... I do not believe that the Measures are the product of some sort of militant feminism, with which some are seeking to associate them.[62]

Thus for senior Tory women in the 1980s and 1990s it was usually important to distance themselves from 'feminism', especially when advocating nominally feminist policies. This was because feminism was held to be inherently radical and left-wing, while feminists were stereotyped as the antithesis of Tory women. As the next section will show, this contrasted sharply with female Conservatives since the turn of the century, when both terms were claimed by Tory women for themselves. This reflected not only different socio-economic realities and the gender relations, but also the changing composition and ideology of the Conservative Party, and the evolution in the nature of 'feminism'.

'Call me an old-fashioned feminist ... ': the 'feministisation' of the conservative party, 2005–2017

With help from David Cameron's 'feminization' policy-designed to increase the number of Conservative female MPs through putting women on an 'A List' from which constituency parties in winnable seats were expected to draw prospective candidates-the number of female Tories in the Commons increased dramatically from 2005, rising to 70 by the time of the 2017 General Election.[63] At the same time, the language and policies used in terms of 'women's issues' evolved. The 2001 and 2005 manifestos did not mention 'women' at all, and concentrated on 'strong families'. By 2010, despite the continued focus on 'families', there was a pledge to 'focus particularly on the rights of women, children and disabled people', foreshadowing the language change by the 2015 manifesto, which spoke of making the economy 'more inclusive' and the desire to see 'full, genuine gender equality'.

Not content with more women on FTSE100 boards and more female MPs, the 2015 manifesto pledged to 'lift the number of women on national sports governing bodies to at least 25% by 2017, and seek to increase participation in sport by women and girls'. It also noted that in government the Conservatives had 'made protecting women and girls from violence and supporting victims and survivors of sexual violence a key priority ... and led the world in promoting women's rights and tackling sexual violence in conflict'. The party also promised to 'continue to lead efforts to tackle violence against women and girls, end FGM and combat early and forced marriage, both at home and abroad'. Thus by 2015 we can see a change in the language utilised in Conservative manifestos, from focusing on career opportunities and family values to less traditional conservative issues such as sexual violence and genital mutilation.[64]

Concurrent with the increase in female representation among the Parliamentary Conservative Party and the changing language of the manifestos, female Conservative MPs began to explicitly refer to themselves as feminists and claim the mantle of feminism for themselves. They attempted to deny the Left a monopoly of feminist language and causes, and use 'feminism' as a means to attack Labour and other left-wing MPs. In an article in *The Guardian* newspaper in 2012, Andrea Leadsom and Amber Rudd argued in response to Labour MP Harriett Harman's claim 'you cannot be a feminist and a Conservative': 'Sisters, we will not take this lying down with our blue rosettes. [Harman] is wrong both historically and politically ... Equality and choice are at the heart of feminism'. They went on to note the historic sexism of the labour movement, as demonstrated through issues such as the wage disparities at the Dagenham Ford motorcar plant in the 1960s.[65] Here we can see the use of traditional feminist language ('sisters') linked with the anti-discriminatory but individualist and anti-statist rhetoric central to the Conservative Party from 2010 to 2016.

Baroness Miller, responding to an article in the socialist periodical Tribune that attacked feminist campaigners for reform of religious laws, including the Baroness' sister, stated that she did not 'regard the term "feminist" as something to be ashamed of'.[66] Eleanor Laing MP began a speech by quoting Jenni Murray, 'the excellent presenter of "Woman's Hour" on the BBC, [who said] earlier this week, "I will be very sparing in my use of the F-word. I will try very hard not to mention feminism."' She then claimed she was 'being goaded into mentioning feminism' by Labour MPs:

> I will mention it and I will also mention equality. However, although the concepts of feminism and equality are good to talk about, they are not what this debate, the motion and our aims are really about. I prefer to talk about empowerment. The point of empowering women, rather than just helping them or saying that they ought to be equal, is that doing so and giving them the practical skills that they need can make a difference in the societies in which they live and operate. It may come as a surprise to know that women earn only 10% of the world's income, even though they work two thirds of the world's working hours—and I bet that does not include looking after the children. I am not being narrow-minded and concentrating on feminism, and I do not argue that men have got everything wrong and that women can put it all right, but I do argue that wasting the potential skills and abilities of half the world's population because of discrimination is simply appalling.[67]

Similarly, during a discussion on the incomes of pensioners, Harriet Baldwin MP hoped that 'like me, the hon. Gentleman [Scottish National Party's Robert Mullin] is a passionate feminist and thinks it important that men and women have the same pension age'.[68] Here we can see how the deliberate attempt of the Labour party under Tony Blair to recruit more women MPs encouraged more explicit expressions of feminism from the Conservative benches, from women who wished to prove that their party was as in tune with changing times as the Left.

Tracey Crouch MP, noted that:

> Over the weekend, I read the online comment that "only leftwing feministas care" about the Modern Slavery Bill. I can tell you, Madam Deputy Speaker, that it would be considered unparliamentary to repeat the first response that sprang to the mind of this right winger.[69]

Fiona Bruce MP, chair of the Conservative's human rights commission, said of China that 'among those who are also in secret detention is Wang Yu, a fearless defender of feminist activists and the victims of rape'.[70] This was in a list of people detained by the Chinese government, and the implication was that feminist activism was something the whole House believed was right and proper. In a debate on sexual violence in war, Jackie Doyle-Price MP paid tribute to Flora Brovina, 'a Member of Parliament in Kosovo and a well-known Albanian feminist and poet'.[71]

Many Tory women who came round to the idea of feminism did so through what might be described as 'liberal feminism'; that is to say, barriers should be removed, and equality will follow. Jessica Lee, MP, in a speech praising Julie Bentley, the Chief Executive of the Girl Guides. Lee described Bentley as a 'fantastic leader' who 'described the girl guides as "the ultimate feminist organisation"' and noted how one of her choices on Desert Island Disks was 'Aretha Franklin singing "Sisters Are Doin' It for Themselves", which, perhaps, makes our point'.[72] Lee's words here were based on the assumptions that feminism is something to be proud of, and something that can be co-opted for the Right. In the same debate, Baroness Seccombe claimed that

> When one hears some of the more strident, feminist demands, I think of one lady who said to me: "I had no idea there was a glass ceiling until I heard it crunching beneath my feet". That is a wonderful attitude and something that we should all emulate ... We often hear that women can have it all or cannot have it all—they cannot have a career and a home. As so many noble Baronesses in your Lordships' House have shown, you can'.[73]

Lee's and Seccombe's words exemplify the kind of anti-discriminatory, individualist feminism of contemporary Conservative women, focussed on combining career advancement and a traditional family, and overcoming obstacles and structural disadvantage through willpower and determination.

In addition to the 'liberal' and 'neo-liberal' feminism of Jessica Lee, Eleanor Laing and Baroness Seccombe, some female Tories advanced what might be considered 'conservative feminism'. Speaking in favour of her bill to restrict abortion to the first twenty weeks of a pregnancy, Nadine Dorries MP claimed that she moved 'the feminist argument':

> As the mother of three young adult daughters, I am a strong believer in a woman's right to choose. Never, ever would I want to see a return to the bad old days of backstreet abortionists, or restricted access to early abortion.

She insisted that she did not champion this issue from a religious perspective, but rather:

> From the perspective of compassion, humanity and civility. I believe in the right to choose, but, provocatively, I would like to throw this in: what about the female baby, post-20 weeks? I often hear the argument, "It is a woman's right to choose." What about healthy female babies who are aborted at 24 weeks?

With this interjection Dorries borrowed a 'conservative feminist' argument more usually found in the United States, namely that aborted female foetuses were women too and that championing their cause could be seen as advancing women's rights. She continued by attempting to draw a dichotomy between privileged, well-educated radical women and 'ordinary' practitioners of common sense:

> Not every women makes the decision because she went to university and marched up and down streets in Oxford and chanted about women's rights. Lots of women are actually incredibly vulnerable. It seems to me as though many of the women who make the feminist "women's right to choose" argument have no regard whatever for those women.[74]

This invocation of an out-of-touch liberal elite juxtaposed with common sense conservatives would become a well-worn right-wing trope in the 2010s, and it demonstrates the variety of ways in which feminism has been utilised by women of the Right. Note the difference between Dorries' denigration of Oxford feminists and Angela McRobbie's point about the 'anti-feminist endorsement of female individualisation [which] is embodied in the figure of ... glamorous high-achievers destined for Oxford or Cambridge'.[75] Similarly, the former Conservative MP Louise Mensch has called for a 'reality-based feminism', and stressed the difference between practical, career-minded women and the abstract and philosophical feminists of the Left.[76]

In a debate on International Women's Day, Baroness Browning conceded that 'If I was asked to describe myself, I would say that I am a feminist but I also believe that men are from Mars and women are from Venus'.[77] In addition to abortion and traditional gender roles, 'conservative feminist' arguments were often put forward in attempts to restrict access to pornography and police public morality. The 1992 election manifesto stated that Britain had 'the toughest anti-pornography laws in Western Europe, and we will keep them that way'.[78] Two decades later, in a debate about the online protection of children, for example, Claire Perry MP claimed that she 'came to this agenda as a mother, a feminist and someone who is deeply concerned about the long-term social experiment we are conducting with our young children'.[79] In a similar vein to Dorries, Jackie Doyle-Price MP argued that:

> Although lifestyles have changed over time and women tend to work more than stay at home, we should not discriminate against those whose lifestyles do not fit that profile … I make a wider point that much action in public policy is sending out a sign that society does not value women who do not work full time. I consider that regrettable, and I speak as someone who is as much of a feminist as anyone else. We must recognise that running a home is every bit as valuable as anything else a woman might do'.[80]

During a 2012 debate in the House of Commons, Anna Soubry MP asked for forgiveness for 'Speaking … as an old feminist'. She then suggested that

> one of the ironies of the feminist movement is that … there is even more pressure on young women to aspire to a certain body image. Equally, we have a terrible celebrity culture. We could have good, strong role models for women, but young women aspire to what the media too often put forward.[81]

In a later contribution to the same debate, Soubry once again identified herself as

> an old feminist and the mother of two daughters, aged 20 and 21. All my life, I have been opposed to any form of stereotyping, whether it is based on gender, sexual preferences, colour of skin, race, religion or whatever.[82]

Three years later, Soubry prefaced an interjection with the qualifier: 'Call me an old-fashioned feminist, but … '.[83] Her use of the phrases 'old feminist' and 'old-fashioned feminist' is interesting, as it appears to designate not merely the longevity of her feminism but also the *type* of feminism. That is to say, one that believes women and girls should not aspire to a certain body image, and in the importance of 'positive role models'.

The previous two sections have demonstrated the changing relationship between prominent Tory women and feminism over the past three decades. In the 1979–2005 period, Conservative Parliamentarians consistently denied that they were feminists and spoke of feminism in desultory terms. In stark contrast, from 2005 onwards-and especially since the 2010 General Election-Tory woman have increasingly claimed that they are feminists, and sought to utilise 'feminism' for political ends. The Conservative Party itself has changed in this period, from a handful of women MPs in the 1980s to 90 by the 2017 General Election. At the same time, the nature of 'Conservatism' in Britain has evolved, from the neoliberalism and moral rectitude that characterised Thatcherism, to the more socially liberal Conservative Party of the 2010s. However, it what ways has 'feminism' changed in this same period, and how does this relate to the Tory co-option of the term?

Is this what a feminist looks like?: the changing nature of 'feminism', 1979–2017

In 2004, Angela McRobbie wrote that 'across these many channels of communication feminism is routinely disparaged'. Echoing Judith Butler, she asked 'why is feminism so hated?

Why do young women recoil in horror at the very idea of the feminist?'[84] By 2017, in contrast, 'feminism' was in vogue, with a broad variety of women (and men) eager to declare that they were feminists. What changed?

As early as 1999, Lynne Segal described a new feminism that was a 'mainstream, majority movement in which women—from the Spice Girls to Cherie Blair and her husband's hundred new women MPs—can celebrate their own sudden power and achievements'. For Segal this was 'a form of power-feminism, applauding women's growing success, identification with their jobs and their ability to help each other'.[85] In 2013 McRobbie wrote that

> what has emerged recently is a perhaps unexpected rehabilitation of feminism as a broad woman, which can be usefully deployed by those modernising forces of the right, centre and also centre left, where previously such an association would be shunned.

Similarly, Nancy Fraser has argued that second wave feminism 'unwittingly supplied' succour for capitalism and that 'when pursued in contexts marked by gross disparities in economic position, reforms aimed at affirming distinctiveness tend to devolve into empty gestures'.[86] In her survey of third wave feminism, Elizabeth Evans argued that 'the promotion of values typically associated with individual growth and self-advancement are widespread [in feminism] in both the US and Britain' and that 'freedom, choice and empowerment have been redefined: freedom to pursue individual ends free from the state is emphasised, choice is understood as consumerism within the market-place, whilst empowerment manifests itself through entrepreneurialism and consumerism'.[87]

However, the apparent co-partnership of neoliberalism and certain aspects of modern feminism does not necessarily mean that feminism has been bastardised and utilised cynically for political purposes. Webb and Childs have noted that, in the developed world at least, 'liberal feminism is [now] the most mainstream form of feminism', and that this is perfectly 'consistent with the British Conservatives' newfound emphasis on individual equality'.[88] As this essay has demonstrated of women at the apex of the party, Webb and Childs found that the Tory grassroots are also 'consistent with liberal feminist objectives. In respect of broad outlook on gender roles and relations, the members are moderate on the whole, but women show a significantly greater sympathy than men for progressive liberal feminist positions'.[89] Furthermore, they claimed that Tory women are more 'economically "wet", more centrist, less post-materialist and more one-nation' than their male counterparts. They also argued that women members are more pre-disposed to feminism than men are, whether in terms of equal opportunities, women's suitability for politics, the impact of women's paid work on family life and childcare. This suggests that claims to feminism by female Tories are not merely a tactical adjustment for electoral advantage.[90] In addition, given the historical systemic sexism on the British Left, and the continued issues with sexual abuse and misogyny on both the hard Left and in the Labour Party, a neoliberal, anti-statist, anti-Left feminism is not at all a contradiction in terms.

The rise of female economic independence and the 'popularisation' of feminism (that is to say its disassociation with New Left radicalism and they claims to feminism by a broad swathe of contemporary women) has forced the Right to embrace certain feminist ideas. This embrace of feminism, along with the broader liberalisation of the Tory Party under David Cameron, has allowed it to reach hitherto unresponsive voters, many of whom were also eager to reduce taxes and state spending. Even so, McRobbie's claim that there was a deliberate intention to 're-vitalise and modernise the conservative agenda through adopting a weak version of feminism which in turn permits a new kind of more attentive address to women' is difficult to substantiate. The adoption of feminism by many Tory women is of a piece with their individualist, anti-statist views, and is no doubt sincerely held by many. Their understanding of feminism is perfectly compatible with Conservatism and was not adopted purely for pragmatic reasons. Furthermore, there was an electoral desire for anti-statist policies in 2010 and 2015, and while the new-found feminism of the Tories may have assuaged the concerns of some liberal voters, it is difficult to argue that the supposed feminism of the Conservative Party was an importer vote-winner at either of those elections.

It used to be Tory that women would offer practical solutions and run from the word feminist, but by the Twenty First century they began to assert their own brand of feminism despite facilitating policies that were arguably anti-feminist. As they have not combined this semantic change with policies that substantially improve the position of women, it undermines the meaning of the word. Hence the claim to feminism by women such as Anna Soubry can be both sincerely felt, and a calculated projection of an image for political gain.

Given the novelty of Conservative claims to feminism, set against a long history of decrying and attempting to distance themselves from the ideology and its practioners, it is not overly cynical to argue that, in most cases, Tory feminists are motivated more by electoral advantage than by deeply-held conversions. A similar process has taken place with many men on the Right, who over the past fifteen years have used women's rights and LGBT issues as a means to attack certain religio-ethnic communities, despite their history of using sexist and homophobic language, and advocating reactionary gender and sexual policies.[91] The pragmatic nature of the embrace of feminism by some female Tories is reinforced by the one constant in Conservative women's language towards feminism over the past three decades: to treat it as an abstract concept that can be taken to mean whatever they wish. The great advantage to politicians of social liberalism is that it is free—they do not have to spend, nor undermine systematic privilege, in order to claim to be a feminist: they merely need to aver that they are.

Notes

1. The Labour Party has had two interim or acting women leaders: Margaret Beckett, after the sudden death of John Smith in 1994, and Harriet Harman, after the resignations of Gordon Brown in 2010 and Ed Miliband in 2015.
2. Angela McRobbie, 'Feminism, Family, and the New "Mediated" Maternalism', *New Formations* 80 (2013): 120.
3. G.E. Maguire, *Conservative Women. A History of Women and the Conservative Party, 1874–1997* (London: Macmillan, 1998), 176.
4. *The Observer*, 1 December, 1974 and the *Hornsey Journal*, 21 April 1978.
5. Dame Margery Corbett-Ashby Memorial Lecture, 'Women in a Changing World', at the Institute of Electrical Engineers, London, 26 July 1982.
6. Paul Johnson, 'Failure of the Feminists', *The* Spectator, March 12, 2011.
7. Patrick Cosgrave, *Thatcher: The First Term* (London: Bodley Head, 1985), 5.
8. Valerie Bryson and Timothy Heppell, 'Conservatism and Feminism: The Case of the British Conservative Party', *Journal of Political Ideologies* 15 (2010): 37–8.

9. See, for example, Natasha Walter, *The New Feminism* (London: Little Brown, 1998); Ann Brooks, *Postfeminisms: Feminism, Cultural Theory and Cultural Forms* (London: Routledge, 1997); Nancy Fraser, 'Feminism, Capitalism, and the Cunning of History', *New Left Review* 56 (2009): 97–116 and Nancy Fraser, *Fortunes of Feminism: From Stage-managed Capitalism to Neoliberal Crisis* (London: Verso, 2013); Stacey Gillis and Rebecca Munford, 'Genealogies and Generations: the Politics and Praxis of Third Wave Feminism', *Women's History Review* 13 (2004): 165–82; Andrea Cornwall, Jasmine Gideon and Kalpana Wilson, 'Reclaiming Feminism: Gender and Neoliberalism', *IDS Bulletin* 39 (2008): 1–9; Catherine Rottenberg, 'The Rise of Neoliberal Feminism', *Cultural Studies* (2013): 1–20; Angela McRobbie, 'Postfeminism and Popular Culture', *Feminist Media Studies* 4 (2004): 255–64 and Angela McRobbie, *The Aftermath of Feminism: Gender, Culture and Social Change* (London: Sage, 2008); Jo Littler, 'The Rise of the "Yummy Mummy": Popular Conservatism and the Neoliberal Maternal in Contemporary British Culture', *Communication, Culture and Critique* 6 (2013): 227–43.

For scholarship specifically concerning the co-option of 'feminism' by the political Right in the United States, see Judith Stacey, 'The New Conservative Feminism', *Feminist Studies* 9 (1983): 559–83; Ellen Flournoy, 'No, It's Not a Joke: The Christian Right's Appropriation of Feminism', *Rethinking Marxism* 25 (2013): 350–66; and Katie Gibson and Amy Heyse, 'Depoliticizing Feminism: Frontier Mythology and Sarah Palin's "The Rise of The Mama Grizzlies"', *Western Journal of Communication* 78 (2014): 97–117.

10. Beatrix Campbell, *The Iron Ladies: Why Do Women Vote Tory?* (London: Virago, 1987), 53.
11. McRobbie, 'Feminism, Family, and the New "Mediated" Maternalism', 119.
12. Rosie Campbell and Sarah Childs, 'Conservatism, Feminisation and the Representation of Women in UK Politics', *British Politics* 10 (2005): 149.
13. Paul Webb and Sarah Childs, 'Gender Politics and Conservatism: The View from the British Conservative Party Grassroots', *Government and Opposition* 47 (2012): 21–48.
14. Bryson and Heppell, 'Conservatism and Feminism', 31–2.
15. Sarah Childs and Paul Webb, *Sex, Gender and the Conservative Party: From Iron Lady to Kitten Heels* (Basingstoke: Palgrave Macmillan, 2012), 91.
16. Such as Amber Rudd enduring fifteen minutes of heckling while attempting to make a speech at a UK Feminista rally in 2012. Given the recalibration of the welfare state between 1979 and 2010, Tory reforms such as the closing of Sure Start centres and the introduction of Universal Credit are believed to disproportionately hurt women. See Campbell and Childs, 'Conservatism, Feminisation and the Representation of Women', 149.
17. On this see and Jasbir Puar, *Terrorist Assemblages* (Durham, NC: Duke University Press, 2007).
18. Maguire, *Conservative Women*, 84–5.
19. Ibid., 88 and 100–1.
20. Conservative Party Archives (CPA), Bodleian Library, University of Oxford: CCO3/1/29 – World Origin of Mothers of All Nations.
21. CPA: CCO60/4/12 – General – 1974.
22. Campbell, *The Iron Ladies*, 291.
23. Ibid., 75.
24. For a discussion of the relationship between the Left and the gay rights movement, but also on the broader relationship between Labour and the politics of gender and sexuality, see Lucy Robinson, *Gay Men and the Left in Post-War Britain* (Manchester: Manchester University Press, 2007).
25. Laura Beers, 'Thatcher and the Women's Vote', in *Making Thatcher's Britain*, ed. Ben Jackson and Robert Saunders (2012), 125.
26. Campbell, *The Iron Ladies*, 192. Emphasis in the original.
27. Ibid., 104.
28. HL Deb 26 February 1992, vol 536, cols 308-9.
29. HL Deb 29 February 1996, vol 569, col 1708.
30. HL Deb 9 February 1996, vol 569, col 1627.

31. HL Deb 21 July 2010, vol 720, col 1008.
32. HC Deb 9 December 1983, vol 50, cols 629-631.
33. See HL Deb 21 May 1928, vol 71, cols160-206.
34. HC Deb 22 February 1983, vol 54, col 900.
35. HL Deb 05 February 1986, vol 470, cols 1212-3.
36. HC Deb 21 October 1986, vol 102, col 1071.
37. HL Deb 16 July 1992, vol 211, col 1250.
38. HC Deb 6 July 1993, vol 228, col 174.
39. HC Deb 7 May 1993, vol 224, col 406.
40. HL Deb 8 May 2000, vol 612, col 1257.
41. Webb and Childs, 'Gender Politics and Conservatism', 24.
42. Ibid., 40.
43. HC Deb 6 November 1985, vol 468, col 10.
44. HL Deb 23 February 1994, vol 552, col 654
45. HC Deb 4 February 1991, vol 185, col 38.
46. HL Deb 26 February 1992, vol 536, cols 282-3.
47. HC Deb 23 October 1987, vol 120, col 1030.
48. HC Deb 21 January 1992, vol 202, col 186.
49. Bryson and Heppell, 'Conservatism and Feminism', 34.
50. HL Deb 7 March 2013, vol 743, col 1629.
51. HC Deb 10 June 1988, vol 134, cols 1111-2.
52. HC Deb 27 June 1985, vol 81, cols 1123-5.
53. HL Deb 10 March 1994, vol 239, cols 467-9.
54. HC Deb 11 November 1982, vol 31, col 733.
55. HL Deb 26 July 1982, vol 443, col 1511.
56. Conservative Women's Policy Group, *Women in the World Today* (2008).
57. Conservative Party Election Manifesto, 2017.
58. HC Deb 26 March 1985, vol 76, col 387.
59. See Pat Thane, *Foundations of the Welfare State* (London: Longman, 1992) and Jose Harris, 'Political Thought and the Welfare State, 1870–1940', Past and Present 135 (1992): 116–41.
60. Conservative Party Manifesto, 1992.
61. HL Deb 15 May 1985, vol 463, col 1232.
62. HC Deb 29 October 1993, vol 230, cols 1133-5. Although it should be noted that Emma Nicholson would go on to leave the Conservative Party and join the Liberal Democrats.
63. https://fullfact.org/law/women-mps-pmqs (accessed 13 October 2017).
64. Conservative Party Manifesto, 2015.
65. Andrea Leadsom and Amber Rudd, 'Tory Feminists: The True Blue Sisterhood', *The Guardian*, January 8, 2012.
66. HL Deb 30 June 2000, vol 614, col 1252.
67. HC Deb 10 March 2011, vol 524, col 1084.
68. HC Deb 17 November 2015, vol 602, col 136WH.
69. HC Deb 8 July 2014, vol 584, col 196.
70. HC Deb 22 October 2015, vol 600, col 1126.
71. HC Deb 14 February 2013, vol 558, col 1148.
72. HC Deb 5 March 2015, vol 593, col 1122.
73. HL Deb 21 July 2010, vol 720, col 1021.
74. HC Deb 31 October 2012, vol 552, col 74WH-75WH.
75. Angela McRobbie, 'Post Feminism and Popular Culture', *Feminist Media Studies* 4 (2004): 257.
76. Louise Mensch, 'How About Some Reality-based Feminism?', *The Guardian*, May 30, 2013.
77. HL Deb 1 March 2012, vol 735, col 1474.
78. Conservative Party Election Manifesto, 1992.
79. HC Deb 12 June 2013, vol 564, col 375.
80. HC Deb 17 June 2013, vol 564, col 695.

81. HC Deb 26 June 2012, vol 547, col 8WH.
82. HC Deb 26 June 2012, vol 547, col 11WH.
83. HC Deb 30 June 2015, vol 597, col 1328.
84. McRobbie, 'Post Feminism and Popular Culture', 258.
85. Lynne Segal, *Why Feminism? Gender, Psychology, Politics* (New York: Colombia University Press, 1999), 228.
86. Fraser, 'Feminism, Capitalism, and the Cunning of History', 111 and Nancy Fraser, 'Social Justice in an Age of Identity Politics', in *Redistribution or Recognition? A Political-Philosophical Exchange*, eds. Nancy Fraser and Axel Honneth (London: Verso, 2003), 65–6.
87. Elizabeth Evans, *The Politics of Third Wave Feminisms: Neoliberalism, Intersectionality, and the State in Britain and the US* (Basingstoke: Palgrave Macmillan, 2012), 42.
88. Webb and Childs, 'Gender, Politics and Conservatism', 26.
89. Ibid., 46–7. Note that the website Conservative Woman, which provides a platform for female Tory members, is resolutely anti-feminist, also its content appears to be more right-wing than the mainstream of Conservative thought.
90. Campbell and Childs, 'Conservatism, Feminisation and the Representation of Women', 163.
91. On the use of feminism to attack Muslim, Arab and South Asian men, see Gargi Bhattacharyya, *Dangerous Brown Men: Exploiting Sex, Violence and Feminism in the War on Terror* (London: Zed Books, 2008).

Acknowledgements

I would like to thank the two anonymous reviewers for their time and for their helpful and constructive remarks, which have improved the final article considerably. I would also like to thank Julie Gottlieb, Clarisse Berthezène, and Catherine Rottenberg for encouraging my interest in different aspects of conservative or neoliberalism feminism, and the Kreitman Foundation at Ben Gurion University of the Negev, for generously funding my research on this topic.

Disclosure statement

No potential conflict of interest was reported by the authors.

The Iron Ladies revisited
Julie Gottlieb interview with journalist, writer and political activist Beatrix Campbell

Julie V. Gottlieb and Beatrix Campbell

ABSTRACT

Beatrix Campbell was one of the first feminists to try to make sense of women's support for Prime Minister Margaret Thatcher and their mobilisation for the Conservative Party since the beginning of the twentieth century. Her book *The Iron Ladies: Why Do Women Vote Tory?* (1987) was groundbreaking when it was published, and it is still highly informative and instructive in making sense of women's leadership and support for the Tory Party today. In correspondence and in conversation with historian Julie V. Gottlieb, Campbell revisited *The Iron Ladies* at just the time when a second Conservative woman, Theresa May, became Prime Minister.

Beatrix Campbell's career in journalism and political activism spans the Campaign for Nuclear Disarmament, the Communist Party, the Women's Liberation Movement, Gay Liberation and the Green Party. As a leading figure in the Second Wave, and co-founder with Nell Myers of the Stratford, East London, Women's Liberation Group, and among the women Communists members who in 1972 founded *Red Flag*, the urgency for activism was signalled by the advent of Margaret Thatcher as Prime Minister and the almost immediate socio-economic and cultural impact of Thatcherism in the 1980s. Campbell helped define the decade with two highly nuanced, courageous, and seminal books based on her own field work and interviews, *Wigan Pier Revisited: Poverty and Politics in the Eighties* (1984) and *The Iron Ladies: Why Do Women Vote Tory?* (1987). Both books were published by Virago, the former winning the Cheltenham Literature Festival Prize, and the latter the Fawcett Society Prize. She was offered an OBE in 2009 for 'services to equal opportunities', and she is as active as ever in progressive/ radical politics and journalism.

The Iron Ladies was a popular success and it reached a wide audience in the late 1980s but this in no way diminishes its importance and value for scholars. The depth and breadth of the research, together with the fact that there were no other studies that covered the same terrain, meant that the book quickly established itself as the cornerstone of the scholarship on British Conservative women.

Campbell and Gottlieb got in touch soon after the launch of the 'Rethinking Right-Wing Women' project in the summer of 2015. Developing from their correspondence and lively discussions, Campbell's contribution to this special is in the form of a thought piece and reminiscence prompted by Gottlieb's questions. The initial idea behind this 'Viewpoint' piece was that it would mark the anniversary of Campbell's groundbreaking book, presenting the opportunity to revisit *The Iron Ladies* thirty years after publication, just as Campbell had revisited Wigan Pier almost four decades after Orwell's own expose.

What they could not have predicted when they first considered this piece was that Campbell's process of remembering, of recapturing the genesis and experience of writing her book, and of reflecting on its meaning and resonances, would occur against the backdrop of a crisis as least as acute and bewildering as that of the early 1980s. Moreover, this viewpoint was written during the first months of the tenure of Britain's second woman Prime Minister, and again a Tory 'lady', Theresa May. It should be noted then that this viewpoint is from the vantage point of 2016 and the first part of 2017, and before the 8 June General Election of that year.

JG: How and why did you write *The Iron Ladies*?

The book didn't begin with me. It would never have occurred to me. The idea came from my publisher Ursula Owen at the feminist publishing house, Virago. We had a woman Prime Minister, the most audacious adversary that progressive politics had faced in a generation. Virago was spot on. At the beginning of the 1980s Ursula had commissioned *Wigan Pier Revisited (1984)* a rendezvous, so to say, with George Orwell's odyssey of dispossessed England in the 1930s. That adventure was across familiar territory: it was about the condition of the English working class—my class—refracted through the new politics of women's liberation, and living through the shock of Thatcherism's rampage. The book was reportage—I'm a reporter, it is what I do—and it was perfectly timed, it came out in 1984 to coincide with Orwell's eponymous dystopia.

The Iron Ladies was an utterly unfamiliar political landscape to me. My family was working class, Communists in a small Cumbrian city on England's border with Scotland. We didn't have the experience of some Metropolitan party members, of living in a bubble of sublime brethren. We knew all sorts, including Christians and even Liberals. But Tories, I doubt it. To be candid, my ignorance was profound and probably a combination of unmitigated class hatred and political piety—an inversion of John Major's mantra: understand a little less, condemn a little more.

That disposition was, of course, challenged by the rise of Thatcherism after her election as party leader in 1975, and by the marvellous investigation of the new conjuncture pioneered by *Marxism Today* and the great intellectuals Andrew Gamble and Stuart Hall. In the 1980s I was working as a reporter with the London magazines *Time Out* and then *City Limits* (as well as writing for *Marxism Today*) and covered the great flowering of radical municipal politics in the capital and the metropolitan cities, pioneered by the leader of London Labour, Ken Livingstone.

The Conservatives in County Hall, the seat of the Greater London Council and the Inner London Education Authority, may not have loved the new regime, but they were inevitably part of it, and they had to withstand the outbreak of hostilities by the government on the other side of the Thames, in the House of Commons.

JG: What or who first motivated you to research Conservative women?

Virago's suggestion had the frisson of risk: how to do something I didn't know how to do, how to *be interested* in Tory women. Lest we forget, the greatest Tory woman of them all, Margaret Thatcher herself, wasn't interested in Tory women. Political science wasn't interested in Tory women either. The Conservative Party depended on the women—couldn't win power without them—but it wasn't interested in them. The standard texts were no help: the long-standing gender gap—women voters' somewhat greater adhesion to the Conservatives—attracted little or no attention. It was taken for granted, not so much explained away as footnoted away, treated as self-evident, a manifestation of women's allegedly natural conservatism—instinctive, passive, inaccessible to reason—and of their Anglicanism, as if their Christianity could also be explained away as innate moralism and mysticism.

This purportedly *natural* conservatism was reiterated in the wake of the 2008 banking crisis: women would not have behaved like the Viking financiers, women wouldn't have taken those risks! Risk-aversion could not explain the radicalism of Margaret Thatcher, however. Furthermore, the voting gender gap in Britain was not echoed in the US where, historically, the Democrats attracted more women voters than the Republicans. It was apparent then that there was no simple correlation between women's votes and their political opinions. Brexit and the Trump presidential election bombshell reprised that seeming paradox: why do people vote contrary to their interests?

Researching the book revealed that women were not, and did not expect to be, animated by parties that would advance their gender interest because none of them did. How did that affect my own thinking? It converged with an imperative shared by many on the Left and within feminism, particularly those influenced by Gramcscian thinking: having a critique of the Right could never be enough; we had to comprehend what it was that worked, how hegemony worked. And it cured me—I hope—of piety.

JG: How did you reconcile your politics and your feminism with your research and your personal encounters with Tory women? Did your own political perspective determine the structure of the book?

The work fell into three sections: reading about the Tory party's history; the contemporary psephology, which showed—contrary to expectations and prevailing myths—that women could no longer be taken for granted by the Tories, and interviewing Tory women themselves. The late Raphael Samuel, the pioneering Labour historian and *History Workshop Journal* editor, fizzed with excitement at Virago's proposal. When I consulted him, he said: the Primrose League, you must do the Primrose League.[1] Bless Raphael Samuel, I still recall this small passionate man in his small kitchen in Spitalfields, ambient tobacco, wood panels, and dense, generous enthusiasm about history. It was perfect advice.

The Primrose League was a mass movement launched in the 1880s before the Tories became a mass party. A rich—and underrated—history by Janet Henderson Robb and Moisei Ostrogorski's *Democracy and the Organisation of Political Parties* (1902) show how a network formed by elite men was swiftly captured by women and transformed into a mass movement. The women had formed 'in less than ten years a formidable Tory militia, which surpasses the regular army of the Tory party.'[2] Janet Robb's pioneering history of the Primrose League argued that it did what the Tory elite failed to do—create a mass, urban movement to participate in the glories of empire.[3] The archive in the Bodleian Library showed how resourceful elite women seized the time, took over the League, and fashioned a mighty electoral machine to manage an expanding male electorate; the archive also revealed the elite men's resentment, jealousy and determined domination of Conservatism, themes that infused Tory culture thereafter.

They were not unique to the Right. The rise of the Tory woman could not be understood without reference to the decline and fall of the Liberals and the rise of the Labour movement, and its mighty partner, the Co-operative movement. It remains one of the tragedies of British socialism that the Co-operative movement and the Co-operative Women's Guilds—so envied by the Right—were subordinate to what I have described as the 'men's movement', the trade unions. British Labourism was a patriarchal firmament that faced women with an aching paradox: the only mass movement committed to equality sought it for men at the expense of women. Given the misogyny of the party-political landscape, where women weren't hailed *as women,* but only as agents of the patriarchal family, why wouldn't women vote Conservative?

JG: How does *Iron Ladies* compare with other feminists' writing about women on the Right, such as Andrea Dworkin?

Andrea Dworkin's *Right-Wing Women* (1983) was a hugely influential critique of the American right-wing woman, but her furious eloquence did not translate across the Atlantic too well. Dworkin's book was less an engagement with the history of women and Right-wing politics in the US than with populist fervour on the Religious right, the repudiation of equality, abortion and sexual liberation. Dworkin was a potent presence in radical feminist thinking, but I'm not sure that this text had much impact on political scientists.

Religion was and is more potent in US popular politics than in the UK, with the exception of the armed conflict in Northern Ireland. Despite the survival of Anglicanism as the Established church, and the influence of non-conformist religion in the making of Labourism, evangelical Christianity has not matched the resonance of evangelism—progressive black, or regressive white—in the US.

Evangelical Christian mobilisation in the US since the 1980s maintained faith-based, counter-revolutionary vigour in party politics that has no equivalent in the UK. The moralist insurgencies of hard Right populism in Britain the 1940s, the 1960s and again in the 1980s were certainly bold and media savvy, but during the reign of Thatcherism had little leverage in the Conservative Party itself.

The Housewives League peaked in the 1940s as a right-wing Christian mobilisation against the Labour government and post-war rationing. Later Christian crusades against abortion, teenage girls' access to contraception, and sex in popular culture—led by Mary Whitehouse and Victoria Gillick—were inflammatory but had almost no traction in the Conservative Party women's organisation which, like Margaret Thatcher herself, was pro-choice.

Mary Whitehouse was a Christian supporter of Moral Re-Armament, a hard right crusade against socialism, who became a household name as the scourge of sex and violence in popular culture. Victoria Gillick, a Catholic mother of 10 children, campaigned against government guidance published in 1980 making contraception available to teen-aged girls without parental consent. She took her case all the way to the House of Lords, where the law lords ruled against her in 1985.

Andrea Dworkin rightly stresses women's fear of men's violence as a current running through right-wing women's movements. But nuance, qualification and complication are not her thing. I don't share her view that women's adhesion to the right expressed a search for *men's* protection. I prefer the interpretation offered by my friend Frankie Rickford who had been a fellow reporter on the *Morning Star* (and part of the feminist network in the Communist Party) who saw Tory law-and-order discourse as a more diffuse vector for fear of male violence and a space for women's rage. It can also be seen as a demand that *the state* take the side of women.

JG: In what ways is the history of British Conservative women unique to the British national and imperial context?

In Britain, 'law and order' was the site of historic clashes between Tory modernisers and the women's organisation in the 1950s and 1960s. In 1955 the Labour MP Sydney Silverman successfully proposed in Parliament the abolition of capital punishment. Abolition was not enacted for another decade, following the election of a Labour government, however the Conservative government felt obliged to yield to the great movement for reform and introduced a compromise in 1957. The manoeuvre was associated with the modernisation of the Tories, their historic compromise with the welfare state, and a deep sensibility in a younger generation of Tory leaders that there could be no return to the pre-war disdain for working class interests.

'Law and order' was a thoroughly gendered discourse in this profoundly patriarchal culture—it was where women enunciated their critique of masculinity. The 'law and order debate, one of the rowdy rituals of Tory conferences, was dubbed 'a debate 'entirely for the ladies.'[4] Their speeches were narratives of men's beastliness.

This was the context in which they were revealed as visceral and intransigent, as belonging to another time, as if they were a rump of hell's grannies. Their deference to the top men stopped here. Their resistance to the reform of the criminal justice system generated their reputation as the 'blue rinsed brigade' and 'hangers and floggers'. Undoubtedly, their punishment rhetoric resonated in popular culture, but they were unloved among the modernising mandarins. They weren't cool or contemporary and they lacked charm. When I asked Edward Heath, who had been defeated by Margaret Thatcher, about the Tory women's organisation, he became bilious—I can still see him, in his Salisbury home, gesticulating angrily, as if screwing the lid on a boiling cauldron of womanly furies. His contempt was palpable, as if crime and punishment—so important to Tory populism—was an atavistic oracle intruding upon the calm, corporate manners of political management.

JG: What was the critical reception of *The Iron Ladies*, and how do you feel it advanced or effected your career at the time and since?

At the time there were a few—very few—skeptical voices: how could a feminist, not to mention a leftie, not only waste time on them, but get on with them, or at least peacefully co-exist well enough to secure their co-operation? This was, of course, familiar—in another moment I might have said the same to myself, but I'd have been wrong. Journalists, historians, anthropologists always have to work out how best to engage people, whoever they are. But this was the only occasion that provoked not only the question but the scent of risk. The question is still asked. It is very odd. Perhaps it comes from a suspicion that either I would be disrespectful, or they would, or that I'd be seduced and lose my marbles.

In any case, the election of Margaret Thatcher as leader in 1975 had changed everything. It rendered the question irrelevant, after all 1975 was International Women's Year, how could we *not* think about her paradoxical persona and the Conservative dialectic—the Tory Party as a gendered project, a patriarchal party, led by a woman.

I say that now, though, of course, it was less clear then just how deep Thatcherism would go, just how much neo-liberalism would diminish the conditions in which women's political agenda could be realised—themes I address in my book *End of Equality*.

JG: You were interviewed by a number of news outlets when Thatcher died in April 2013. What is your assessment of the impact and legacy of Thatcher and, thinking more about the very contemporary setting, the so-called 'feminisation' of the Conservative party under David Cameron, and of course the rise of Theresa May?

It is still common enough to address Thatcher as a *woman* politician without addressing the politics of gender. David Cannadine's 2017 book, *Margaret Thatcher* exemplifies the tendency: he refers to her admiration for her father, but has nothing to say about her relentless disengagement from her mute, doormat mother. He repeats the story in Penny Junor's revealing book, *Margaret Thatcher*, published in 1984, that instantly after the birth of her twins, whilst still in her hospital bed, Thatcher resolved not to be defeated by motherhood; she would take her bar exams, without exploring the implications, indicating that her own engagement with motherhood was precarious, not to say disassociated.

I think femininity was what Thatcher performed, it was the frock she wore; but she eschewed any concessions to equality, to the world of women except to invoke patriarchal rhetoric of home and hearth. She didn't extend solidarity to women colleagues. I think she associated female experience—and feminism—with sacrifice, subordination and defeat, and she disparaged feminism for drawing attention to that.

Thatcher's power also clarified the urgency of exercising what the feminist intellectual Cynthia Enloe calls 'feminist curiosity'.[5] That could not be exercised by referring only to archives or texts: it meant going to the women themselves. Women as women were scarcely written into Tory history or contemporary programmes; they were hailed, if at all, as the matrons of home and hearth, as domestic bursars. And the Conservative Party's discourse was not explicit about its patriarchal imperatives.

Journalism, like other forms of ethnography or historical inquiry, is never objective. Journalists are always positioned. But having a standpoint is not compromised by comprehension. The research did—for me at least—enlist empathy. Since this story could not be written without Conservative women themselves—they were its subject—it had to engage them and try to see the world as they saw it. Empathy didn't mean abandoning critique, it did not mean becoming one of them, it just meant standing in their shoes, or, as the book puts it, asking the question: 'How does Conservatism enable women to make sense of themselves and their world?'

This was not sociological research, there would be no samples, no balance, no tests of representativity, and no tick boxes. But there was method: women were interviewed in London the Midlands and the Borders; in Parliament and local government; they were rural and urban, young and old, white and black. There was a template for our conversations; it included their own biographies and their opinions and responses to a cluster of questions addressed to everyone.

JG: Can you share something more about the process of researching and writing the book? What was it like interviewing women whose political ideas were so opposed to your own?

I interviewed the leading figures in the Conservative women's organisation, women ministers and parliamentarians, regional and local activists and members. There was no difficulty with access, although at the beginning of the process nothing could be assumed—after all the party was at war with the purported 'enemy within' who were, of course, my people. And the party did its research, so they knew exactly who they were inviting across their threshold. The most important conversation in this respect was with Emma Nicholson, party vice-chair*man* (as she was described then) and the leader of the women's organisation. She was a dynastic Tory, as her people had been in Parliament since Simon de Montfort. She was ebullient, forthright, and modern. She fixed her gaze and asked why this book was being written and why should they co-operate. She responded to the explanation with *yes*. Her concern was merely that it would not be a hatchet job. Critique they didn't object to, contempt ... well, that was a different matter. I understood that.

JG: How did the critical reception of *The Iron Ladies* affect your career?

Not sure I can answer this—as I recall Tory women rather liked the book, not necessarily because they agreed with it but because they recognised themselves in it and they felt they had been taken seriously. Feminist political scientists, psephologists, were interested. I might be wrong, but I never had a sense of Left-wing engagement with it. There was, I remember, one socialist-feminist review that said (probably because the book wasn't nasty) that I'd supped with the devil. Silly.

Virago had been absolutely on the button to commission such a book—we were in the midst of an incendiary crusade against progressive politics, with horrible consequences for feminism. It had been widely assumed that Thatcher was uniquely alluring to women but it was more complicated than that. Her appeal to enough of the 'labour aristocracy' to wound Labour's social base was decisive. How could we not investigate this thoroughly gendered project? And how could we not be interested in what it was about Conservatism that connected with women when, structurally, it offered them so little?

There was another kind of resistance to the theme of women representing patriarchal projects. Typically Queen Elizabeth II and Margaret Thatcher are routinely claimed for some kind of quasi-feminism because they are strong and powerful, when in fact, what they represent is a feminine—not feminist—affirmation, or embodiment of thoroughly patriarchal institutions and ideologies.

The point about Thatcher was that she never affirmed powerful women, and she didn't intervene against women's relative powerlessness—she did not connect with women as women. It is routine to locate her political inspiration in her father, a Tory alderman. But I think it is equally important to address what Thatcher might have taken from her mother—the mute, downtrodden, perhaps depressed servant to the Thatcher household, the proverbial doormat. Thatcher was not inspired by her mother.

To have connected with women would have taken her to pain and subordination. And perhaps to feminism. That she would not do.

Thatcher absolutely resisted the counsel of one of her political advisers—and admirers —Patrick Cosgrave. He was alert to gender politics and to the shifting demographics of the 1970s. His polling in the 1970s suggested to him that Thatcher should use her sex to engage with women who had been touched by the women's movement. But she wouldn't.[6]

Nor did she expand women's political space or discourse. On the contrary—for example, in her speech in 1982 in honour of the suffrage campaigner Dame Margery Ashby—Thatcher, far from celebrating her feminism, referred only to the 'privilege' of being a wife and mother.

My interviews with Tory women politicians and candidates were very revealing about this: they didn't think she promoted women, they didn't think that she created political space for women. Nor did they believe that she shared their discontents about the sheer difficulties they encountered. They had expected her to. Being there was Thatcher's gift to women.

She scorned feminism. However, she *did* gender, sometimes with irony, but always in the service of men, masculinity and a patriarchal division of labour. Thatcher addressed women only as wives or mothers sequestered in domesticity. She reserved greatness for herself. She could do anything a man could do. She could wage war and make breakfast. No, she could do *more* than any man could do.

JG: One could say Thatcher was the Annie Get Your Gun of British politics then?

Yes, that is a good way of thinking about it. Her critics sometimes misread the way that she performed gender—most marvellously Fluck and Law in *Spitting Image*, the satirical puppet show for grown-ups: she was clad in a manly pinstriped suit and used a gentlemen's urinal. It was very funny, indeed it became iconic and at its peak attracted millions of viewers. But even they said they knew that it was tricky.

JG: *The Iron Ladies* is much cited by historians in this field and will always be a cornerstone in the historiography. Does this surprise you? What was the intended readership for the book?

That is wonderful—though I wasn't aware of it. I'd be interested to know more.

JG: As we have reached the 30th anniversary of the publication of *The Iron Ladies*, how do you make sense of the long history of Conservative women?

A comparison between Thatcher and her successors is inescapable but unhelpful—not least because Theresa May is managing a world that Thatcher helped to make. The sheer audacity of Thatcher's rupture—her assault on her own party's historic compromise with an interventionist, expanded welfare state, her monetarism, her insurgency against organised labour and her reassertion of the Anglo-American relationship as the world's centre of gravity—was mesmerising. She was the beneficiary of what the historian Ben Jackson describes as the 'archipelago of think tanks' circling Central Office in the 1970s, and, of course, her friendship with Sir Keith Joseph, who set up the Centre for Policy studies.

Thatcher embarked on a radical intellectual critique of the post-war consensus and her adhesion to economic liberalism, which is well-known. It is worth recalling that before 1975, that project, advanced by the Institute of Economic Affairs, was regarded as far right and idiosyncratic.

Nevertheless, Thatcher's project was pragmatic, contingent and tactical. Her achievement was less the coherence of her programme, than the creation of new political terrain that gave Thatcherism an afterlife beyond Thatcher herself. Stuart Hall and Andrew Gamble, writing in *Marxism Today* in the 1980s, were insistent that she was creating a new political project without parallel in Europe.

Little did we know then just how much Thatcherism would change everything. Gamble, writing in *The Guardian* on 14 October 2005, reminds us that although she almost wrecked her own party and its 'great governing tradition', her successes helped to disable old Labour and incubate New Labour. And New Labour, he suggests, was perhaps 'the more lasting ideological architect of the post-industrial era.' We might add that Brexit was also Thatcher's bequest.

Ironically, Thatcher's successors in her own party found themselves trying, in vain, to mitigate the mess bequeathed by her revolution: the pauperisation of the bottom 10%, accelerating inequalities unknown for a century, the slow death of local government, the end of an 'entrepreneurial state', the economy's dependence on financial gambling and property profiteering, and the enduring fissures on the right over Europe.

David Cameron in 2008 proclaimed a rhetorical triangulation that would have horrified his heroine: 'If you care about poverty, if you care about inequality ... forget about the Labour Party ... If you count yourself a progressive, a true progressive, only we can achieve real change.'[7]

JG: How do you make sense of Theresa May and her place in the women's history of the Conservative Party, and in the gender history of Britain?

Theresa May's colours were clear during the great migration crisis, when she was Home Secretary: she was unyielding toward refugees. In 2015, when thousands were risking—or losing—their lives in hazardous Mediterranean crossings, May refused to participate in any European re-settlement strategy. She inherited a party that was not only disunited by Brexit in 2016, but bested by UKIP. Theresa May was no Thatcherite when she enlisted the 'one nation' discourse with even more explicit appeals to those who experienced discrimination and disadvantage: 'if you're poor ... if you're black ... if you're a white working class boy ... if you're at a state school ... if you're a woman ... if you're young ... '—everyone that is, who wasn't a middle-class white man—then the Tories were there for you: her mission, she said, was to 'make Britain a country that works for everyone'.

What she meant, of course, was British only! With no immigration—an impossible dream, and one that had to be abandoned after the Brexit poll.

Tories were not Thatcherite now, it seemed, except that they all were. None could restore to their party its 'great governing tradition' because Thatcherism has so successfully uncoupled public governance from the institutions: if the trains didn't run, if towns were flooded, if child care or elder care cost an arm and a leg, if London became unliveable even if it were the only city to prosper, then so what, it wasn't the government's fault.

Nevertheless, May was confronted by a perfect storm of troubles that doomed her to be defensive and opaque where Thatcherism had been offensive. The proliferation of devolved governments and national parties constituted an imminent threat to the Tories' treasured 'governing tradition'.

This was an effect of the post-1979 democratic deficit. Scotland and Wales were not Thatcher territory but they had endured, disproportionately, the costs of Thatcherism. 'Big House Unionism', the Conservative Party's partner in Northern Ireland, its party of government between 1921 and 1972, when direct rule was restored, scarcely survived the ruinous armed conflict that Thatcherism, without doubt, prolonged. In the 2015 General Election the Ulster Unionists sent only two (out of 18) Northern Ireland MPs to Westminster.

JB: How would you relate your current project on patriarchy to your older work on Tory women? What are the continuities but also the discontinuities here? What will it take to plug the gender gap?

The current project (in collaboration with Rahila Gupta) is asking the questions: why and where does patriarchy thrive, and why and where does feminism thrive. We're asking why doesn't patriarchy die? Behind those questions is the clear evidence that the goal of gender equality remains elusive, and that gender oppression finds new contexts and platforms. There is no evolutionary road to equality.

The impact of Thatcherism and the globalisation of capitalism has been decisive. Gender inequalities accelerated at the end of the Cold War in the old Communist Bloc, spectacularly so in Russia and China, compounded by the decline of their welfare states. The impact of neo-liberalism on India since the 1990s has been to re-instate or modernise patriarchal cultures. These regions are home to half the world's population. They exemplify a new global sexual division of labour.

In western Europe the protracted decline of welfare states, de-regulation of financial systems, the proliferation of precarious employment, make it difficult to imagine by what means an already unsustainable socio-sexual contract could be ousted by a more democratic and egalitarian sexual settlement.

There is a liberal notion—very Thatcherite—that all you have to do is lean in and win, that girls achieve as well as and indeed better than boys in the education system, and all they need to do is toughen up and galvanise their ambition. But that individualises gender inquality and renders invisible sexual culture and the division of labour, particularly unpaid labour. Welfare states were not conceived as guarantors of gender equality, but they became crucial sources of employment and services for women and they have been decisive mediators between women and men, a wedge through patriarchal structures. The neo-liberal assault on welfarism and strong local government is a patriarchal project. This represents a problem for conservative women, of course, and many of them are alive to that, though it doesn't seem to have affected their Parliamentary voting record.

Historically women had tended to be more Tory than men, but in 2015 a new gender-generation gap was clear: Labour led among women under 50.

The Conservatives knew they had a problem with women, and both Cameron and May promised to present a more feminine—if not exactly feminist—face. But both recoiled from compulsion—all-women candidate panels, or quotas. Theresa May supported the Women2Women campaign launched in 2005 to increase the dismal number of Tory women MPs (only 9% of the Parliamentary party). It proposed an A-list to ensure that half of the Tories' target seats would go to women. The A-list was dropped, however.

The Conservatives didn't learn from their own party's history: after World War I the Tories managed the challenge of universal suffrage by introducing structural reform. They were confronted by the enviable development of the Co-operative movement— one of the largest manufacturing, trading and consumer organisations in the country since the first co-ops were created in the political tumult of the 1840s. By the end of the 1920s there were 6 million members of 1000 Co-operative societies and there were co-op shops in every town.

The Conservative Party admitted women to its national conference for the first time in 1920. Alert to criticism of their massive but mute presence, compared to the activism of women in the co-op movement, the Tories set about training women agents and imposed quotas for conference delegations: a third had to be women. Nearly a century later the Tories couldn't bring themselves to enforce equality.

One of the most memorable images of the 2015 general election—lamentably, one of the few—was a group hug by Nicola Sturgeon, Scotland's First Minister, the Greens' Nathalie Bennett and Plaid Cymru's Leanne Wood at the end of a televised hustings in April. It was 'a hug that almost stole the show' commented the *Daily Telegraph's* correspondent Claire Cohen. Cameron's promise flared up in his face: the Brexit referendum became a vector of 'posh boys' obloquy, reckless plotting and of xenophobic furies swirling around the entire political firmament.

The Prime Minister's flame-throwing engulfed not only Cameron himself but the entire Westminster Establishment. May emerged from the smoke, seemingly saintly, untainted by the posh boys' coarse ambition. If commentators wanted to represent May as the inheritor of Thatcher's legacy, as only the second woman Prime Minister, the comparison was undone by the presence of a coterie of women political leaders in the twenty-first century. Whatever May's qualities, she would never enjoy—or endure—Thatcher's solitary status as the one woman, the only one, the exception, the greatest. Women were leading political parties and governments in all the jurisdictions of the United Kingdom and Northern Ireland. In England, Caroline Lucas was leader of the Green Party and frequently named as 'best MP'—including the Political Studies Association 'most influential MP'; Plaid Cymru in Wales was led by Leanne Wood, a feminist, socialist and republican. Scotland had Nichola Sturgeon, an adroit national champion, a feminist, on the left, who, unlike Thatcher the great divider, appeared as the voice and soul of Scottish society: working-class, educated, humane, capable and witty.

Theresa May was now not the only one, she was not even the first among equals. She might, just, have joined that TV hug and it would certainly have been embraced by the Scottish Tories' own leader, Ruth Davidson, who seemed to be achieving 'that which was once deemed to be impossible—detoxifying the Tory brand in Scotland', according to Scottish journalist Kevin McKenna.

Davidson is gay, like Scottish Labour's leader Kezia Dugdale and the SNP's Mhairi Black, who beat Labour in Paisley and become the youngest MP in the House of

Commons in 2015. This troika would have been inconceivable in Thatcher's political habitat—a cold house for gays: Section 28 of the 1988 Local Government Act, banned local authorities' promotion of homosexuality or 'the acceptability of homosexuality as a pretended family relationship.'[8]

These Scottish politicians, in particular, were emblematic of the surprising country that Scotland—and the UK—had become.

Theresa May would not be uncomfortable with these women—though she had not been a champion of gay rights—and she proclaimed herself a feminist, something Thatcher would never do. (Not that this seemed to define her voting habits. She was not significantly feminist on abortion or equal pay). Still, May positioned herself among, rather than above, Tory women. She was now not the only woman party leader in the UK, nor was she the 'first among equals'. Unlike Scotland's Nicola Sturgeon or the Green MP Caroline Lucas, whose popularity resonated way beyond their own parties' social base, May cut a lonely figure at home and abroad.

She was snared by the long-term global calamities bequeathed by Thatcherism and the neo-liberal hegemony; the hazards of climate change and proliferating wars; if Brexit was bad enough—it had opened the door to Downing Street but sent tumbrils clattering through her government—she was then chastened by the messianic populism of Donald Trump. 'Hug them close', the mantra of Thatcher's and Blair's approach to the Anglo-American special relationship, was not going to be comfortable. Where Thatcher had been an unashamedly divisive leader, Theresa May had proclaimed herself—impossibly—a leader of national unity at a time when, thanks to Thatcherism, the future of United Kingdom could no longer be guaranteed.

Theresa May was elected to Parliament in 1997 and in 2002, as chair, welcomed her party conference audience with a caution: there was a lot to do, she said, the party was still seen as 'just plain unattractive' and worse, 'people call us the nasty party'. After the Brexit referendum in 2016, she might have said the same thing. Indeed she herself was a leader who, it appeared, was prepared to let people drown in the Mediterranean rather than find shelter on her 'sceptered isle'. But by then there seemed to be no shame in leading the nasty party.

Notes

1. The Primrose League was established by the Tory Party in 1883, in memory of Benjamin Disraeli. It was the first Conservative party organisation to admit women. In this way women were politicised and mobilised by the Conservatives decades before they had the vote. See Philippe Vervaecke (2007) The Primrose League and Women's Suffrage, 1883–1918, in M. Boussahba-Bravard (Ed.) *Suffrage Outside Suffragism* (London: Macmillan), pp. 180–201.
2. M. Ostrogorski (1902) *Democracy and the Organisation of Political Parties* (London).
3. J. Robb (1968) *The Primrose League 1988–1906* (New York).
4. *The Iron Ladies*, p. 7.
5. C. Enloe (2004) *The Curious Feminist: searching for women in a new age of empire* (Berkeley: University of California Press).
6. P. Cosgrave (1985) *Thatcher: The First Term* (London: Bodley Head).
7. We are the Champions of Progressive Ideals, *The Independent*, 9 May 2008.
8. Local Government Act 1988, section 28.

Disclosure statement

No potential conflict of interest was reported by the authors.

Index